Competing by Design

Competing by Design

The Power of Organizational Architecture

DAVID A. NADLER AND MICHAEL L. TUSHMAN

WITH MARK B. NADLER

New York   Oxford

OXFORD UNIVERSITY PRESS

1997

Oxford University Press

Oxford   New York
Athens   Auckland   Bangkok   Bogotá   Bombay
Buenos Aires   Calcutta   Cape Town   Dar es Salaam
Delhi   Florence   Hong Kong   Istanbul   Karachi
Kuala Lumpur   Madras   Madrid   Melbourne
Mexico City   Nairobi   Paris   Singapore
Taipei   Tokyo   Toronto

and associated companies in
Berlin   Ibadan

Library of Congress Cataloging-in-Publication Data
Nadler, David.
Competing by design: the power
of organizational architecture /
by David A. Nadler and Michael L. Tushman
with Mark B. Nadler.
p.   cm.
Includes bibliographical references and index.
ISBN 0-19-509917-6
1. Organizational effectiveness.
2. Organizational change—Management.
3. Corporate reorganizations—Management.
4. Competition.   I. Tushman, Michael.
II. Nadler, Mark B.   III. Title.
HD58.9.N33   1997   658.4'02—dc20   96-41167

3   5   7   9   8   6   4   2

Printed in the United States of America
on acid-free paper

This book is dedicated to our children—
Amy, Cara, Katharine, Jonathan, and Rachel—
sources of great joy to us over the years.

Preface

Let's do a few quick mental calculations.

See if you can come up with a rough estimate of how much time you've spent in the past year thinking and talking about competitive advantage. Remember to include time spent in attending meetings and seminars, reading and writing memos, digesting reports, and articles—and maybe even scanning a few books.

Now try to remember how much time you've spent working on reorganizations, restructurings, and redesigns—those dictated from above as well as those you've initiated yourself.

Finally, put the two together and try to come up with a report card. Grade yourself on (1) how much of the organizational redesign was directly related to your search for competitive advantage; (2) how many restructurings were implemented with an eye towards others that would likely follow; (3) how many restructurings you had to abandon, fix or replace within twelve months; and (4) how many actually achieved the competitive goals you originally had in mind.

Unless you're incredibly lucky or superbly skilled, your honest self-appraisal will be less than dazzling. You're not unusual. After more than forty years of combined experience with more than fifty organizations of all kinds throughout the world, we've come to realize that organizational design is at once one of the most common—and one of the most commonly mishandled—of all business activities.

We believe this book can help—whether you're a CEO or a department head, whether you're looking for ways to redesign a corporation or restructure a factory. It is based on our notion of "organizational architecture," which simply boils down to this: The traditional search for competitive advantage in terms of specific products, technology, markets, or production processes is obsolete. You won't find it there any more. The only real, sustainable source of competitive advantage lies, instead, in an organization's "architecture"—the way in which it structures and coordinates its people and processes in order to maximize its unique capabilities over the long haul, regardless of continuous shifts in the competitive landscape.

Operating with that overall blueprint, we describe in this book the concepts, processes, and practical tools for translating the theory of "architecture" into practical lessons in successful design at every level of the organization. Throughout, we've consistently attempted to tightly link a coherent, time-tested theory with concrete examples taken from actual experience.

We first wrote about this approach to design in 1987, when we co-authored *Strategic Organization Design*, a book that enjoyed wide acceptance in academic and educational circles. In the decade since then, we have been using and refining these concepts in a wide range of change situations. We have tested our ideas in the marketplace and learned from practical experience. In the decade since our first book was published, we have seen our ideas and lessons put to use in one organization after another. As a result, what began simply as an attempt to update the first book became a much more ambitious endeavor and resulted in a much different book. *Competing by Design* is not only based on more contemporary developments in business and management; it reflects concepts sharpened by years of experience and refinement. As a result, in comparison with our earlier effort, this book is intended for practical use by a much wider audience, including executives and managers at organizations of all kinds.

Acknowledgments

Our thinking on this issue was profoundly shaped by several of our academic mentors—Paul Lawrence and Jay Lorsch at the Harvard Business School and Jay Galbraith, now at the University of Southern California—who influenced, inspired and supported our early efforts. In addition, many of our concepts, particularly those involving participation and the coupling of research with practice, were shaped by our mentors, colleagues, and dear friends, Ed Lawler and Tom Allen. We will always be in debt to each of them.

Our work on organizational architecture, executive teams, and change builds on that of many others. Charles O'Reilly and Jeffrey Pfeffer, both at Stanford, have been wonderful friends and colleagues over the past twenty years, and their ideas pervade our book. At Columbia, Mike has been nourished by superb students, executive education participants, and faculty colleagues. In particular, Don Hambrick, Joel Brockner, Ruth Wagemen, Eric Abrahamson, Schon Beechler, Jerry Davis, Chris Ahmadjian, Kirby Warren, and Danny Miller have been of particular assistance in helping us connect our ideas to practice. While visiting at INSEAD and MIT, Mike got important feedback from Deborah Ancona, Charlie Galunic, Martin Gargiulo, Rick Rummelt and Henry Mintzberg. Finally, Andy Van de Ven, David Whetten, Lex Donaldson, and George Huber have all pushed us to deepen and extend our work on organization architecture and managing change.

Since its founding more than sixteen years ago, the Delta Consulting Group has been our laboratory for developing design concepts and tools. Over the years, many of our Delta colleagues have helped to shape and refine this approach to design through their work with clients. It would take more space than we have here to mention them all. But several colleagues—both past and present—merit special thanks for their role in developing these concepts and tools. These include David Bliss, Marc Gerstein, Rick Hardin, Michael Kitson, Terry Limpert, Kathy Morris, Chuck Raben, Robert Shaw, Marilyn Showers, Janet Spencer, Roselinde Torres, and Elise Walton.

In particular, Marilyn Showers, Michael Kitson, Rick Hardin, and Chuck Raben were of great assistance in helping to develop case material and concepts that appear for the first time in this book.

Finally, and perhaps most importantly, we want to acknowledge our clients, who have truly been our partners in learning over the years. Again, it would be impossible to mention all of them here. But we do want to note several individuals and companies whose active collaboration has been of particular value over the years.

Paul Allaire and Bill Buehler at Xerox have been partners in some of our most ambitious design work, and have urged us on to continue learning new concepts. Paul has often described Xerox as a laboratory for Delta—and it has been.

From the beginning, AT&T has been involved in our work. Many AT&T managers and executives, both past and present—and especially Bob Allen—have supported our efforts. Similarly, our clients at AT&T who joined its spin-off, Lucent Technologies—including Bill Marx, Rich McGinn, and Carly Fiorina—have continued to support our efforts since the break-up.

For more than a decade, Corning has been an active partner in our learning. In particular, Jamie Houghton, Roger Ackerman, and the late Jim Riesbeck were all of tremendous help over the years.

We also offer our special thanks to all those at GTE, Kaiser Permanente, and Citibank who also made special contributions.

C.K. Chow and his colleagues in the Industrial Gases Division at BOC helped us extend our work on the challenges of developing and implementing global matrix organizaitons. For ten years, Guido Spichty has helped us test and refine our ideas on organization architectures throughout Ciba Geigy (now Novartis). We have learned much from Alex Krauer, Glenn Bradley, Kurt Huber, Uwe Eisenlohr, Pierre Urech, Michael Jacoby, and Rolf Meyer. We thank them and many others throughout Ciba for helping us mesh the concepts of organization design with the realities of shaping executive teams and managing change.

To all of the clients with whom we've worked, and especially to those named above, we express our gratitude for your faith in us and for enabling us to learn together.

Finally, we owe a very special debt to our collaborator, Mark Nadler. When Mark first joined this effort, we were planning on a simple rewrite of our 1987 book. His vision of a new, broader, and much more accessible book inspired us to take on a more ambitious goal. Time and again, we were amazed by his ability to take our concepts and experiences and make them come alive on the page. His years in both the local and business press and his management experience in the newspaper industry all combined to make him a very special and valued partner in this project. Thanks, Mark.

New York, N.Y.
Cambridge, Mass.
October 1996

Contents

Competing by Design

1

A Blueprint for Change

BOC Industrial Gases: Awakening a Competitive Giant

For more than a century, the Industrial Gases Division of BOC, a huge British conglomerate, had joined the march of industrial progress across the British Empire. Its 35,000 people worked in fifteen countries around the globe to produce and deliver oxygen, nitrogen, helium, and a wide variety of industrial gases to manufacturers of products ranging from steel and food to microchips.

Industrial Gases maintained a steady, if unremarkable, course until 1993. Then, in a sharp break with its staid British traditions, the company elevated C. K. Chow to its top post. Chow, head of Industrial Gases' Hong Kong subsidiary, was an aggressive entrepreneur with a strong belief that the sluggish giant had lost touch with the competitive realities of the late twentieth century.

As he settled into the corporate headquarters outside London and surveyed the worldwide operation, Chow's concern only grew deeper. He saw an organization resistant to new ideas, focused on internal concerns rather than on customer needs, and fixated on geographic boundaries that discouraged collaboration (see Figure 1-1). While the operation faced no imminent crisis, it was clearly an underperformer, seemingly content to pursue business as usual in a world where markets and technology were constantly changing. He came to believe that two particular problems, if left unresolved, might soon become critical.

3

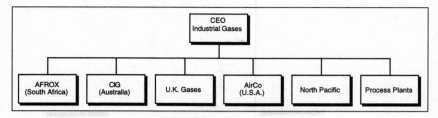

Figure 1-1 BOC (Pre-Restructuring)

First, Industrial Gases was slow to develop new technology and slow to diffuse it throughout the company. A new manufacturing or delivery process developed by the company's Australian subsidiary might take years to show up at the other Industrial Gases operations. In the meantime, competitors were copying the Australian breakthroughs and using them to gain advantage over Industrial Gases subsidiaries in other countries.

Second, from a historical standpoint, the industrial gases business had been intensely local; plants were located right next to steel mills, for instance, and few customers had global operations. By the early 1990s, that was changing. Major microchip producers, such as Intel and IBM, had little patience for dealing separately with BOC in a dozen different countries; they wanted to streamline their relationships and have just one BOC contact—and if they couldn't, they were more than willing to take their business elsewhere.

Convinced that the company's plodding performance was rooted in fundamental organizational problems, Chow secluded himself with the dozen members of his senior team near the ancient village of Runnymede. There, they spent days thrashing out the company's problems and hammering out a new vision for the future. They resolved that in order to be truly competitive in a full range of local and worldwide markets, they would have to become "the most customer-focused" company in the industrial gases business "through innovation and service created by working together around the globe."

At first, the senior team was excited. Then came a painful letdown, as they realistically set their grand vision alongside the jolting reality of the self-satisfied relic Industrial Gases had become. The truth was that the company was neither technologically innovative nor customer focused; it didn't think or act globally.

Their challenge was clear: In order to fulfill their strategic vision, they would have to dramatically redesign virtually every aspect of the company.

Introduction

The story of C. K. Chow's campaign to reshape BOC's Industrial Gases Division illustrates the defining goal of modern-day business—the search for competitive advantage. As everyone in business knows, it's a lot harder than it used to be—and getting tougher all the time.

On one hand, in practically every industry and business sector, competition is more intense than ever. The quickening pace of technological innovation, rising consumer expectations, government deregulation, global markets—all those factors and more create opportunities for new competitors who suddenly change the basic rules of the game with new products, production processes, distribution patterns, and marketing strategies.

At the same time, most of the old, reliable sources of competitive advantage are drying up. No longer can companies located in a handful of money centers rely on exclusive access to capital; no longer can the Xeroxes and Polaroids of the world rely on the exclusive, proprietary technology that once assured them of a virtual monopoly. Markets that were once the exclusive domain of local producers are now fair game for competitors headquartered halfway around the globe. And highly skilled employees, their loyalty shaken by years of corporate cutbacks and downsizing, feel free to offer their services to the highest bidder.

In the war for competitive advantage, the rules of engagement have been thoroughly transformed. The strategies employed by General Motors, IBM, and AT&T to maintain their seemingly unassailable positions of dominance in the 1960s and 1970s are as obsolete today as the full-dress cavalry charge.

In this volatile environment where instability is the norm, we're convinced that the last remaining source of truly sustainable competitive advantage lies in what we've come to describe as "organizational capabilities"—the unique ways in which each organization structures its work and motivates its people to achieve clearly articulated strategic objectives. These capabilities combine an organization's core competencies—technological innovation, customer focus, low-cost manufacturing of high-quality products, or whatever they might be—with the ability to sustain and adapt those competencies in the fulfillment of long-term objectives despite changing competition, altered strategies, and the loss of key employees.

What does that mean for managers? Two things. First, it means they have to understand the concepts and learn the skills involved in designing their organizations in ways that unleash and exploit their inherent competitive strengths. Too many managers, for too long, have thought about design simply in terms of rearranging the boxes and lines on the organizational chart. We have seen one company after another in which successive rounds of destabilizing restructurings did nothing to change the fundamental patterns of performance.

Second, managers have to recognize that truly effective organization design is a never-ending process. Constant change in the competitive environment will require continuous modification of strategic objectives; consequently, design, too, will have to keep changing to ensure that the organization remains aligned with its strategy. This implies that managers engaged in design will always be aiming at moving targets. At the same time, however, the most effective designs will be flexible enough to accommodate change without requiring perpetual upheaval.

Consequently, it's essential for every manager to possess, at the very least, a rudimentary understanding of the concepts and dynamics of organization design. At some levels, managers will be expected to implement elements of designs developed by others. But with growing frequency, managers will be involved in their own designs at various levels of the organization. The truth is that continuous design, at one level or another, will become a fact of life, and the successful managers will be those who can understand it, embrace it, explain it to others, and help make it happen.

The purpose of this book is to provide managers, at every level and in every kind of organization, with a set of powerful yet fairly simple tools for using strategic organization design to gain competitive advantage—for competing by design. Drawing on specific cases to illustrate the design process in practice—in both successful and unsuccessful situations—we describe the basic components of design and explain how they can be creatively assembled in a remarkable variety of configurations in order to achieve each organization's unique strategic objectives. We present a design process, explore the key decisions managers face, and present some guiding principles for incorporating the design function as a continuing process in organizations that are constantly looking to the future.

We hope that by the time readers have finished our book, they will have mastered the key concepts and acquired the essential tools they will need to creatively reassess the design of their own operations—a company, a manufacturing plant, a business division, or whatever—in an entirely new way. They should have the ability to determine precisely how the design is preventing the organization from meeting its strategic objectives. They should have a road map for devising a deliberate and disciplined process for reshaping the design. And ideally, they should be able to look at the organization's design from a fresh perspective, with a sharp focus on seeking out opportunities for leveraging competitive advantage.

The underlying theme of this book is that organization design can be an invaluable tool for shaping the overall look and feel of an organization—in short, the way it gets things done. Those broad dimensions of structure, capacity, and performance form the general outline of organizational architecture; strategic organization design fills in the specific features of how work is organized and coordinated. The concept of architecture is essential to our entire perspective on strategic organization design, and that is where we begin our discussion.

The Key Concept: Organizational Architecture

In 1918 Henry Ford's new Dearborn assembly plant stood proudly as one of the architectural marvels of the industrial age. Incorporating the latest assembly-line technology, it anchored the massive, 2,000-acre River Rouge manufacturing colossus that was the envy of the industrialized world. But time passed; industrial architecture progressed, new technologies emerged, and River Rouge became an anachronism requiring massive overhaul.

And yet, incredibly, the fundamental concepts of organizational architecture that found their physical expression in the hundreds of decaying plants that litter the Rust Belt live on. Those early-twentieth-century notions of steep hierarchies, powerful centralized bureaucracies, and narrowly defined jobs have proved more durable than the physical structures they spawned. They are truly anachronisms today in a competitive environment light-years removed from Henry Ford's Detroit.

Today, more and more companies are coming to realize that they can't hope to compete successfully in the twenty-first century with organizations based on nineteenth-century designs. Radically different organizational architectures are emerging in much the same fashion as new schools of physical architecture (Nadler, Gerstein, and Shaw 1992).

Essentially, four factors contribute to the development of new architectural designs. The first is *purpose,* or the basic function for which a building is intended. In the late 1880s, for example, the emergence of large retailers led to demands for an entirely new kind of building, the commercial loft, where acres of merchandise could be put on public display in accessible, open spaces.

The second factor is *structural materials*. Obviously, the availability of materials plays a huge role in framing the architect's vision of possible solutions to particular design problems. The development of structural steel, for example, allowed the construction of skyscrapers that were impossible to build with traditional load-bearing walls, which required broad bases that could support only a few upper floors.

The architect merges the building's purpose with the available structural materials to develop the third element of architectural design—an *architectural style*. When a new purpose, such as the need to centralize and coordinate the activity of large numbers of office workers, calls for a new solution involving new materials— structural steel, for instance—the result is a new architectural style—in this case, the modern skyscraper.

Finally, there's the element of *collateral technology*. These technologies aren't essential to the construction of the building, but without them the building can't really fulfill its purpose. Theoretically, it would have been possible to build the Empire State Building without elevators or ventilation systems—but it's hard to imagine anyone working there for long under those conditions.

Now consider the parallels with organizations. In the late 1800s, new industries—the railroads, in particular—found it necessary for the first time to coordinate and control the activities of large, widely dispersed workforces, to monitor huge inventories of expensive equipment, and to plan long-term capital investments (Yates 1992). That need for control and coordination represented a new business *purpose.*

The essential *structural materials* for meeting the new purpose were found in the emerging information technologies of that time— the typewriter, carbon paper, the early duplicating machine, the vertical file. They allowed for the unprecedented generation, collection, and retrievable storage of written information.

The combination of new purposes and structural materials led to the *organizational design* now commonly referred to as the machine bureaucracy, with its narrowly defined jobs, small spans of control, functional divisions, and steep hierarchy. The development of *collateral technologies*—namely, the disciplines and techniques of scientific management—firmly positioned machine bureaucracy as the prevailing design of its time.

Today, we're seeing the emergence of new organizational architectures in a period of change unmatched by anything since the development of the machine bureaucracy nearly a century ago. Once again, new purposes, structural materials, and collateral technologies are converging to produce entirely new concepts of design.

A host of changes in the external business environment—technological innovation, global markets, consumer expectations, and governmental involvement—are redefining traditional notions of purpose. Rather than seeking designs that emphasize coordination and control, what organizations need now is speed, innovation, customer focus, and radically improved productivity.

Two structural materials are making this shift possible. The first is *information technology*, which makes it possible for companies to make timely information available to thousands of people simultaneously no matter where they're located. Not only does information technology demolish traditional constraints of time and geography; it enhances collaboration and teamwork, eliminates the need for entire levels of bureaucracy that were created largely to process information, and provides new ways for organizations to build and share their collective knowledge. The second technology is the innovative use of *teams*—not in the traditional sense, but as a basic building block of the new architecture, relying upon people to use their collective knowledge, judgment, skill, and creativity to perform a variety of jobs and functions, rather than just one, in concert with their colleagues.

In order to perform effectively, the new architectures require new collateral technologies. In particular, they demand new leadership skills, new methods for selecting and developing key people, new human resources approaches to assessment and reward, and new techniques for enhancing the organization's capacity for collective learning.

Together, these new purposes, structural materials, and collateral technologies have merged to foster the development of a new organizational architecture. It is characterized by greater autonomy at every level of the organization, starting with increased self-management by individuals and teams. It involves the creation of self-contained units, which are accountable for a wide range of strategic objectives, and structural designs that can quickly adapt to rapid changes in the business environment. It shatters the rigid boundaries that traditionally separated one division from another, or even one company from its suppliers and competitors, and provides more flexible relationships and alliances. Moreover, it is an architecture keenly sensitive to both the technical and the social aspects of the organization—both the "hardware" and the "software," to borrow an analogy from technology architecture.

In this book, we consider a number of leading companies in the United States and around the world that are developing their own versions of the new architecture. One of the leaders has been Xerox, which underwent a dramatic redesign in 1992. Like other leading companies, Xerox was clearly conscious of the need for a transformation that would transcend the routine modifications that had routinely passed for redesign. As CEO Paul A. Allaire explained:

> The change we are making now is more profound than anything we've done before. We have embarked on a process to change completely the way we manage the company. Changing the structure of the organization is only a part of that. In fact, the term "reorganization" doesn't really capture what we are trying to do at Xerox. We are redesigning the "organizational architecture" of the entire company (Howard 1992).

That is the essence of architectural design—rethinking and reshaping the very fabric of the enterprise, both its technical processes and its social relationships.

Design as a Management Tool

The concept of organizational architecture involves a fairly global perspective on strategic change and helps provide a larger, historical context for our discussion. But the fact of the matter is that design is a basic tool available to almost every manager, not just the CEO and the senior team. No vision for change at the corporate level can succeed unless managers throughout the corporation fully understand and "buy into" the underlying concepts of the redesign. At each level, managers must translate the overall vision into a consistent design within their own area of responsibility. Successful managers are neither bystanders nor victims; they stretch themselves to comprehend, embrace, and advance the redesign principles developed for the organization as a whole.

Indeed, there's nothing new about the popularity of redesign as a management tool. One manager involved in the Xerox redesign of 1992 remarked to us early in the process that he had already witnessed six major reorganizations during his time with the company, none of which had succeeded in changing how the company was run. So what is it about redesign that makes it so attractive? Why are the histories of so many companies marked by successive—and often unsuccessful—reorganizations? Why have so many managers come to view redesign as one of the key leverage points for change?

First, design is one of the few levers for change available to most managers. Strategic change is generally the responsibility of a small group of senior executives and can't be employed too often without throwing the organization into massive confusion. Wholesale changes in personnel are generally impractical and severely destabilizing. And changes in underlying organizational culture are complex and take extensive periods of time. Design, in contrast, can be done at numerous levels, can be completed in a reasonably short period of time, and, at least superficially, can be implemented quickly and with relatively little pain and discomfort.

Beyond that, design draws much of its appeal from its enormous—though often unachieved—potential for massively changing patterns of performance. Consider Corning Inc.; as a result of a major reorganization in the mid-1980s, two previously insignificant operations—including fiber optics—were elevated to the status of full-fledged business units with their own identities, leadership, resources, and strategic goals. Less than ten years later, what had only been "tiny little pesky businesses," in the words of chairman James R. Houghton, were together piling up more than half the corporation's operating profit.

In addition, design can grab the organization's attention and focus it squarely on particular issues. In the mid-1980s, when Xerox decided to make the quality of its products and services an absolute priority, it took the early step of creating the positions of vice presidents for quality at the corporate level and in all the operating units. The creation of those jobs, the important levels at which they were placed in the organization, and the caliber of people appointed to them all sent a clear signal that something serious was going on.

Another reason that redesign has such allure is that it offers managers—particularly those just starting out in a new position—a clear opportunity to put their personal stamp on an operation. That's what Walter Shipley did in 1995 as he went about designing the organization of the largest bank in the United States, which was about to emerge from the merger of Chemical and Chase Manhattan banks. Determined to create a collegial relationship among the merged institutions' senior executives, Shipley carefully chose the word "partnership" to describe the governing structure of five top officials, including himself, sitting at the helm of the new enterprise.

Similarly, design can be used to shape an organization's tone, or operating style. At Corning, Houghton became convinced that dramatic and lasting change was impossible unless he could develop a broad cadre of managers who shared his vision and values. So beyond his eight-member management committee, Houghton established a corporate policy group of thirty executives who met four or five times a year. Then he extended leadership out to a third concentric circle by creating a corporate management group that consisted of the 130 top managers in the corporation, who met annually. The new formal structures underscored Houghton's conceptual commitment to more inclusive leadership.

Design can sometimes signal a sharp change in strategic emphasis. In 1993, Randall Tobias became CEO of Eli Lilly & Co., an underperformer in the health care industry with resources dispersed in activities that ranged from selling drugs to designing surgical tools to basic medical research. Tobias came to the conclusion that if the company was to excel in any areas, it would have to abandon others where it had no chance of becoming a world-class player. Accordingly, all of Lilly's activities were restructured around five disease areas, such as oncology and central nervous systems disorders.

Finally, managers are frequently forced to become involved in redesign by mergers, acquisitions, or divestitures, which place them in the role of designers and redesigners as pieces of organizations are either combined or desegregated. For example, literally hundreds of managers were assigned to various design tasks in the wake of AT&T's decision to split itself into three independent companies.

Consequently, it's not surprising that design and redesign are common occurrences in the life of most organizations. Whether it's a new manager restructuring a small department or Ford Motor Company CEO Alex Trotman reconfiguring the company's worldwide engineering and design activities into three new vehicle program centers, organizational design is important and pervasive. With the possible exception of individual leadership, no management tool offers so much potential for fomenting substantive change. Design decisions define where an organization will channel its resources. They define jobs, shape work processes, motivate performance, and, perhaps most important, shape the patterns of informal interactions and relationships that develop over time.

Why So Many Redesigns Fail

And yet, despite the incredible impact design changes can have, appalling numbers of them are done poorly; some, like the 1984 General Motors restructuring (which we'll examine shortly), were outright disasters. For every well-planned, carefully implemented success, there have been dozens of flops that helped speed an organization's decline. At the very least, poorly conceived and badly enacted reorganizations typically cause confusion, divert energy, and diminish effectiveness as measured by almost any indicator. For every design that displays a spark of genius or a truly new insight into social organization, there are ten misguided efforts that reflect no more thought than a couple of sketches on napkins over lunch.

Given the importance of organization design, the obvious question becomes: Why is so much of it done so badly? The answer lies in both the traditional theory and the contemporary practice of design.

For years, academia's guidance in this area generally took the form of lofty prescriptions by classical management theorists. Starting in the late 1960s and continuing through the 1970s, the literature focused on more solidly grounded approaches to understanding organization structure. This research provided some valuable insights but didn't provide the guidance managers needed as they faced specific design decisions. There's been some progress in recent years, but, on the whole, the academic literature is still of little practical use to most managers.

Instead, managers have had to rely either on their own common sense or on the recommendations of management consultants. These approaches, while pragmatic, involve some dangerous pitfalls. To begin with, they sometimes focus exclusively on the technical aspects of design—the formal organizational structures—while giving only a backward glance to the social, cultural, and political implications of the redesign. As a result, many of these designs never make it past the recommendation stage and end up as sets of overhead transparencies in binders, permanently planted on bookshelves. Even worse, as we see, some of these designs actually reach the implementation stage.

There's a second category of design that focuses myopically on personal and social issues. These designs are often intuitive reactions to immediate personal and political problems, rather than methodical responses to strategic demands. Too often, the underlying rationale for a crucial design decision turns out to be, "Well, we had to come up with a decent job for everybody on the team." That may avoid some unpleasant personal conflict, but it saddles the organization with a redesign based on minor tinkering with the current structure, rather than the radical overhaul that might have been called for. Merely reshuffling the deck without changing the game is a purely political exercise that accomplishes nothing in terms of substantially improving competitive performance.

Third, many of these designs are driven by solutions rather than problems. "Let's find something to reengineer" was a demand that went forth from corporate offices all over the United States in recent years. After much time and great expense, most companies finally came to understand that reengineering was a somewhat limited and potentially dangerous tool for rethinking specific work processes, rather than a comprehensive strategy for redesign. But the reengineering craze illustrates an all too frequent approach to design: A manager or consultant becomes enamored of the latest design idea to hit the bookshelves, business magazines, and seminar circuit and then searches eagerly for some place to try it out. These solutions in search of symptoms have little to do with the serious search for competitive advantage and everything to do with the managerial faddism that continues to plague American business.

A Balanced Perspective

In this book, we present a comprehensive, balanced approach to design that recognizes the technical requirements, human dynamics, and strategic demands of successful design in any organization or business unit. Our underlying themes can be summarized as follows:

1. Organization design is an essential and ongoing part of each manager's job.
2. Organization design emanates from an overall vision for the organization, embodied in a strategic plan with a clear set of strategic objectives. The goal of organization design is to fashion a set of formal structures and processes that, together with an appropriate informal operating environment, will give people the skills, direction and motivation to do the work necessary to achieve the strategic objectives.
3. As managers make design decisions, they must constantly balance the two aspects of the organization—the effectiveness of the design in terms of performing the work required by the strategic objectives and the design's impact on individuals, group relationships, and the political dynamics of the organization. Both are crucial, and maintaining the proper balance presents managers with a never-ending stream of design-related decisions.
4. The ultimate goal of design is to use creatively the new structural materials and collateral technologies to achieve a fundamentally new architecture that will focus and unleash the competitive strengths embedded in each organization.

It's worthwhile to emphasize the importance of the second item. It is not our intention in this book to discuss the entire strategy-making process from beginning to end. Indeed, we deal in considerable detail with the issues and processes involved in developing sound organizational strategies in some of our other works. This book confines itself to the design process that begins once the organization and its leaders have articulated an overall vision, developed and communicated a clear strategy, and fashioned a set of specific strategic objectives. It is at that point that design becomes an essential tool for transforming strategy into reality.

This book, then, focuses on three critical aspects of organization design. Using a specific company to illustrate the issues raised in each chapter, we first provide some basic concepts for thinking about organizations and the implications of organization design. Second, we consider the range of design decisions managers can expect to face. Finally, we propose some proven processes for making sound decisions about organization design.

We begin in Chapter 2 by presenting an overall model of how organizations work and how the relationships among the key components—the design—contribute to overall performance. We continue along those lines in Chapter 3 by explaining the fundamental elements and basic terms associated with organizational architecture and design. Chapter 4 introduces the important notion of the organization as a mechanism for processing information and explores the implications for various forms of design.

In Chapter 5, we begin addressing the key decisions involved in the design, presenting the basic alternatives for grouping people and their work. Then, in Chapter 6, we move on to the systems and processes that are available for linking and coordinating work at each level of the organization. In Chapter 7, we step back and consider the issue of design at the enterprise level. We look at the creative ways in which companies such as Xerox, Sun Microsystems, and Corning have created new architectures to unleash their full competitive advantage by fundamentally reshaping their internal structures and processes and by seeking out new strategic alliances with partners, customers, and suppliers. Chapter 8 shifts the focus once again, this time to microlevel design, with an examination of the emerging architecture of High-Performance Work Systems and a discussion of process reengineering.

In Chapter 9, we examine the critical steps in the design process, tracing the process used to restructure dramatically the Northern California region of Kaiser Permanente Hospitals and Health Plan, the country's largest HMO. That leads directly to the issues involved in implementing new designs and reshaping organizational culture, which we address in Chapter 10. In Chapter 11, we analyze design as an ongoing process, rather than a single event, and explain the important implications that approach holds for organizational leaders and managers.

We conclude in Chapter 12 by synthesizing the various propositions presented throughout the book into ten fundamental themes that can help guide managers in their future design efforts. These themes also provide a general framework for the book and are useful to keep in mind as we go forward:

1. Organizational capabilities represent the last truly sustainable source of competitive advantage.
2. Organizational architecture provides a conceptual framework for employing strategic design to develop organizational capabilities.
3. At every level of the organization, design constitutes one of the most powerful tools for shaping performance.
4. Regardless of its scope or scale, there are certain fundamental concepts that apply to design at every level.
5. There is a logical sequence of actions and decisions that applies to the design process at any level of the organization.
6. There are no perfect designs; the design process requires the weighing of choices and the balancing of trade-offs.
7. The best designs draw on the knowledge, experience, and expertise of people throughout the organization.
8. Even the best designs can be derailed by ill-planned, poorly executed implementation.
9. As continual redesign becomes a fact of life, successful organizations will learn to create flexible architectures that can accommodate constant change.
10. Flexible architectures and designs that leverage competitive strengths will themselves become the ultimate competitive weapons.

BOC Industrial Gases Revisited

Industrial Gases' response to impending threats was, in many ways, a textbook case of strategic redesign. Using a process that relied on massive participation by managers throughout the company, they first diagnosed the gaps between their strategic objectives and their organization's capacity to meet those objectives and then set about redesigning the basic architecture of the organization.

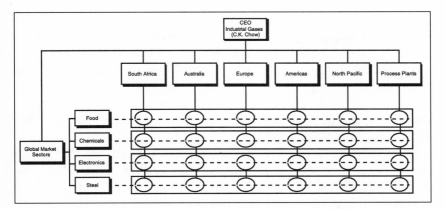

Figure 1-2 BOC (Post-Restructuring). (*Note:* Simplified structure)

First, they redesigned the formal structure by developing a "global matrix" (see Figure 1-2). In other words, while retaining the existing structure of separate operations in each country, the company also appointed global product managers for each major sector of its business, such as food, steel, and chemicals, with responsibilities cutting across national boundaries. At the same time, they initiated an intensive program to provide the top 500 managers with the skills and insights required by the new culture of cooperation and teamwork. Within two years, the improvements were clear; the rate of innovation was drastically improved, and Industrial Gases was once again winning major supply contracts from global customers.

As we see in later chapters, Industrial Gases was just one of many companies that developed dual sets of structures—in this case, structures based on product lines and geography—in order to capitalize simultaneously on three areas of competitive strength. First, by retaining its traditional structure of semiautonomous subsidiaries in each country in which it operates, Industrial Gases was able to continue addressing the unique demands of widely varying customers and markets. Second, the global product lines made it possible to meet the needs of large customers who demanded one-stop shopping for their worldwide needs. Finally, the product-line structure provided a focus—by assigning responsibility to specific managers who would be accountable for meeting goals—on developing, disseminating, and building on new technology.

In other words, Industrial Gases was recognizing and nurturing its traditional organizational capacities for technological innovation and customer focus. What it had to do was revamp the aging design

and culture that were stifling those very capacities. The old architecture had been adequate in the days when companies could sit for
years on their exclusive technology and when markets and customers were so local that there was no need for managers in one
country to deal with anyone but the home office. But Industrial
Gases fell prey to precisely the trends we have discussed—the rapid
pace of technological change and the growing prevalence of global
customers and competitors.

Rather than shifting a few senior executives from one job to
another or rearranging a few reporting relationships, C. K. Chow and
Industrial Gases chose to create a dramatically new structure and
then helped managers learn to collaborate in unprecedented ways. In
the process, they succeeded in designing and building a new and
competitively powerful organizational architecture.

But every successful design process, including Chow's, begins
with a basic understanding of how the organization functions and
the variables that can be reconfigured to provide a profoundly new
look and feel. In Chapter 2, we begin our exploration of those underlying concepts of how organizations actually work.

Bibliography

There has been substantial research on the question of organization
design and its relationship to organization performance. Examples of
this work include:

Bartlett, C., and S. Ghoshal. "Matrix Management: Not a Structure, a
    Frame of Mind." *Harvard Business Review* (July 1990): 139–145.
Burns, T., and G. Stalker. *Management of Innovation.* London: Tavis-
    tock, 1961.
Chandler, A. *Strategy and Structure.* Cambridge, Mass.: Harvard Uni-
    versity Press, 1990.
Chandler, A. *Scale and Scope.* Cambridge, Mass.: Harvard University
    Press, 1990.
Daft, R. *Organization Theory and Design,* 2d ed. St. Paul, Minn.: West,
    1986.
Daft, R., and R. Lengel. "Organization Information Requirements,
    Media Richness and Structural Design." *Management Science* 32,
    no. 5 (1986): 554–576.
D'Aveni, R. *Hypercompetition: Managing the Dynamics of Strategic
    Maneuvering.* New York: Free Press, 1994.
Donaldson, L. *American Anti-Management Theories of Organization:
    A Critique of Paradigm Proliferation.* Cambridge: Cambridge Uni-
    versity Press, 1995.

Galbraith, J. *Organization Design.* Reading, Mass.: Addison-Wesley, 1977.

Hedberg, A., P. Nystrom, and W. Starbuck. "Camping on Seesaws: Prescription for Self-Designing Organization." *Administrative Science Quarterly* 21 (1976): 41–65.

Howard, R. "The CEO as Organizational Architect: An Interview with Xerox's Paul Allaire." *Harvard Business Review* (September–October 1992): 106–121.

Hurst, D. *Crisis and Renewal: Meeting the Challenge of Organization Change.* Cambridge, Mass.: Harvard Business School Press, 1995.

Lawrence, P., and D. Dyer. *Renewing American Industry.* New York: Free Press, 1983.

Lawrence, P., and J. Lorsch. *Organization and Environment.* Cambridge, Mass.: Harvard University Press, 1967.

MacKenzie, K. "The Process Approach to Organization Design." *Human System Management* 8 (1989): 31–43.

Miller, D. "The Architecture of Simplicity." *Academy of Management Review* 18 (1993): 116–138.

Mintzberg, H. "The Design School: Reconsidering the Basic Premises of Strategic Management." *Strategic Management Journal* 11 (1990): 171–195.

Nadler, D., Gerstein, M., and R. Shaw. *Organizational Architecture.* San Francisco: Jossey-Bass, 1992.

Nohria, N., and R. Eccles, eds. *Networks and Organizations.* Boston: Harvard Business School Press, 1992.

Perrow, L. *Complex Organizations,* 3d ed. New York: Random House, 1986.

Pfeffer, J. *Organization Design.* Arlington, Ill.: AHM Publications, 1978.

Scott, W. *Organizations: Rational, Natural and Open Systems,* 3d ed. Englewood Cliffs, N.J.: Prentice-Hall, 1992.

Thompson, J. *Organizations in Action.* New York: McGraw-Hill, 1967.

Weick, K. *The Social Psychology of Organizing,* 2d ed. Reading, Mass.: Addison-Wesley, 1979.

Woodward, J. *Industrial Organization.* New York: Oxford University Press, 1962.

Yates, J. *Control through Communication: The Rise of System in American Management.* Baltimore: Johns Hopkins University Press, 1989.

2

Mapping the Organizational Terrain

Xerox Corporation—Designing Organizational "Fit"

By 1991, Xerox was well on its way toward one of the most successful comebacks in U.S. corporate history. Under the leadership of David T. Kearns, Xerox became the first major U.S. company to overcome an onslaught by Japanese competitors. Its intense emphasis on quality had earned the company the first annual Malcolm Baldrige National Quality Award. A massive, systematic rethinking of its strategy was finally focusing Xerox's scattered energy and resources on a sharply defined identity as "The Document Company."

But much remained to be done. As Paul A. Allaire, Kearns's successor, sought to understand the factors that underlay Xerox's continuing problems, he came to the conclusion that the company would have to transform itself into a fundamentally different company—"The New Xerox"—if it was to become truly capable of pursuing its new strategy. The problems inherent in the old Xerox were manifesting themselves in every aspect of the operation.

Despite its new strategy and its successful focus on quality, Xerox continued to operate as a traditional "functional machine" (see Figure 2-1). So many key decisions were bottled up in an all-powerful and overstaffed corporate office that it begged comparison

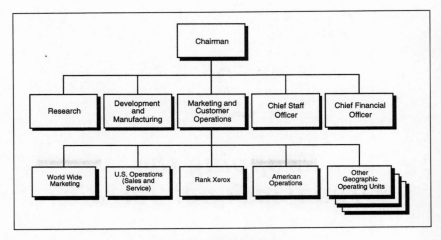

Figure 2-1 Xerox 1991

with the old Central Committee of the Soviet regime. The complexity of the bureaucracy discouraged key operating managers from making important decisions on their own and blurred accountability for the development and delivery of products and services. Everything about Xerox was too slow—technological innovation, the development of products to meet customer needs, and the capacity to adapt to new market conditions. There was still too much focus on internal operations, rather than on customer demands.

In short, despite all its progress, Xerox continued to rumble along as a rigidly centralized, overly complex institution that had failed to unleash the initiative, judgment, creativity, and energy of its people. And its failure to radically change the way the company was run was costing it dearly in terms of productivity, innovation, customer service, and, ultimately, financial performance.

Understanding the Organization

What Paul Allaire faced in 1991 was a classic case of an organization in need of an entirely new architecture. Typically, the radical reshaping of an organization begins with strategy, as executives search for solutions to the problems created by shifting business conditions. But, as is often the case, Xerox discovered that its traditional organization was incapable of implementing its new strategy; the two just didn't fit.

Moreover, Allaire understood this wasn't a problem that would be solved by merely rearranging the boxes on his table of organization. This was truly a case in which the company needed an entirely new architecture that would foster the development of new organizational capabilities—speed, innovation, accountability, customer focus, simplicity, self-management. If the redesign was to be successful, Allaire realized, it would have to result in profound change in each and every aspect of the organization—its work, its formal structures and processes, its culture, and its people.

The kind of fundamental redesign faced by Xerox in 1991—and by increasing numbers of organizations of every description—is enormously difficult under the best of conditions. But it's absolutely impossible unless the design leaders are equipped with a conceptual road map that lays out the complex patterns of interrelationships that are the real substance and soul of their organizations. Our purpose in this chapter is to offer just such a road map—an organization model that literally thousands of executives and managers, including Paul Allaire and his team at Xerox, have used to understand and then reshape the dynamics of their organizations. In Chapter 4, we offer a more refined model that specifically addresses design issues. But that comes later; at this stage, our purpose is to provide a useful way of looking at organizations that goes beyond balance sheets and staffing charts and analyzes the relationships between people, work, formal structures, and informal practices and behavior. From that perspective, we propose a model that is based on the relatively simple premise that each organization is a highly integrated system whose performance is determined by the degree of alignment among its major components.

Our general model also builds directly on the notion of organizational architecture. The right architecture doesn't automatically guarantee perfect alignment, but the wrong architecture will almost certainly lead to failure. Paul Allaire realized that there was little point in creating nine independent business units, whose presidents were supposed to pursue specific segments of the office market with entrepreneurial zeal, if the company at the same time retained a top-heavy, micromanaging corporate office that maintained a stranglehold on practically all decision making. One result of the Xerox redesign was, therefore, an entirely new role for the corporate office, one emphasizing strategy and coordination rather than operational management and control. At the same time, it quickly became apparent that traditional Xerox managers had little experience and few of the personality traits required for entrepreneurial leadership. So another aspect of the design was an entirely new process for assessing and developing qualified candidates for the new jobs.

Figure 2-2 Two Design Perspectives

Strategy/Work Performance	Individual/Social/Cultural
Design supports the implementation of strategy	How will existing people fit into the design?
Design facilitates the flow of work	How will the design affect power relations among different groups?
Design permits effective managerial control	How will the design fit with people's values and beliefs?
Design creates doable, measurable jobs	How will the design affect the tone and operating style of the organization?

What, then, are the most crucial issues and conflicting demands that should be uppermost in the mind of anyone setting out to redesign an organization? Two sets of questions are involved (see Figure 2-2). First, the designer must consider what kind of structure will best enable the organization to manage its work in order to meet its strategic objectives. And second, the designer must take into consideration how those new structures will affect—and, in turn, be influenced by—the culture, politics, and informal behavioral patterns of the people who make up the organization.

Both perspectives, structural and social, are valid, but considering either one in isolation from the other invariably leads to trouble. Focusing exclusively on structures and formal work processes is likely to lead to an organization that looks impressive on paper but somehow can't get the right people doing the right work the right way. Indeed, restructuring done from that perspective is likely to create more problems than it solves. On the other hand, basing organizational design solely on social and cultural issues may well result in a working environment where people eagerly look forward to coming to work each day; the problem is that one day they may show up and find the place locked and shuttered because they were all happily working away on activities that had little to do with the organization's crucial strategic objectives.

These two perspectives reflect sharply contrasting notions about the fundamental purpose of organizations. The strategic/task perspective views organizations purely as mechanisms to perform the work required to execute strategies that, if successful, will create value for customers and shareholders. It perceives organizations essentially as economic mechanisms created to achieve results that would be impossible for individuals working alone. The social/cultural perspective, on the other hand, sees organizations as devices for satisfying the needs, desires, and aspirations of various shareholders, both inside and outside the organization. Consequently, it views organizations as social organisms that exist for the express purpose of meeting individual needs, aiding in the exercise of power, and expressing individual or collective values.

Conceptual Models as Managerial Tools

Clearly, there is some validity to both perspectives; managers engaged in redesign should keep in mind the importance of balancing both. And in order to do that, he or she needs a model—an intellectual tool for sorting out those complex interests while reconfiguring the elements of the organization. This isn't just a theoretical exercise. The selection of a model is critical; in reality, it will guide the designer's analysis and action. Here's why. Problem solving in any organizational situation, including design, involves the collection, analysis and interpretation of information to identify specific problems and appropriate responses. Models—explicit ones that we draw on flip charts or informal ones that we unconsciously keep tucked away in the corners of our minds—influence the kind of information we collect, guide our interpretation and analysis, and shape our ultimate decisions. Indeed, anyone who's at all familiar with an organization already has some kind of model in mind, based on personal experience. In Chapter 1, we mentioned the example of Walter Shipley and his plan to design the Chase Manhattan executive team as a "partnership." Where did he get the idea? Shipley has often said he was impressed with the partnership concept that he learned about from his father, who had been a partner at Brown Brothers Harriman, a well-known investment banking firm. Through those experiences, Shipley had developed a model for thinking about how organizations might be structured.

Shipley's model was explicit. That's not true for most people. Despite vast differences in quality, validity, and sophistication, the organizational models most people carry around in their head are vague and unspoken. But that doesn't prevent them from becoming powerful guides to thought and action.

A Basic View of Organizations

When asked to "draw a picture of an organization," most managers usually respond the same way: They sketch some version of the traditional, pyramid-shaped structure that has characterized hierarchical organizations for centuries. It is a perspective based on a snapshot in time; it focuses on a stable configuration of jobs and work units as the most critical factor in an organization. Certainly, that view provides some helpful ways to conceptualize the enterprise. But in the long run, it's a seriously limited model, one that excludes such critical factors as leadership, external influences, informal behavior, and power relationships. The traditional model captures only a fraction of what's really going on within any complex organization.

Over the past two decades, there's been a growing tendency to replace the traditional static model with one that views the organization as a system. This new perspective stems from repeated observations that social organisms display many of the same characteristics as mechanical and natural systems. In particular, some theorists argue that organizations are better understood if they are thought of as dynamic and "open" social systems.

Think of any organization with which you're familiar—your own, for example. Is the competitive environment it competes in today the same as it was ten or even five years ago? Has the nature of competition been altered by new competitors, different technologies, or government deregulation? Is the organization structured and managed as it was in the past? Do its employees use the same skills, knowledge, and management techniques as they used to? Have customer demands changed in terms of value, quality, delivery, and service? Clearly, every component of the organization, along with the external environment in which it operates, is subject to constant change. And each change has the potential of launching a serious ripple effect.

That pretty well satisfies the definition of a system. More formally, a system is a set of interrelated elements—a change in one element affects the others. Taking it a step further, an *open system* is one that interacts with its environment; it draws input from external sources and transforms it into some form of output. Think of a manufacturing plant as a simple example. The plant consists of different but related components—departments, jobs, technologies, employees. It receives input from the environment—capital, raw materials, production orders, cost control guidelines—and it transforms them into products or output.

Organizations display some of the same characteristics as any basic system. The first is *internal interdependence*. Changes in one component of an organization frequently have repercussions for the others; the pieces are interconnected. In our hypothetical manufac-turing plant, a change in one element—the skill level of the employ-ees, for example—will affect production speed, the quality of the output, and the kind of supervision that's required.

The second characteristic is the *capacity for feedback*. Feedback allows organizations to correct errors and even to change them-selves. In our plant, if data indicate a decline in product quality, managers can use the information to identify factors that are con-tributing to the problem. But human organizations are, after all, only human; the availability of feedback doesn't ensure that it will be used, or used properly.

The third characteristic of systems is sometimes referred to as *equilibrium*. When an event throws the system out of balance, the system's response is to try to right itself. If, for some reason, one work group in our plant were to suddenly increase its output, the system would be seriously out of balance. Its suppliers would have trouble keeping pace, while inventory would start piling up on the other end. One way or another, the system would work itself back into balance; either the pace would be accelerated elsewhere in the plant, or the overachievers would see their staffing or supplies cut back.

Fourth, systems can produce similar outputs using *alternative configurations*. There is no "one best way" to structure the system. This point is particularly critical in the context of organizational design; as we see in Chapter 9, one of the most crucial steps in the design process is the development and consideration of a wide range of alternative designs, from which managers select the most appro-priate option. The challenge is to identify the design that makes the most sense for that particular organization in the context of its unique social and technical demands.

Finally, successful systems are characterized by *adaptation*, the capacity to constantly readjust to the demands of the environment. Our plant might have done a spectacular job of printing circuit boards until the day it shut down because the world was shifting to microchips or until we modified our skills, equipment, and tech-nology to produce something the marketplace wanted. Very simply, any system must constantly adapt to changing environmental con-ditions.

Compared with the old pyramid-shaped drawing, the open-sys-tems theory certainly provides a more helpful way of thinking in a general way about organizations in more complex and dynamic terms. And yet, it's still too abstract to be of much practical use in solving day-to-day organizational problems; what we need is a model that encompasses the general concepts of the open system but provides us with a more pragmatic problem-solving tool.

The Congruence Model

We began building such a model in the mid-1970s, benefiting from the earlier work of noted theorists such as Katz and Kahn and of Seiler and Lorsch, among others. At the same time we were doing our work at Columbia University, Jay Galbraith at MIT and Harold Leavitt at Stanford were proceeding along the same lines. From that collective thinking emerged a new way of looking at organizations that has proven helpful to thousands of managers in scores of organizations over the years. We call this conceptual framework "the congruence model of organizational behavior."

According to this model, the components of any organization exist together in various states of balance and consistency—what we call "fit." The higher the degree of fit—"or congruence"—among the various components, the more effective the organization. This model clearly illustrates the critical role of interdependence within the system and places special emphasis on the transformation process—the means by which the organization converts input into output.

To understand how the entire organization works, it's essential to understand each of its important elements. Those include the input that feeds into the system, in terms of both its external and its internal environment. They encompass the strategies that translate a particular vision about how the organization will interact with its competitive environment into a series of concrete business decisions. They include the output—primarily, the offerings of products and services that the organization is required to produce to meet its strategic objectives. And of particular importance in terms of our model, they include the transformation process—the work and the business processes—that converts resources into offerings. Let's consider each in turn.

Input

The organization's input includes the elements that, at any point in time, make up the "givens" with which it has to work. There are three main categories of input, each of which affects the organization in different ways.

1. *The environment.* Every organization exists within, and is influenced by, a larger environment, which includes people, other organizations, social and economic forces, and legal constraints. More specifically, the environment includes markets (clients or customers), suppliers, governmental and regulatory bodies, technological and economic conditions, labor unions, competitors, financial institutions, and special-interest groups. The environment affects the way organizations operate in three ways.

First, the environment makes demands on the organization. For example, customer requirements and preferences play a large role in determining the quantity, price, and quality of the offerings—the products and/or services—the organization provides. Second, the environment often imposes constraints. These range from limitations imposed by scarce capital or insufficient technology to legal prohibitions rooted in government regulation, court action, or collective-bargaining agreements. Third, the environment provides opportunities, such as the potential for new markets that results from technological innovation, government deregulation, or the removal of trade barriers.

2. *Resources.* The second element of input is the organization's resources. This includes the full range of assets to which it has access—employees, technology, capital, and information. Resources may also include less tangible assets, such as the perception of the organization in the marketplace or a positive organizational climate.

3. *History.* There is considerable evidence that the way an organization functions today is greatly influenced by events in its past. It's impossible to understand fully an organization's capacity to act now or in the future without an appreciation of the developments that shaped it over time—the strategic decisions, behavior of key leaders, response to past crises, and evolution of values and beliefs.

Strategy

Environmental conditions, organizational resources, and history cannot be changed in the short run—these are "givens" that provide the setting within which the organization must operate. Each organization must first develop and articulate a vision of how it intends to compete and what kind of organization it wants to be, given the realities of the environment. From that vision flows the strategy, a set of business decisions about how to allocate scarce resources against the demands, constraints, and opportunities offered by the environment.

More specifically, strategy can be defined as explicit choices about markets, offerings, technology, and distinctive competence. Taking into consideration the threats and opportunities presented by the environment, the organization's strengths and weaknesses, and the pattern of performance suggested by the company's history, managers have to decide what products and services to offer to which markets and how to distinguish their organization from others in ways that will provide sustainable competitive advantage. Then these general, long-term strategic objectives must be refined into a set of internally consistent short-term objectives and supporting strategies.

For managers, these decisions about offerings, markets, and competitive advantage are crucial. Organizations that make the wrong strategic decisions will underperform or fail. No amount of organization design can prop up an ill-conceived strategy. By the same token, no strategy, no matter how dazzling it looks on paper, can succeed unless it's consistent with the structural and cultural capabilities of the organization. The manager's challenge, consequently, is to design and build an organization capable of accomplishing the strategic objectives.

In practice, strategy flows from a shared vision of the organization's future—a coherent idea of its size and architectural shape, its competitive strengths, its relative position of leadership in the market, and its operating culture. Beyond the general view of the future, however, strategy is closely linked to specific, measurable objectives. The guiding aspirations are molded into a strategic intent—a set of specific goals that must be reached if the organization is to fulfill its guiding vision.

Successful organizations embark on periods of major change by molding and articulating that vision and set of objectives, as demonstrated by Xerox's "Leadership Through Quality" program of the mid-1980s and "The Document Company" vision of the 1990s. At Ford, the vision was articulated as Ford 2000, a set of goals for market leadership and superior quality. At Corning, in the 1980s, the redesign work followed a guiding vision known as the Corning Wheel, an entirely new way of looking at the relationships involving the conglomerate's five major areas of activity. And at Sun Microsystems, a radical new architecture built around the notion of Sun and its "planets" was designed in the early 1990s; the idea, which proved immensely successful, was to leverage the competitive potential of the company's internal operations by reconfiguring its traditional internal divisions as a loosely linked network of semiautonomous businesses involving hardware, software, sales, service, and distribution—the "planets" revolving around a central coordinating unit—the "Sun."

In Chapter 7, we examine some of those redesigns in much more detail. For now, it's important to understand that strategic design, in its fullest sense, flows directly from a strategic intent that clearly articulates a vision or set of aspirations for the future course of the organization.

Output

In our organizational model, "output" is a broad term that describes what the organization produces, how it performs, and how effective it is. It refers to not only the organization's effectiveness at creating products and services or providing a certain level of economic return but also the performance of individuals and groups within the organization.

There are three criteria for evaluating performance at the organizational level. First, how successfully has the organization met the objectives specified by its strategy? Second, how well has the organization used its available resources to meet its objectives, and how successfully has it developed new resources rather than "burning up" existing ones? Third, how well does the organization reposition itself to seize new opportunities and ward off threats posed by the changing environment?

Of course, the performance of groups and individuals contributes directly to overall organizational performance. But in certain situations, changes in both individual and collective attitudes and capabilities such as satisfaction, stress, poor morale, or the acquisition of important experience can all be seen as output, or the results of the transformation process.

For the manager involved in organization design, the central issue is the identification of "performance gaps." That entails a comparison of the specific objectives articulated in the "strategic intent"—which we discuss later in this chapter in more detail—with actual output. The "gaps" help spotlight those activities where output is falling short of objectives and provide essential guidelines for figuring out where in the organization the redesign efforts need to be focused.

The Organization as a Transformation Process

The heart of the model is the transformation process, embodied in the organization, which draws upon the input implicit in the environment, resources, and history to produce a set of outputs. The organization contains four key components: the work, the people who perform the work, the formal arrangements that provide structure and direction to their work, and the informal arrangements—sometimes referred to as "culture"—that reflect their values, beliefs, and patterns of behavior (see Figure 2-3). For managers involved in organizational design, the issue is how to find the best way to configure those components to create the output necessary to meet the strategic objectives. To do this, it's essential to understand each of the components of the organization and its relationship to the others:

1. *The work.* We use this general term to describe the basic and inherent activity engaged in by the organization and its units in furtherance of the company's strategy. Since the performance of this work is one of the primary reasons for the organization's existence, any analysis from a design perspective has to start with an understanding of the nature of the tasks to be performed and the patterns of work flow, as well as an assessment of the more complex characteristics of the work—the knowledge or skills it demands, the rewards it offers, and the stress or uncertainty it involves.

2. *The people.* From the standpoint of organizational "fit," the key issue is identifying the important characteristics of the people responsible for the range of tasks involved in the core work. That means looking at the workforce in terms of skills, knowledge, experience, expectations, behavior patterns, and demographics.

3. *Formal organizational arrangements.* These are the explicit structures, processes, systems, and procedures developed to organize work and to guide the activity of individuals in their performance of activities consistent with the strategy.

4. *The informal organization.* Coexisting alongside the formal arrangements is a set of informal, unwritten guidelines that exert a powerful influence on the behavior of groups and individuals. Also referred to as organizational culture and operating environment, the informal organization encompasses a pattern of processes, practices, and political relationships that embodies the values, beliefs, and accepted behavioral norms of the individuals who work for the company. It's not unusual for informal arrangements actually to supplant formal structures and processes that have been in place so long that they've lost their relevance to the realities of the current work environment.

Figure 2-3 The Four Organizational Components

Component	Work	Individual	Formal Organizational Arrangements	Informal Organization
Definition	The basic and inherent work to be done by the organization and its parts	The characteristics of individuals in the organization	The various structures, processes, methods that are formally created to get individuals to perform tasks	The emerging arrangements including structures, processes, relationships
Critical Features of each Component	Degree of uncertainty associated with the work, including such factors as interdependence and routineness	Knowledge and skills individuals have	Grouping of functions, structure of units	Leader behavior
	Types of skill and knowledge demands the work poses	Individual needs and preferences	Coordination and control mechanisms	Norms, values
	Types of rewards the work inherently can provide	Perceptions and expectancies	Job design	Intragroup relations
	Constraints on performance demands inherent in the work (given a strategy)	Background factors	Work environment	Intergroup relations
		Demography	Human resource management systems	Informal working arrangements
			Reward systems	Communication and influence patterns
			Physical location	Key roles
				Climate
				Power, politics

The Concept of Congruence

Because our model, as we said earlier, is based on an "open-systems" approach, it focuses primarily on the relationships and interactions among the components within the organization and on the ways in which those relationships affect performance and output. At any given time, between each of the components of the organization, there is some level of congruence, which we define as the degree to which the needs, demands, goals, objectives, and/or structures of one component are consistent with those of the other.

In other words, congruence is a measure of how well pairs of components fit together. Consider where Xerox was in 1991. The company had determined that it wanted to provide a range of products and services that would meet its customers' complete needs for producing, processing, sharing, storing, and retrieving documents. But nothing in its organizational structure provided for the necessary focus on each element of the document process. Nor, as we mentioned earlier, had it developed a cadre of managers who were well suited by experience or temperament to take on beginning-to-end responsibility for cultivating new markets. The result was a dismally low degree of congruence between the different components of the organization; it lacked the formal structures, personal capabilities, operating environment, and work processes to get the job done. (For an overview of the critical elements of each congruence relationship, see Figure 2-4.)

The Congruence Hypothesis

Each organization as a whole displays a relatively high or low degree of overall congruence. The basic hypothesis of the model is this: Other things being equal, the greater the total degree of congruence, or fit, among the various components, the more effective the organization will be. Put another way, the degree to which the strategy, work, people, structure, and culture are smoothly aligned will determine the organization's ability to compete and succeed.

The basic dynamic of congruence sees the organization as most effective when its pieces fit together. If we also consider strategy, this view expands to include the fit between the organization and its larger environment; an organization is most effective when its strategy is consistent with its environment (in light of organizational resources and history) and when the organizational components fit the tasks necessary to implement that strategy. Again, think of

Figure 2-4 Definitions of Fits

Fit	The Issues
Individual—Organization	How are individual needs met by the organizational arrangements?
	Do individuals hold clear perceptions of organizational structures? Is there a convergence of individual and organizational goals?
Individual—Work	How are individual needs met by the work? Do individuals have skills and abilities to meet work demands?
Individual—Informal Organization	How are individual needs met by the informal organization? How does the informal organization make use of individual resources consistent with informal goals?
Work—Organization	Are organizational arrangements adequate to meet the demands of the work? Do organizational arrangements motivate behavior that is consistent with work demands?
Work—Informal Organization	Does the informal organization structure facilitate work performance? Does it help meet the demands of the work?
Organization—Informal Organization	Are the goals, rewards, and structures of the informal organization consistent with those of the formal organization?

Xerox. The "Document Company" strategy was totally appropriate to the changing competitive environment; the problem was that every aspect of the organization was out of sync with the strategy.

One important element of the congruence hypothesis is that diagnosing organizational problems requires describing the system, identifying problems, and determining the sources of poor fit. The model also implies that various components can be configured in different ways and still achieve some degree of desired output. Therefore, the question becomes one not necessarily of finding the "one best way of managing" but of determining the combinations of components that will lead to the greatest degree of congruence. Another way to think about congruence is to consider it in terms of architecture—in this case, the architecture of technology. It involves three elements:

- *The hardware*—the computers, monitors, keyboards, modems, disk drives, servers, cables, printers, scanners, and other physical pieces of equipment that make up a computer system
- *The software*—the encoded sets of instructions that allow the hardware components to function, both individually and collectively, as a system or network
- *The human interface*—the people who actually select and use the software that makes the hardware perform its assigned functions

Clearly, the effectiveness of each component is dependent on how well it meshes with the rest of the system. Neither hardware nor software is of any use whatsoever in the absence of the other. Some hardware and software are simply incompatible; together, they're as good as useless. Beyond that, there are all kinds of software that will run on all kinds of hardware—but some combinations work much more smoothly than others. And even if you've found the optimal combination of hardware and software, it won't do any good unless the people using it understand how to use the software and the equipment. They've got to have a clear idea of the work they're supposed to perform, and they must be motivated to do it in a swift and conscientious way.

The parallels with organizational architecture are clear. In many organizations, the term "hardware" has become synonymous with the technical/structural axis of the model—the work and the formal structural arrangements. "Software" is analogous to the informal operating environment; like software, you can't actually see or feel or touch it, but you can easily see its powerful impact on the way both the machine and the organization operate. In both cases, it is the skills, motivation, and guiding values and beliefs of the individuals involved that determine how productively the work gets done. In both forms of architecture—technological and organizational—it is the proper fit among all the components that determines the effectiveness of performance.

While the congruence model and the concept of architecture provide a general framework, organization designers will need other, more specific models to help define high and low congruence, particularly in the relationship between the formal organizational arrangements and the other components. In Chapter 4, we describe a model that focuses specifically on those crucial relationships.

In summary, then, what we have just described is a general model for understanding organizations (see Figure 2-5). It embodies a view of the organization as a system and, in particular, as a process that transforms input into output; that process, in turn, is driven by the relationships among the four basic components. The critical dynamic is the fit or congruence among the components. Now let's see how this model can be used to analyze organizational problems.

Analyzing the Organization's Problems

Organizations constantly face changing conditions. Consequently, effective managers must continually identify and solve new problems. This entails gathering data on performance, matching actual performance against goals, identifying the causes of problems, selecting and developing action plans, and, finally, implementing and then evaluating the effectiveness of those plans. Any organization's long-term success requires ongoing problem-solving activities along these lines.

Our experience has led us to develop a general approach to using the congruence model for solving organizational problems that includes the following steps:

1. *Identify symptoms.* In any situation, initial information may reveal symptoms of poor performance without pinpointing real problems and their causes. Still, this information is important because it focuses the search for more complete data.
2. *Specify input.* With the symptoms in mind, the next step is to collect data concerning the organization's environment, its resources, and critical aspects of its history. Input analysis also involves identifying the organization's overall strategy—its core mission, supporting strategies, and objectives.
3. *Identify output.* The third step is to analyze the organization's output at the individual, group, and organizational levels. Output analysis involves defining precisely what output is required at each level to meet the overall strategic objectives and then collecting data to measure precisely what output is actually being achieved.
4. *Identify problems.* The next step is to pinpoint specific gaps between planned and actual output and to identify the associated problems—organizational performance, group functioning, or individual behavior, for example. Where information is available, it's often useful to identify the costs associated with the problems or with the failure to fix them. The costs might be in

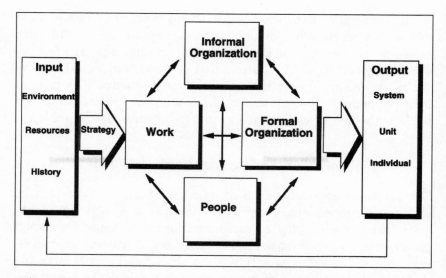

Figure 2-5 A Congruence Model for Diagnosing Organizational Behavior

the form of actual costs, such as increased expenses, or of missed opportunities, such as lost revenue.

5. *Describe organizational components.* This is where analysis goes beyond merely identifying problems and starts to focus on causes. It begins with the collection of data on each of the four major components of the organization. A word of caution: Not all problems have internal causes. Some result from external developments—a shift in the regulatory environment, a new competitor, a major technological breakthrough—that make existing strategies insufficient or obsolete. It's important to consider strategic issues before focusing too narrowly on organizational causes for problems; otherwise, the organization is in danger of merely doing the wrong thing more efficiently.

6. *Assess congruence (fit).* Using the data collected in step 5, the next step is to assess the degree of congruence among the various components.

7. *Generate hypotheses about problem causes.* The next step is to look for correlations between poor congruence and problems that are affecting output. Once these problem areas have been identified, available data are used to test whether poor fit is, indeed, a key factor influencing output and a potential leverage point for forging improvement.

8. *Identify action steps.* The final stage is to identify action steps, which might range from specific changes aimed at relatively obvious problems to more extensive data collection. In addition,

this step requires predicting the consequence of various actions, choosing a course of action, implementing it, and evaluating its impact.

Xerox Revisited

Faced with the awesome task of redesigning the basic architecture of Xerox, Paul Allaire began by appointing a team of managers from throughout the corporation to explore alternative design models used by other organizations and then present him with four recommendations for redesigning Xerox. After the "Future-techture" group completed its assignment, Allaire and his senior team refined the basic model—a sweeping redesign of the core business which we examine in greater detail in Chapter 7.

In essence, Xerox stood the organization on its side; instead of organizing around the traditional functions of product development, production, sales, and service, it created a set of nine independent business units, each offering various products and services aimed at specific segments of the market. The focus was shifted radically from internal operations to customer needs.

After deciding on an overall design, Allaire appointed a second team, the Organization Transition Board (OTB), made up of executives two and three levels below the corporate office, to flesh out the operational plan and to formulate the tactics for implementing it.

At the same time, the OTB devoted considerable time and energy to formulating a list of key dimensions required of managers in the new Xerox. These characteristics—some of them markedly different from the styles and traits exhibited by Xerox managers in the past—then became the guideline for assessing and assigning managers to top positions in the new organization.

The Xerox redesign process succeeded in large part because the executives guiding it were thoroughly conscious of the need to make changes—and consistent changes—in every aspect of the organization. They not only restructured the formal structures and processes—the work and formal arrangements, in terms of our model—but also paid close attention to defining the skills, characteristics, and management styles essential for the managers who would be responsible for building a new operating environment.

The Xerox experience illustrates the relationship of the congruence model to the task of redesign. Management's first job, in most instances, is to develop strategies in the context of the organization's history, resources, environment, and internal capacities. The second step is to implement those strategies through the creation, shaping, and maintaining of an organization. This means constantly defining the key tasks to be performed, making sure that individuals are motivated and capable of performing those tasks, and developing formal and informal organizational arrangements consistent with the strategy, work requirements, culture, and people.

Fundamentally, organization design involves configuring the formal organization to support the implementation of strategy. But just as important, it means designing the proper fit among the formal organization, the work, the people, and the informal operating environment. As we see in Chapter 3, redesigns that seem to make perfect sense on paper frequently crash and burn when subjected to the human dynamics that play such a powerful role in every organization.

Bibliography

There has been substantial writing and research on organizations as social and technical systems, and the concept of fit. See, for example:

Brown, S., and K. Eisenhardt. "Product Development: Past Research, Present Findings and Future Directions." *Academy of Management Journal* 20 (1995): 343–378.

Collins, J., and J. Porras. *Built to Last.* New York: Harper Business, 1995.

Davis, S., and P. Lawrence. *Matrix.* Reading, Mass.: Addison-Wesley, 1977.

Galbraith, J. *Organization Design.* Reading, Mass.: Addison-Wesley, 1977.

Gresov, C. "Exploring Fit and Misfit with Multiple Contingencies." *Administrative Science Quarterly* 343 (1989): 431–453.

Hanna, D. *Designing Organizations for High Performance.* Reading, Mass.: Addison-Wesley, 1988.

Homans, G. *The Human Group.* New York: Harcourt, 1950.

Katz, D., and R. Kahn. *Social Psychology of Organizations.* New York: Wiley, 1966.

Leavitt, H. "Applied Organization Change in Industry." In J. March, *Handbook of Organizations.* Chicago: Rand McNally, 1965.

Lorsch, J., and A. Sheldon. "The Individual in the Organization: A Systems View." In J. Lorsch and P. Lawrence, *Managing Group and Intergroup Relations.* Homewood, Ill.: Irwin, 1972.

March, J., and H. Simon. *Organizations.* New York: Wiley, 1959.

Miles, R., and C. Snow. *Fit, Failure and the Hall of Fame.* New York: Free Press, 1994.

Miller, D. "Configurations of Strategy and Structure." *Strategic Management Journal* 7 (1986): 233–249.

Nadler, D., Gerstein, M., and R. Shaw. *Organization Architecture.* San Francisco: Jossey-Bass, 1992.

Peter, T., and R. Waterman. *In Search of Excellence.* New York: Harper, 1982.

Pfeffer, J. *Competitive Advantage Through People.* Boston, Mass.: Harvard Business School Press, 1994.

Tichy, N. *Managing Strategic Change.* New York: Wiley, 1983.

Van de Ven, A., and R. Drazin. "The Concept of Fit in Contingency Theory." In B. Staw and L. Cummings, eds., *Research in Organization Behavior,* vol. 4. Greenwich, Conn.: JAI Press, 1985.

Weick, K. *Social Psychology of Organizing.* Reading, Mass.: Addison-Wesley, 1969.

3

The Principles of Design

Technicon: Trouble in the Laboratory

In many ways, Technicon was a classic entrepreneurial success story. Launched in a Bronx loft soon after World War II, the company designed, manufactured, and marketed diagnostic equipment for clinical and industrial laboratories. In the late 1960s, Technicon developed and successfully marketed a breakthrough process for analyzing blood samples, human tissue, and industrial chemicals. Sales soared, and the company mushroomed.

But growth brought problems, particularly to the Technical Division, which housed the research and development activities so crucial to the company. Technicon had built its reputation by staying on the leading edge of technological innovation. The division was headed by John Whitehead, grandson of the company's founder and son of the CEO. "We have a bad case of technical constipation," Whitehead told the consultants he'd invited to Technicon's Tarrytown, New York, headquarters. "This division has not brought out a successful new product in two years. Given our competition, if we don't do something about this problem soon, the whole company is going to be in big trouble."

Whitehead described a widespread morale problem; in particular, some of his key research scientists were so demoralized that they were jumping ship to go to work for competitors. Innovation was drying up; the cycle time for new product development had slowed to a crawl. To make matters worse, Technicon, which for years had enjoyed a virtual monopoly in its major diagnostic product lines, suddenly faced growing competition from major players such as DuPont.

In the course of their diagnostic work, the consultants found that the Technical Division consisted of seven departments, with sharp delineation based on disciplines—basic research scientists, engineers, chemists, and so forth (see Figure 3-1). Each project under development was the responsibility of a project director, who was supposed to bring together people from various departments and disciplines as needed.

But in an operation where cooperation was the key to success, the consultants found pervasive mistrust and antagonism among the various disciplines. The lack of teamwork so evident within the lab extended to the division's dealings with the rest of the company, including manufacturing and marketing. Scientists felt little incentive to throw themselves into product development; for one thing, their financial incentives were based on winning new patents and professional recognition, rather than on developing marketable products and processes. Moreover, there was a demoralizing pattern of senior management abruptly halting projects in mid-stream and importing new technology from the outside, both of which left researchers feeling less than excited about starting new projects. And project directors, operating at the mercy of the lab department heads, were often powerless to marshal the resources they needed.

Faced with this array of daunting problems, Whitehead hired a new department head to act effectively as his second in command. Together, they brainstormed the problems and possible solutions. Finally, they called together everyone in the department, and announced a major restructuring—fewer department heads, more power for project managers, and a revised incentive system that would emphasize product integrity rather than technical excellence.

Introduction

The temptation to solve major problems by shutting yourself up in a room and drawing a new organizational chart can be powerfully seductive. It's neat, it's clean, and you don't have to spend time arguing and debating with people who don't understand "the big picture" the way you do. You just draw the new chart, explain to everyone how things are going to change, and send them to their new desks.

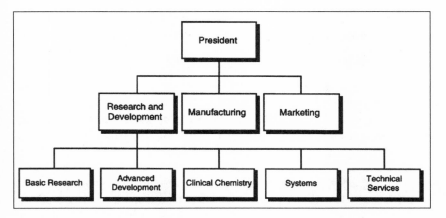

Figure 3-1 Technicon (Pre-Restructure)

John Whitehead certainly thought he could solve the Technicon research lab's problems that way. But it didn't work for Whitehead, and it won't work for other managers, either. The substance and the process of design are too complex and their ramifications too critical—as Whitehead was to learn—to be handled in such an arbitrary manner. (A historical note: In the years following the restructuring, Technicon changed hands several times and operates today as Bayer Diagnostics.)

In this chapter, we continue our exploration of the key concepts of design by building upon the conceptual model we presented in Chapter 2 and looking at some of the difficult design decisions managers have to make. We focus on the role of design within the context of the general organizational model, define the basic elements of design, and deal with the issue of when different forms of design are most appropriate.

Design and the Congruence Model

Assuming there's already an articulated vision and strategy in place, what are the first issues that will confront the manager responsible for implementing that strategy? In general, the manager should be posing some preliminary questions.

1. What changes will the new strategy require in the organization's core work? How will tasks be modified? Will there be new constraints, resources, processes, or technologies involved?

2. Do the organization's people have the skills, interest, characteristics, and capacity to perform the required work in a manner consistent with the strategy?

3. How will the new work requirements be affected by the explicit structures and processes that make up the formal organizational arrangements?

4. Are the values, beliefs, behavior patterns, and leadership styles associated with the culture, or informal organization, likely to aid or to hinder the performance of the new work?

In practice, once the work requirements are defined, managers tend to gravitate toward the formal organizational arrangements as the most obvious tool for implementing change. Why? First, structural arrangements are substantially easier to modify than either individual or collective human behavior. Except in new organizations, a manager usually inherits a group of people. There are limits to how extensively and quickly their attitudes, values, skills, and capacities can be changed. Similarly, there are limits on the extent to which people can be replaced or reassigned. Recruiting new people is time-consuming—and risky. Moreover, filling major positions from the outside undermines the psychological contracts, or implicit understandings, that people have about their career advancement and job security. Even in the best of situations, significant changes in the composition of organizational groups takes a substantial amount of time.

Fundamental changes in the informal organization are even more complex and time-consuming. An organizational culture takes years to develop; the more fully developed the culture, the more resistant to change it becomes, as the people it attracts and nurtures construct a tight web of shared values and beliefs. As we see in chapters 10 and 11, changing culture is much more easily said than done.

The second reason that managers are drawn to formal organizational arrangements as a tool for change is that modifications in structures and processes can directly alter patterns of activity, behavior, and performance. Indeed, the formal organizational arrangements can profoundly influence the other components, both directly and indirectly. For example, formal job definitions, hiring processes, and training programs can, over time, significantly shape people's capacity to perform various tasks. The organizational structure, the composition of key advisory groups, and the design of the measurement and rewards system can greatly influence how people perceive and perform their jobs.

The organizational arrangements affect people's performance in three primary ways:

1. Organizational arrangements can *motivate behavior.* Through the definition of jobs, the creation of goals, the development of measures, and the use of reward systems, people can be directed and energized to behave in certain ways.

2. Organizational arrangements can *facilitate behavior.* Once someone is motivated to behave in a certain way, the arrangements can help him or her do so. By providing methods and procedures, by placing the person in proximity to others with whom the person needs to communicate, and by providing necessary information, the formal organization can help people perform tasks.

3. Organizational arrangements can *constrain behavior.* By limiting information, by instituting formal procedures, and by separating certain groups or units from each other, the formal organization can limit what people can do and prevent them from spending time and energy on important activities.

Taken together, motivation, facilitation and constraint offer powerful tools for influencing individual behavior. When combined in a thoughtful, systematic way with the impact the formal arrangements can have on informal culture, the opportunities for change are immense.

Defining the Basic Terms

Before moving on to a more detailed discussion of design, let's clarify some of the basic terms.

In the context of our congruence model, the term "formal organizational arrangements" includes the explicit and relatively stable aspects of the organization, which fall into three broad categories. The first category involves *structures*, the formal patterns of relationships between groups and individuals. Grouping all of the sales people into a single department is a structure, for example, as is the reporting relationship of each sales manager to a vice president for sales.

The second category involves *processes*, a specifically defined sequence of steps, activities or operational methods. Manufacturing, for example, can be a process or series of processes; order fulfillment is a business process involving a set sequence of activities involving warehousing, distribution, order taking, billing, and delivery.

The third category consists of the formal structures known as *systems*, applications of either physical or social technologies that enable the performance of work. Human Resources systems, for example, involve specific sets of policies and practices that directly influence how work gets done and by whom. Information systems incorporate various forms of technology to process and channel various forms of information to the appropriate people and work units.

The congruence model highlights the fact that in any organization, there are both formal and informal structures and processes. As we have mentioned, however, the formal structures, processes, and systems are much more amenable to direct manipulation.

In this context, our definition of design is as follows: *Organization design involves decisions about the configuration of the formal organizational arrangements, including the formal structures, processes, and systems that make up an organization.* The goal of the organization designer is to develop and implement a set of formal organizational arrangements that will, over time, lead to congruence, or good fit, among all the components of the organization: strategy, work, people, the informal organization, and the formal organizational arrangements.

While the concepts of structure, process, and systems are useful for definition, they are not particularly helpful in making actual design decisions. In concrete terms, what do they involve? It is hard to develop an all-inclusive list of every possible element, but Figure 3-2 lists the types of design features (both structures and processes) around which managers frequently make decisions.

When we talk about organization design, then, we are talking about managers' decisions about the nature, shape, content, and features of the design elements included in Figure 3-2. To some extent, managers are making design decisions all the time. Every time a specific job is assigned, a procedure created, a method altered, or a job moved, the organization design is being changed. There's nothing necessarily wrong with that; in fact, constant fine-tuning is part of any manager's job. Think of the manager as the skipper of a boat, and envision the sails, rigging, and rudder as the components of a design process, tools for guiding the boat's course and speed. Those navigational tools allow the captain and the manager alike to make both minor adjustments or dramatic changes in course. There are times, of course, when major course changes are imperative. Just as a change in wind and currents or the presence of another boat may require a significant change in how the sailboat is configured, there frequently are times when the manager must make major changes in the formal organization and must devote significant attention to making design decisions.

Figure 3-2 What is Included in Organization Design?

1. Composition of organizational units	*Strategic*
2. Reporting relationships among units	*Organization*
3. Other structural connections between units	*Design*
4. Organization-wide information, measurement, and control systems	
5. Organization-wide methods and procedures	
6. Organization-wide work technologies	
7. Subunit work resources (tools, materials)	*Operational*
8. Subunit reward systems	*Design*
9. Subunit physical work environment	
10. Individual job design	

When to Redesign?

The congruence model offers a clear way of understanding when a significant redesign is called for. Simply put, when the organization evolves to the point at which there are substantial congruence problems between the formal organizational arrangements and the other components, then it's time to seriously consider a major redesign. It's even more advantageous, when possible, to use the model to anticipate the need for redesign by analyzing the probable impact any impending change might have on organizational congruence. There are several situations that typically justify a major redesign:

- *Strategic shifts.* Strategic changes may occur as a result of environmental factors (such as competition, regulation, or new technology), changes in resources, or problems of organizational performance. Such changes may involve a redefinition of the business, the markets, the product-service offerings, or the competitive basis of the organization. These shifts require individuals in the organization to redirect their efforts and to apply resources differently. As a consequence, design changes may be appropriate to ensure that the work is consistent with the new strategy.

  Consider the BOC Industrial Gases case we introduced in Chapter 1. The development of global markets made BOC's traditional hyper-local focus an anachronism, a structural holdover from the days when customers' needs could be met exclusively by a local supplier. Add to that the impact of information technology, which made innovations available to competitors almost immediately, regardless of where they operated. The result was a strategic shift that necessitated a new structure unfettered by geographic boundaries.

- *Redefinition of work.* Redesign may be required to meet changes in the organization's core work. Sometimes that's the result of an altered strategy. In other situations, the work is altered by new technologies or shifts in the cost, quality, or availability of resources. A common example is the introduction of new technology in office systems. Digitized information changes not only the way people perform individual tasks but the information-processing relationships; the configuration of computer networks, for example, plays a major role in either erecting or erasing boundaries between individuals and groups. The elimination of time and geography as barriers to shared work plays a major role in determining organizations' structures and processes.

- *Cultural/political change.* Some redesigns are implemented for the express purpose of reshaping the informal organization. As we said earlier, changing the formal organization is sometimes the most effective way to influence the informal operating environment.

  In the 1980s, after pouring billions of dollars into the most advanced technology money could buy, U.S. automakers finally figured out that the success of their Japanese competitors had more to do with their workers' sense of responsibility and commitment to quality than with expensive robotic spray painters and delivery carts. But in order to change the factory culture, the automakers decided, they had to start by changing the factory. So they began designing new plants and redesigning old ones with the specific intent of creating a new environment characterized by high levels of employee involvement, participation in problem solving, teamwork, and commitment to high-quality products. Rarely were any of these plants designed without substantial changes in the typical formal manufacturing structures; these projects nearly always included features such as flattened hierarchies, wider spans of control and new structures to formalize employee involvement.

- *Growth.* One of the events that commonly leads to redesign is an organization's growth in size or scope. When organizations are relatively small, when most people know each other, and when the relationships are face to face and personal, many of the mechanisms for motivating, facilitating, and constraining behavior can be informal. There is no need to invest time, effort, and energy in the creation of formal arrangements. As an organization (or a part of an organization) grows, however, these informal arrangements may get overloaded or overburdened. As new tasks and strategies are taken on (a natural part of growth), the formal arrangements may no longer be congruent with the rest of the organization.

- *Staffing changes.* Since effective organizational arrangements are designed with individuals in mind, changes in the staff—either wholesale changes throughout the organization or a small number of changes in key positions—require a rethinking of the organization design. The most graphic examples of this occur through the natural processes of management succession. As a new manager and a new set of players come to lead an organization, the arrangements that used to fit the needs, skills, talents, and capacities of the previous team may no longer make sense. Similarly, major changes within the work force—changes in needs, preferences, skill levels, education, and values—may also call for substantial redesign.

- *Ineffective organization design.* The cases mentioned so far are largely situations encountered in the normal growth, evolution, and maturation of an organization. Sometimes, however, redesign is necessary because of performance problems created by the gradual emergence of poor organizational fit. These symptoms frequently indicate problems related to organization design:

- **Lack of coordination**—Cross-unit projects don't get finished, work units are unclear about their responsibilities, some groups seem to be isolated and out of step with the rest of the organization.
- **Excessive conflict**—Relationships among internal groups are characterized by needless friction.
- **Unclear roles**—Individuals or groups are uncertain about what is expected of them, or where their jobs end and others' begin. Functions may overlap, or work may fall "into the cracks" between units. When roles are unclear, decision making may be tedious, prolonged, and inefficient.
- **Misused resources**—Resources don't get to the people who need them. Specialized unit functions or individual skills may not be fully utilized.
- **Poor work flow**—Disruptions and cumbersome processes inhibit the effective flow of work throughout the organization.
- **Reduced responsiveness**—The organization cannot respond quickly or appropriately to changes in the environment, to new market needs, or to product characteristics.
- **Proliferation of extraorganizational units**—The organization comes to rely excessively on task forces, committees, and special project groups to deal with every significant new challenge. This may indicate that the basic design is inadequate or, at the very least, is widely perceived as inadequate.

Although these symptoms may reflect a number of problems stemming from different causes, they frequently indicate underlying problems in the organization's design, suggesting the necessity to at least consider a redesign. If the signs seem to be pointing in that direction, it becomes important to collect relevant data in order to verify the true cause. As we see in Chapter 9, in the redesign at Kaiser Permanente's Northern California region, extensive time was spent on determining how the organization was failing to meeting its strategic objectives and which aspects of the design were getting in the way of success.

Types of Design Decisions

Once the organization has decided that redesign is in order, it's important for everyone involved in the decision-making process to keep in mind the various types of design decisions that must be made at different times, by different people, and with different criteria. Typically, managers tend to focus on a few of the boxes and lines at the top of the organization and then treat the rest of the operation as an afterthought.

In practice, there are two basic approaches to making design decisions. The first type, *top-down*, deals almost exclusively with the organization's top levels, focusing primarily on their composition and reporting relationships. Regardless of how well or how systematically these decisions are made, these projects are insufficient because they ignore so much of the organization. While there may be changes or new directions at the top, the rest of the organization is doing the old work with the old structures and processes. The results are all too common: never-ending waves of top-level restructuring that have only minor impact outside the executive offices.

A second approach is to start with the work being performed at the most basic level at which the organization manufactures its product or performs its service and do the redesign working *bottom-up*. This approach is advocated by many job design theorists and has been used extensively by internal staff groups within organizations. The work is identified, jobs are built around the work, work flows are constructed, and supervisory and support jobs are created to facilitate the work flow. These are then collected into work units and groups. The process is repeated as the design proceeds up through the organization.

The bottom-up approach typically runs into several problems. First, there is an inevitable mismatch at the point where the bottom-up design meets the top levels of the organization, where a different design process has been at work. When the two clash, the top-down

Figure 3-3 Strategic and Operational Design

	Strategic	Operational
What type of decision?	Basic architecture/ shape of the organization	Management and operational processes, work flows, jobs, measures
What part of the organization?	Top 2–4 levels	All levels as necessary
Direction?	Top-down	Bottom-up
Driven by?	Strategy	Operational concerns (cost/quality/time)

perspective usually wins. As a result, some technically excellent designs either never get implemented or are planted in hostile ground where they never have the chance to develop. Moreover, because they lack strategic perspective, bottom-up designs run the risk of simply making people more effective at performing the wrong work.

Our experience strongly suggests that neither of these approaches, taken alone, is sufficient. Organization design needs to be done both ways—designing top-down to implement the strategy and then, within the context of that design, designing from the bottom up to improve basic work processes and create meaningful and motivating jobs for individuals.

One way of thinking about this is to identify two basic types of design decisions to be made with different criteria, by different people, and at different points in time (see Figure 3-3). *Strategic organization design* is driven by strategy and provides the basic architecture that will dictate how the organization goes about pursuing its strategic objectives. Within that overall framework, the detailed *operational design* of jobs, work units, and operational processes are shaped by concerns such as cost, quality, time to market, and employee involvement. In that sense, operational design can also be thought of as *microlevel design*, which we examine in much greater detail in Chapter 8. Briefly, however, there are three basic approaches to microlevel design. The first is the traditional approach of scientific management: breaking tasks down to their smallest components, defining jobs as narrowly as possibly, then exerting tight structural and managerial control. The second approach is process design, popularized in recent years under the label "process reengineering." Its emphasis is on the design of work processes—sequences of related

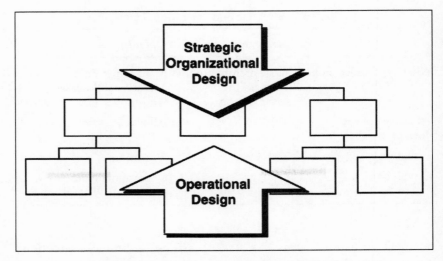

Figure 3-4 Top-Down and Bottom-Up Design

activities that, together, create a product or service of value to the customer, rather than on traditional configurations of work and jobs. The third approach, known as High-Performance Work Systems (HPWS), represents the convergence of new thinking on process design, along with new perspectives on the enormous potential of self-managed teams whose members share a broad range of responsibilities. In Chapter 8, we take a close look at how this form of microlevel design actually works in one of Corning's most efficient and most profitable manufacturing plants.

The important point here is that organization design should always be pursued at several levels within the organization (see Figure 3-4). Strategic design works from the top down, establishing an architectural frame for the organization as a whole. Operational design works from the bottom up, fleshing out the essential details for each subunit within the organization. Ideally, operational design should flow from, and be consistent with, the overall strategic design.

Technicon Revisited

Let's go back to the situation at the Technicon research and development lab. John Whitehead and his new deputy have just announced a restructuring that involves reducing the number of department heads, strengthening the roles of project managers, and revising incentives to reward more directly the development of marketable products (see Figure 3-5).

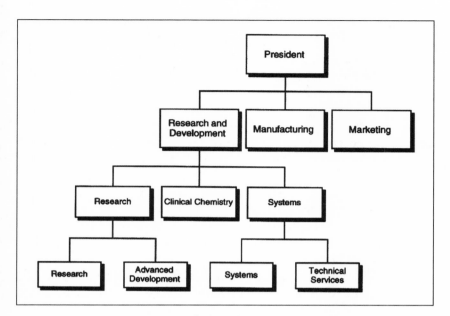

Figure 3-5 Technicon (Post-Restructure)

What was the outcome? Disaster.

The powerful department heads, having been totally excluded from the redesign process, were enraged and found all sorts of ways to render it ineffective. Throughout the lab, people were expected to become more cooperative and teamwork-oriented, without any work being done to change the atmosphere or teach essential skills in conflict resolution or teamwork. Relationships between the lab and the rest of the company, and within the lab itself, continued to deteriorate. The lab's performance, already poor, got even worse. Within nine months, the new number two had become so frustrated with continuing resistance to the change that he left the company. Not long thereafter, the company was sold.

What went wrong? On the surface, lab chief John Whitehead seemed to be making the right structural moves at the top of the division. But in retrospect, he acknowledged that he'd stumbled badly in two respects. First, his redesign addressed only two components of his organization: the work and the formal arrangements. He completely ignored the informal, cultural issues of politics, power relationships, the traditional role of department heads, and the professional relationships among various disciplines. And he'd expected people to start acting in entirely new ways without helping them gain new skills or adopt new attitudes. Second, spurred by an understandable sense of urgency, he had made the classic mistake of creating a redesign behind closed doors without the participation of the key people who would be responsible for making it work. Consequently, they responded in classic fashion; feeling powerless and disenfranchised, they fought back with passive-aggressive behavior, scuttling the redesign by refusing to make it work.

In this chapter, we've tried to provide some basic perspectives, concepts, and definitions related to organization design. We have linked design to our general model of organizational performance and discussed what is included in the definition of organizational design. We have identified those situations in which significant redesign may be necessary and, in particular, the symptoms that may indicate design problems. Finally, we have provided a way of thinking about the two general types of design decisions—strategic organizational design and operational organization design.

That distinction brings us to a fork in the road—and in this book, our primary focus now becomes strategic design. By no means do we mean to imply that operational design is not important; indeed, it is a critical aspect of design. And as we proceed with our discussion of strategic design, we will frequently refer to related operational design issues and explore how to link the two.

Nevertheless, we now sharpen our focus on how to make effective strategic design decisions. One common method, of course, is trial and error. In practice, managers try different designs by implementing them and seeing how they work. This is a costly, risky, and ultimately unnecessary approach. We know enough about organizations and design to work through some of the options and eliminate designs that clearly will be unsuitable or only marginally effective. We can even judge designs and compare their impact before committing to their implementation.

To do this, we need some tools, which we provide in the next three chapters. In Chapter 4, we discuss a more specific model for thinking about design decisions. In Chapters 5 and 6, we examine some of the key decisions in strategic organizational design and discuss some of the options available to managers.

Bibliography

When to engage in organization design efforts and the distinction between strategic and operational design have been discussed by several authors, including the following:

Bartlett, C., and S. Ghoshal. *Managing Across Borders.* Boston, Mass.: Harvard Business School Press, 1991.

Beer, M., R. Eisenhardt, and B. Spector. *The Critical Path to Corporate Renewal.* Boston, Mass.: Harvard Business School Press, 1980.

Gyllenhammer, P. *Dignity at Work.* Stockholm: Streiffert, 1985.

Hanlon, M., D. Nadler, and D. Gladstein. *Attempting Work Reform.* New York: Wiley, 1985.

Lawler, E. *Pay and Organization Development.* Reading, Mass.: Addison-Wesley, 1981.

Lucas, H. *The T-Form Organization.* San Francisco: Jossey-Bass, 1996.

O'Toole, J. *Work in America.* Cambridge, Mass.: MIT Press, 1973.

Quinn, J. B. *Intelligent Enterprise.* New York: Free Press, 1992.

4

The Crucial Design Issues

HTP—When the Pieces Don't Fit

A company we'll call High Technology Products, Inc. (HTP), had long been a leader in the field of electronic products.* It built its leadership on product innovation. Through smart investments in research and technology, it became known as the innovator in its field, and HTP products had long been regarded as the industry standard. For years, in fact, HTP developed and maintained such a significant lead in basic technology (protected by patents in some cases) that it was able to sell new products simply on the basis of one-page product announcements. Customers would willingly wait months and pay a premium for an HTP product because it was uniquely state of the art.

As the company diversified, the Advanced Products Group (see Figure 4-1), headed by Executive Vice President Sam Tucker, remained at the heart of the business. Reporting to him were five vice presidents, each heading a major division:

- Research—responsible for basic research in electronics and other disciplines relevant to the HTP product line.
- Product Development and Engineering—developed the Research

*At the request of company officials, we have agreed not to use the actual name of HTP, which has since become part of another corporation.

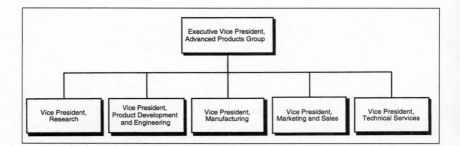

Figure 4-1 High Technology Products Inc. (HTP) Organization Chart

  Division's work, when possible, into products, applications, and new features ready for manufacturing.
- Manufacturing—responsible for production, including preproduction, engineering, purchasing, and distribution.
- Marketing and Sales—responsible for selling HTP products, primarily through a small but technically well-versed direct sales force.
- Technical Service—responsible for installation, maintenance, and some limited customer support in the field.

  Over a five-year period, and particularly in the last two, HTP had encountered difficult times. With the maturation of some of its product lines, HTP lost much of its competitive edge. New competition entered the scene, including some particularly tough foreign competitors. In some product areas, where the pace of change had been particularly fast, HTP found itself in the unusual and unpleasant position of just being one of the pack—or even lagging behind it—instead of being the leader.

  Faced with new choices that encouraged higher expectations, customers had become more demanding. They wanted more product support, they were impatient about slow deliveries, and they were less willing to pay a premium for HTP equipment when the competition was providing comparable products at much lower prices. In addition, customers' complaints about poor quality were mounting. Overall, customers were getting more explicit about their needs and more insistent about their expectations. As a result, HTP was forced to develop special features, configurations, and packages to meet specific customer requirements—a radical departure from the days when HTP customers were willing to accept whatever the company offered and then wait months for it to arrive.

  Sam Tucker had grown increasingly alarmed about the array of problems facing his group. Being relatively new in his job, he spent several months getting to know the market and taking a look at internal operations. The results of his analysis were frightening.

The group had experienced major problems in developing the product and getting it out the door. Foul-ups had become common; most recently, a new product had been introduced with much fanfare, despite the fact that Manufacturing was half a year away from turning out the new product in volume.

Sam had also become aware of the intense conflicts brewing between the divisions. Marketing and Sales personnel were constantly complaining about the lack of good products and about Product Development and Engineering's refusal to talk with them about competition, customer needs, or problems with scheduling and distribution. Manufacturing complained that Marketing and Sales had unrealistic expectations. Product Development people argued that if they listened to Marketing and Sales and copied every low-budget innovation introduced by competitors, they would continue to fritter away HTP's technological lead and reputation. Meanwhile, the Technical Services Division complained about the increasing number of machine failures in the field. Finally, Tucker had just been out to the Research Division headquarters to hear a presentation on the increasing turnover rate among technical personnel and scientists, who seemed to be frustrated by how few of their ideas were being translated into products.

After thinking about the events inside the company during the past year, Tucker was amazed to learn that things were much worse in the marketplace. He was beginning to think that maybe it was time to restructure the organization, to redesign it from the ground up. He felt that the basic pieces were still in place—the technology was good, the people were excellent, the name was still valuable, and the product strategy was fundamentally sound. The basic pieces were right, but, for some reason, they just weren't fitting together.

Introduction

Sam Tucker was coming to the realization that he might be facing some critical problems involving organization design. While he seemed to have skilled people and the basic elements of an effective strategy, something had gone seriously wrong, and the symptoms were pointing toward design. A pattern of arrangements that had once fit together smoothly had somehow slipped out of sync.

Sam's primary task was to figure out which element—or elements—no longer fit as well as in the past. To do that, he had to go beyond the general concepts of congruence and organizational systems; he needed tools to help him weigh the relative effectiveness of various designs in performing different kinds of work. He needed help both in diagnosing the shortcomings of his current organization and in developing a new design that would address his problems.

In this chapter, we describe a systematic approach to understanding the kinds of organization design decisions faced by Sam Tucker and thousands of other executives and managers. First, we provide some background on various approaches to design decisions, and then we introduce the specific model that we apply throughout the rest of the book.

Approaches to Design Decision Making

For centuries, leaders of all kinds of organizations have sought models to guide their decisions about the best way to structure their armies, churches, governments, mercantile groups, or what-have-you. But it has only been within the past century or so that significant attempts have been made to work out some generalized rules for designing organizations.

In the late nineteenth and early twentieth centuries, most writers on organization management were searching for a set of universal design principles. They were looking for the "one best way" to structure an organization. They developed models composed of sets of rules, such as the notion that the ideal span of control is six subordinates. The general bias was that organizations would work better when there were highly formalized and rational procedures, rules, and methods. Jobs should be kept simple so that workers could be interchangeable; decisions would be made at the top of the organization, while people at the bottom automatically carried out those decisions.

These principles-of-management writers focused on the formal aspects of organizations, and their underlying model was the machine. If the right working parts could be designed and produced to specification, then the machine would work. In terms of our congruence perspective, these writers focused almost singlemindedly on the fit between work and formal arrangements; they were hoping to identify universally applicable formulas for designing organizations that would fit any task.

From the late 1940s through the 1960s, a second approach became popular. This perspective properly criticized the classical management theorists for failing to consider what we would call the individual and cultural elements of organizational life. These theorists advocated creating organizations that were much less formal and in which decision making was widely shared, communication and information flowed freely, and people at the bottom of the organization had a significant say in how things were done. These later theorists were similar to their predecessors in that they also saw their approach as universal; they, too, were prescribing what they believed was "the one best way" to organize in each and every situation.

A third approach emerged in 1960 and remained popular into the 1970s. This approach stemmed from empirical research into whether there was in reality any relationship between an organization's design and its effectiveness. The researchers did, indeed, find such a relationship—but in patterns significantly different from those suggested by either of the earlier approaches. What their research indicated was that different situations called for different forms of design; rather than discovering a universal approach to design, they determined that design decisions are contingent on a variety of factors that vary from one situation to another. Their perspective has become known as the *contingency approach* and marks a sharp break with previous attempts to find an all-purpose supermodel.

Still, these researchers struggled for years to find a set of rules to help identify which kinds of designs to use in particular situations. They tried various approaches. Some research indicated that the most effective type of design was contingent on the technology involved. Other researchers looked to the environment, while still others focused on the specific work process.

Then, in the early 1970s, the design theorist Jay Galbraith proposed a concept that seemed to integrate many of the different contingency approaches. He proposed that if one thought about organizations as information-processing systems—mechanisms that moved information to people so that they could do their work and accomplish tasks—it would be possible to develop some general rules for thinking about the contingencies of design. While the debate about design continues and the research work goes on, this information-processing theory has proved to be useful in making real design decisions. It has earned considerable acceptance in both academic and managerial circles and serves as the basis of the design model we use in this book.

A Model for Organization Design

Let's begin by considering precisely what it is that an effective organization design is intended to accomplish.

First, it should create *benefits of scale*. This creates value by bringing together sets of individuals or groups who perform similar jobs, moving beyond the inefficient structure of "cottage industries." The economies and advantages of grouping similar work accrue from specialization, shared support, and the leveraging of shared resources.

Second, organization design *shapes behavior*. The design of work, together with the formal arrangements for getting that work done, focuses the attention of individuals on particular tasks, motivates their performance, enables and empowers them in the performance of their jobs, and constrains behavior that might be counterproductive.

Most important for the modern organization, design shapes the patterns of *information processing*. In a sense, information processing has become the single most important function within any organization. In some large companies, no more than 10 percent of the employees actually touch the product that goes out the factory door or deal directly with a customer. There's only one thing you can point to that everybody needs, everybody uses, everybody consumes or generates—or both—in the course of his or her daily work, and that's information—information about markets, resources, output, behavior, procedures, processes, and performance. Any given pattern of organization arrangements will collect, channel, and disperse information in certain ways. It follows, then, that the key to design is constructing information-processing patterns within an organization that most closely match the information-processing requirements of its work. We can think about this in terms of three basic propositions that underlie our model.

1. *Different tasks pose different information-processing requirements.* Different kinds of work require different patterns of information movement. Let's go back to the HTP case, which opened this chapter, to look at two different situations (see Figure 4-2).

Scenario One describes the old strategy and work situation that used to exist at HTP. Prior to the changes in competition, customers, and technology, the work of the Advanced Products Group in HTP was relatively straightforward. The whole group was charged with developing technologically sophisticated and innovative products, which could be produced and sold to customers. In this scenario, the

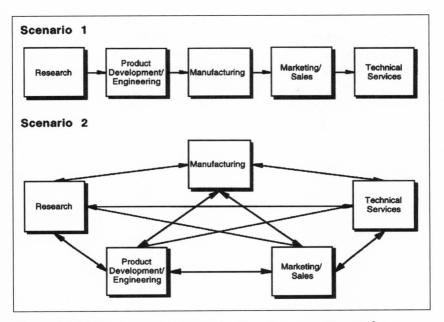

Figure 4-2 HTP Information-Processing Requirements: Two Task Scenarios

Research Division focused on basic investigation. When they found something with potential applications, they passed it on to the Product Development Division, which in turn transformed the technology into a product and then passed it on to Manufacturing, which figured out how to build it. Once the product was in production, Marketing and Sales introduced it to customers. After the completion of sales, the Technical Services Division provided support in the field.

In Figure 4-2, Scenario One illustrates the fairly simple flow of information required by the traditional work demands. For example, once Product Development received information about the new technology, it didn't have much reason for further contact with Research on that subject. Similarly, Product Development was finished with a product once they handed it off to Manufacturing. The information flow required for this kind of work is merely a progression of hand-offs down the line from one division to the next—an informational "bucket brigade," in a sense.

Now consider Scenario Two in Figure 4-2, which describes the information flows ideally required to meet the new competitive demands on the Advanced Products Group. Because of heightened competition, the loss of a commanding technological lead, and new customer demands, the work of Product Development, Manufacturing, and Marketing have to change. Rather than continuing to develop products in a comfortable vacuum, the Product Development Division should be in close contact with the Marketing people to understand the constantly shifting customer demands. They also need to know what products and services competitors are offering and at what price so that they can work with Manufacturing to see if the product can be made at a reasonable cost. Product Development also needs information from Technical Services about the performance of the products in the field and about customers' problems and concerns.

Given the dynamic nature of the marketplace, the exchange of internal information has to be continuous. With competitors constantly turning up the pressure with new products, lower prices, and shorter delivery times, the divisions that make up the Advanced Products Group must exchange more information and at a quicker pace than ever before. Clearly, the changing demands of the work have profoundly altered the required pace and patterns of information processing. That's because the new work differs from the old in three important ways:

- *Predictability.* In the old days, when HTP dictated customer requirements, it was reasonably easy to predict customer response to new products. In fact, very little happened in the marketplace that HTP didn't already know about. Now, all that has changed. Bombarded by new and surprising developments, HTP needs the capacity to gather and process new information much faster.

- *External focus.* When HTP dominated the market and controlled the technology, little that occurred in the outside world was of much consequence to it. Now, information about competitors, products, technologies, distribution patterns, and marketing strategies are absolutely vital.

- *Task interdependence.* As we saw earlier, when HTP controlled the market and periodically developed a few standard products, each division was minimally dependent on the others. But in the new environment, the divisions suddenly find themselves intensely dependent on one another. Product Development looks to Marketing for competitive intelligence and customer information; conversely, Marketing is dependent on Product Development and Manufacturing to modify product features and production schedules to enable Technical Services to promise competitive features and delivery times. In a multitude of ways, the divisions are finding that their work relies upon information that can only be provided by the others.

What is important to note is that all three of these changes—increased unpredictability, greater external focus, and expanded interdependence—tend to increase significantly the degree of uncertainty involved in the work at hand. As the future becomes less clear, there is a greater need to get information more quickly to those who need it. And it becomes more important than ever to exchange information in order to coordinate efforts and make necessary adjustments. All of which says that different types of work—and changes in work—can present very different kinds of information-processing requirements.

2. *Different organization designs provide different types of information-processing capacity.* Formal structures and processes facilitate the movement of information in various ways. Three elements of organization design play a major role in determining how information is moved.

- *Grouping* involves the aggregation of work functions, positions, and individuals into work units. Grouping takes place whenever a structure is created involving units, departments, divisions, groups, or even whole companies within larger holding companies. Grouping explicitly places some jobs (and thus people) together in the same units and implicitly separates some jobs and people; in that sense, it is a double-edged sword. On one hand, grouping eases the flow of information within the boundaries of the group by providing a common language, a common goal, and, indeed, even a common view of the world. The group becomes an identifiable subculture of the larger organization, and the sharing and processing of information become easier. But the boundaries inevitably become barriers, making it more difficult to share information outside the group and often engendering conflict, competition, and a lack of cooperation among groups. In HTP example, the basic grouping reflected in the structure of the divisions makes it difficult to handle the information-sharing requirements of Scenario Two.

- *Structural linking* describes the formal relationships among groups separated by structural boundaries. The most common way of connecting groups is through the hierarchy, with two groups, for example, reporting to the same manager (thus becoming two units in a larger, higher-level group). But there are a variety of other linking techniques, such as cross-unit groups, integrators, and planning teams (all of which are described in detail in Chapter 6). The point is that the creation of structural links allows for the movement of information among otherwise disparate groups, thus creating numerous alternatives for configuring the information-processing capacity of the organization as a whole. For example, if HTP were to create teams within the Advanced Products Group, each dedicated to developing and marketing distinct products and with responsibilities that crossed the traditional boundaries of the group's five divisions, the organization's capacity to move information would change dramatically.

• *Systems and processes* are designed with groupings and linkages in mind to support the movement of information among groups. These devices can range from information, control, and reward systems to formal processes and meetings. In HTP, for example, project review processes, or meetings, and special accelerated product planning and development processes could be used to enhance the flow of information.

The key point is that each combination of groupings, linkages, processes, and systems produces an organizational design with a markedly different capacity for processing information.

3. *Organization effectiveness is greatest when the information-processing capacities of the structure fit the information-processing requirements of the work.* This final proposition provides the key to making design decisions. Other things being equal, organizations function more effectively when the design is shaped to meet the information-processing needs posed by the work to be done. It's helpful to step back and view all this once again in the context of the larger organizational model we described in Chapter 2. In that sense, the requirements of the work—benefits of scale, particular forms of behavior, and, most important, information processing—can be described as the design criteria; those are the needs our design has to meet. The formal organization arrangements—grouping, linkages, processes, and systems—represent the capacity of the organization, at a given time and operating with a particular design, to fulfill those requirements. The extent to which the design's capacity matches its requirements dictates the degree of fit. Clearly, the greater the fit between the design criteria and the design capacity—or, to put it another way, between work and the formal organizational arrangements—the more effective the organization will be.

This model for organization design provides some general direction for making organization design decisions. At the most basic level,

Step One is to analyze the work required by the strategy for the purpose of identifying the particular information-processing needs it imposes. Step Two is the construction of an organization design that meets those needs. Consequently, organization design invariably involves decisions about groupings, linkages, processes and systems.

HTP Revisited

If Sam Tucker at HTP had examined his situation using the concepts we've just discussed, he would have found that the changing nature of the work had created new and complex information-processing requirements that far exceeded the capabilities of his existing structure. Since these requirements were inherent in the work, the strategy, and the competitive environment, Sam would have had little choice: He had to change the basic design of the organization so that it could acquire the capacity to move essential information among the appropriate individuals and groups.

Sam might have thought about altering the organization in two ways (see Figure 4-3). First, he could retain the current set of groups within the organization (Product Development, Technical Services, and so on) but create more effective mechanisms to coordinate and link the activities that cut across these lines. This could be done through a combination of structural linking and management/operational processes. Second, he could consider reconfiguring the basic groups within the organization; these might be smaller units based on products or markets. He could also combine that approach with the current structure. Before he made a choice, however, he needed to understand more about the range of options available and the relative advantages and disadvantages associated with each. Those are precisely the considerations we look at in the remainder of this book.

In this chapter we have presented a specific model for making design decisions. We have traced the background of design theory and used the information-processing perspective to develop a way of looking at work, at organization design, and, finally, at the relationship between them. We are moving toward the application of the model in a sequence of design decisions, starting with analysis of the strategy and work and moving toward specific design decisions. First, however, we look at some of the specific options available to the designer when making decisions about grouping, structural linking, and processes.

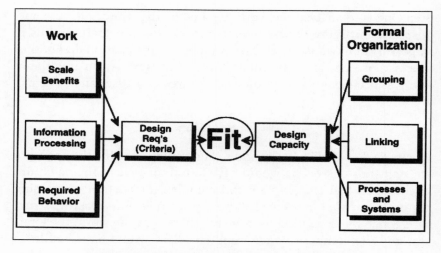

Figure 4-3 The Information-Processing Model

Bibliography

The contingency model of organization design and information processing ideas have been discussed by many writers, including:

Donaldson, L. "Strategy and Structural Adjustment to Regain Fit and Performance." *Journal of Management Studies* 24 (1987): 1–24.

Galbraith, J. *Designing Complex Organizations.* Reading, Mass.: Addison-Wesley, 1973.

Gresov, C. "Exploring Fit and Misfit with Multiple Contingencies." *Administrative Science Quarterly* 34 (1989): 431–453.

Hanna, D. *Designing Organizations for High Performance.* Reading, Mass.: Addison-Wesley, 1988.

Lawrence, P., and J. Lorsch. *Organization and Environment.* Cambridge, Mass.: Harvard University Press, 1967.

Lucas, H. *The T-Form Organization.* San Francisco: Jossey-Bass, 1996.

Miles, R., and C. Snow. *Fit, Failure and the Hall of Fame.* New York: Free Press, 1994.

Miller, D. "The Architecture of Simplicity." *Academy of Management Review* 18 (1993): 116–138.

Pennings, H. "Structural Contingency Theory." *Organization Studies* 8 (1987): 223–240.

Thompson, J. *Organizations in Action.* New York: McGraw-Hill, 1967.

Tushman, M., and D. Nadler. "Information Processing as an Integrating Concept in Organization Design." *Academy of Management Review* 3 (1978): 613–624.

5

Choosing a Basic Structure— Strategic Groups

SMH Swatch—Creating Order from Chaos

After dominating the worldwide watch industry for more than a century, the Swiss found themselves in the late 1970s on the verge of disaster.

New technologies involving quartz, batteries, microelectronics, and digital timepieces had allowed low-cost manufacturers in Japan, Hong Kong, and the United States to underprice their Swiss competitors and wrest control of both the low- and mid-range segments of the market. In 1983, as the two giants of the Swiss industry—SSIH and ASUAG—faced insolvency, Swiss bankers took over and asked Nicholas Hayek to advise them on how to save the combined operation, known as SMH. Hayek, a Lebanese immigrant and the founder of one of Switzerland's leading consulting firms, agreed; two years later, the banks induced him to purchase a controlling stake in SMH and to become its CEO.

The operation Hayek took over was an agglomeration of more than 100 different brands, including Omega, Longines, Rado, Tissot, and Hamilton, each with its own research and development, manufacturing, and marketing operations. "It was crazy," Hayek later recalled (Taylor 1993).

Hayek immediately set his sights on winning back the mass market for watches, building his strategy around an intensive campaign to make the innovative, inexpensively priced Swatch one of the most popular watches in the world. He announced an astounding goal: Within 10 years, 10 percent of the world would be wearing Swatch watches. Moreover, the watches would be produced in Switzerland, which has the dubious distinction of having the world's highest labor costs.

Now, after developing a comprehensive strategy of growth and sharply delineated product lines, it was time for Hayek to redesign the jumbled structure of SMH Swatch into an entirely new organization that would restore the Swiss to their previous position of market leadership.

Nicholas Hayek was grappling with the most fundamental question in organization design: Given a wide array of products aimed at a broad range of customers in countries around the globe, and with functional operations ranging from research and development to manufacturing to marketing to sales, what would be the most effective way to group the company's activities? Should he reorganize SMH along the traditional functional lines of research, production, and marketing? Should he maintain some form of grouping along product lines? Should it become more market-focused, or should it be organized along geographic lines? Or was there some combination of those groupings that might make sense?

Those decisions were crucial; from them would flow all the other aspects of design—linkages, processes, systems, and operational design issues involving the allocation of resources and assignment of people. Indeed, in any design situation, the choices begin with strategic grouping. In this chapter, we describe the various options for grouping, explore their particular strengths and weaknesses, and explain strategic grouping's relationship to business unit strategy and the demands of information processing.

Keep in mind that grouping, while at the core of organization design, must be accompanied by a second set of decisions involving linking mechanisms to coordinate interdependent activities. Because grouping, by definition, separates some activities at the same time that it combines others, linkages are essential to bridging the structural gaps. Consequently, every set of grouping decisions must be accompanied by a complementary set of linkages, which is the focus of our attention in Chapter 6.

Introduction

Strategic grouping is the most important step in the design process. The grouping decisions made at the top of the organization dictate the basic framework within which all other organizational design decisions are made. Grouping gathers together some tasks, functions, or disciplines, while pushing others apart; in essence, it focuses the organization. People grouped together are better able to discuss, plan, and perform the necessary tasks. They also become more skilled and specialized as they dedicate their efforts to a limited range of activities. Since grouping affects people's ability to communicate with each other, it also influences the organization's information-processing capacity; information becomes easier to process within grouping boundaries but more difficult to process between one group and another. In short, grouping decisions determine what the organization will be able to do well and deemphasize other work. By providing basic coordination through common supervision, resources, and systems, grouping decisions give shape to what work gets done, and how.

Strategic grouping involves two related questions: (1) What is the basic form of the organization, and (2) given the organization's form, how specialized or differentiated are the organizational components? At SMH, for example, Nicholas Hayek had to decide first what the basic grouping should be—function, product, or geography—and then determine how specialized each unit should be. Should the marketing unit, for instance, handle every watch from the $40 Swatch to the $200,000 Blancpain? Should it devise global marketing strategies or specific strategies for Europe, the United States, and Japan—or should those be left up to managers in each country?

The initial choice in strategic grouping—the shape of the core organization—is a direct outgrowth of the organization's or unit's strategy. As we see later in this chapter, certain forms of organizational grouping are better suited to achieving particular strategies. Management's job, obviously, is to choose the strategic form best suited to meeting the demands of its own unique strategy.

While it's up to senior management to make the key decisions concerning the overall shape of the enterprise, strategic grouping requires coordinated efforts by managers throughout the organization. Thus, it is the first problem to be confronted by *any* manager involved in decisions about organization design.

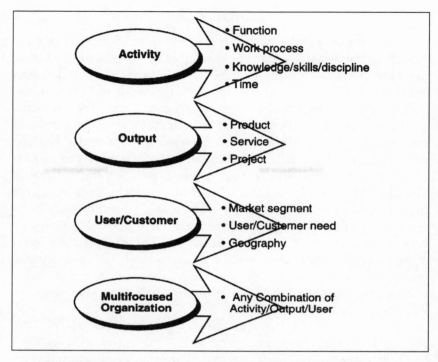

Figure 5-1 Organization Form Options (or Grouping Alternatives)

Strategic Grouping: The Basic Forms

Regardless of where in the organization grouping takes place, the set of basic options is really quite limited. Different levels of the organization can be grouped according to different criteria. But the truth is that there are only three basic forms of grouping, which can be combined and modified to produce creative variations. While these generic alternatives rarely exist in pure form, they accurately represent the range of alternatives (see Figure 5-1).

1. *Grouping by activity* brings together individuals who share similar functions, disciplines, skills, or work processes. In traditional functional organizations, for example, everyone involved in manufacturing is grouped together, as are all the people involved in product development, marketing, and sales (as illustrated by the Xerox organizational chart in Figure 2-1). Grouping by activity can also involve disciplines; a research lab, for example, might group all the chemists in one department and all the biologists in another.

Grouping by activity also applies to the element of time. At its most basic level, this applies to the structuring of twenty-four-hour

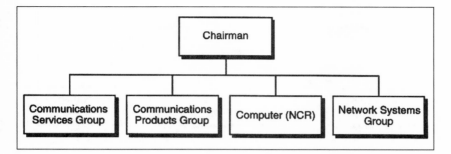

Figure 5-2 Grouping by Output (AT&T Early 1990s)

operations into separate shifts, each with its own supervisors. But it also relates to more complex situations, where various people are working according to different timetables. As we saw in the Technicon case, within the same research lab some scientists were assigned to a department that concentrated on basic research and long-term projects, while a separate department focused on quick turnaround testing and evaluation of new innovations to assess their potential marketability.

In organizations characterized by activity groupings, the goals, positions of influence, rewards, and control systems tend to be based on performance of specific tasks; the emphasis is on the quality of work, rather than on sales volume or customer satisfaction ratings.

2. *Grouping by output* organizes people on the basis of the service or product they provide. The people within each group perform a variety of tasks, employ various skills, and use widely varying processes, but they are all contributors to the same final output. A classic illustration is the product organization, typified by AT&T's structure in the early 1990s. During that period, the operations were segmented into communications services, communications products, computers, and network systems (see Figure 5-2). Another example is our opening case, SMH; when Nicholas Hayek entered the scene in 1983, SMH consisted of more than 100 different brands, each operating essentially as a semiautonomous unit with its own product development, manufacturing, and marketing functions.

In output-focused organizations, the primary goals focus on the product or service. Influence is dominated by those concerned with output integrity, and rewards, promotion, and controls are dominated by product, project, and/or service considerations.

3. *Grouping by user, customer, or geography* gathers together people who perform different kinds of work and produce different

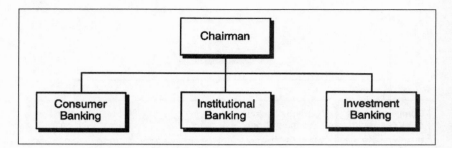

Figure 5-3 Grouping by Customers (Citicorp)

outputs but serve the same customers. Grouping by market or market segment is another way of addressing the same issue. For example, telephone companies traditionally structured their operations on the basis of which customers were served—residential or business. Another version of the same concept is geographic grouping. Think back to the BOC case in Chapter 1, in which the Industrial Gases group was essentially an amalgam of fifteen semiautonomous operating units in various countries. It's not uncommon for multinational firms to be divided into domestic and international groups, each subdivided by geographic region (see Figure 5-3). Each market, user, and/or geographic area has the requisite resources to produce products specialized to its defined market. Grouping by user or client focuses the unit on user/market/geographic considerations. User goals are emphasized, influence is dominated by those concerned with user needs, and rewards and controls are dominated by user assessments of value.

Traditional organizations typically employed either a single form of grouping or distinctly different forms of grouping at various levels. But the increasingly complex nature of competition frequently makes more demands on an organization than can be satisfied with a single grouping pattern. The result has been the growing popularity of mixed groupings and matrix patterns—combinations of groupings that focus simultaneous emphasis on multiple strategic priorities. Consider SMH, for example. There were undeniable benefits of scale to be derived from using the same factories to produce several different brands of watches; from a manufacturing standpoint, a centralized, functional grouping seemed to make the most sense. But marketing an Omega or Longines had little in common with selling Swatches, so a decentralized product grouping might make the most sense for marketing, sales, and distribution. And in SMH's global operation, it was essential to understand the dramatically different markets in each country, so some form of geographic grouping was required.

These matrix groupings are particularly common at the enterprise level, where grouping decisions provide an architectural framework for the entire organization. It's at that level that design decisions most often involve multiple—and, sometimes, seemingly contradictory—strategic objectives. ABB, the Swiss-based global engineering giant, is built around the notion of "Think globally, act locally"; Sun Microsystems, one of the most successful of the Silicon Valley startups, based its reorganization in the early 1990s on the idea of business units that would be "loosely coupled but closely aligned." We delve into these issues in much greater detail in Chapter 7, but, for purposes of this discussion, it's important to note the growing popularity of—and the need for—matrix grouping patterns at the enterprise level.

Grouping Options: Strengths and Weaknesses

Because each form of grouping focuses the organization in different ways, each involves a distinct set of strengths and weaknesses. Although the effectiveness of any option is closely tied to the specific situation in which it is applied, there are some general considerations that can be used to help assess the potential impact of each form of grouping.

1. *To what extent does the option maximize the utilization of resources?* Grouping by activity and function maximizes resources because individuals performing the same function or activity can share resources, develop specialized capabilities, and develop a large critical mass of expertise. If lowering production costs is a strategic goal, functional grouping offers clear advantages; while it has other shortcomings, it is the simplest way to crunch costs through centralized mass production.

Grouping by output, user, or geography, on the other hand, inevitably results in the duplication of resources. People, equipment, and work processes must be specialized by product, market, or location. In a product organization such as SMH, for example, each brand had its own manufacturing, marketing, and sales operation, each duplicating, to one extent or another, the efforts of the parallel departments for the other brands.

2. *How does grouping affect specialization and economies of scale?* Grouping by activity, again, offers the benefits of critical mass and the capacity for specialization in important ways for professionals. Grouping all the chemists in a research lab together, for example, allows each to take advantage of the collective knowledge base; at the same time, it allows for further specialization within the broader discipline, with some, for example, specializing in physical chemistry. This combination of large critical mass and activity-based specialization permits increased economies of scale as activity-focused areas perform the same functions repeatedly. The benefits of scale economies diminish, however, when a functional group becomes so large that it begins to incur the expenses of increased bureaucracy, extensive support staff, and increased organizational inertia.

Grouping by output or user dedicates resources to focused areas. Rather than specializing by activity or discipline, people are assigned to work on particular products or market segments. So our chemists, to extend the example, rather than all being assigned to one department in the research lab, might well be separated and assigned to work in various departments on particular products or projects, surrounded by biologists, engineers, and people from other disciplines who are working on the same products. Output and user organizations do not have the economies of scale or large professional reference groups seen in activity groupings; instead, their more limited resources are specialized and focused on particular products and markets.

3. *How does the grouping form affect measurement and control issues?* Grouping by activity or function makes it relatively easy to design measures and controls based on functional, disciplinary, and work considerations—how good is this person's chemistry? What is the quality of that person's market research? From a functional standpoint, is the manufacturing department meeting production quotas?

Output groupings also make it relatively easy to monitor the quality and quantity of work. Are products being developed and manufactured according to established schedules? Are products meeting specific quality standards? Are sales forces meeting their goals? User groupings make measurement and control trickier; the criteria must be based on success at meeting prescribed customer needs or market requirements. Consequently, there's less emphasis on more traditional measures of performance and output and a greater need to create assessments based on unique sets of customer-based criteria.

4. *How does the grouping form affect the development of individuals and the organization's capacity to use its human resources?* Grouping by activity fosters the development of professional identity and skills as individuals become experts at general functions or specific disciplines. But there's a trade-off; as professional specialization increases, there's considerable risk that individuals will develop a narrower organizational perspective. Our chemists, for example, will tend to identify exclusively with other chemists, rather than with the entire research lab, let alone with the company as a whole. As that sense of identification and affiliation narrows, the likelihood of conflict among specialized groups increases.

Output and user groupings, on the other hand, lessen the opportunities for specialization by discipline, while exposing individuals to colleagues from a broader range of disciplines from throughout the organization. The good news is that this increases the individual's sensitivity to general management issues; the bad news is that a more global perspective may, over time, dull employees' disciplinary associations and lead to their technical obsolescence. Loyalty to a particular brand, rather than to the company as a whole, can also be a double-edged sword; while it may intensify focus on the success of a particular product, it may inhibit cooperation and collaboration that might be in the company's best interests.

5. *How does the grouping form affect the final output of the organization?* Each form offers its own advantages. Functional groupings are the most effective way to create low-cost products through mass production. Activity groupings create specialists and relatively large areas of functional or disciplinary excellence. Grouping by output facilitates the integration of various functions and disciplines in the development and distribution of products. And grouping by user allows the organization to become more attentive to customer needs and helps transcend traditional functional boundaries.

6. *How responsive is each organization form to important competitive demands?* Groupings based on function and activity encourage innovation within a discipline or in an internal process, but they're not particularly attuned to market needs. Product and user-based organizations, in contrast, respond much more rapidly to changes in the marketplace but are less focused on breakthrough innovation, either in their functional processes or in areas of basic research.

Figure 5-4 Consequences of Grouping Options

	Organization Form		
Activity (Functional/ Discipline)	*Output (Product/ Service)*	*User (Market, Geography)*	*Multifocused (Product/ Market, etc.)*
Benefits:	*Benefits:*		*Benefits:*
Colleagueship for technical specialists	High product, service, market, or geographic visibility		Focused attention to multiple objectives
Supports substantial critical mass by function/discipline	Focused coordination by product, service, market, or geography		Coordination and specialization
	Relatively easy cross-functional communication		
Costs:	*Costs:*		*Costs:*
Poor inter-unit coordination	Duplication of resources		Substantial conflict
Decisions pile at top	Lose critical mass, specialization by function, discipline		Costly to implement and design
Restricted view of whole	Difficult to allocate pooled resources		Highly unstable

Source: R. Duncan, "What is the Right Organization Structure?" *Organization Dynamics* (Winter 1979).

Clearly, there is no universally ideal choice of grouping patterns. Each strategic grouping option comes with its own set of strengths and weaknesses (see Figure 5-4). Most broadly, activity-based organizations buy scale economies and functional excellence at the cost of integration. These forms tend to be innovative in technologies or functions but less responsive to markets, users, and clients. Output and user-based organizations buy integration at the cost of specialization. They are attentive to the markets they serve but less responsive to fundamental changes in underlying disciplinary or functional areas.

Consequently, it's easy to understand why so many organizations attempt to develop mixed and matrix patterns in an attempt to reap the benefits of multiple forms of strategic grouping. But it's important to remember that along with complexity comes potential confusion, higher costs, and a significantly heightened potential for conflict. As we see in Chapter 6, the advantages offered by those hybrid forms must be carefully weighed against the various costs of implementing and managing their complex structures, systems, and cultures.

Grouping Forms: How to Decide

Given the relative advantages and disadvantages of each organizational form, how does an executive or group of managers go about deciding which forms to use at each level of the organization? The driving factor, at each and every level, is the same: strategy and vision. Whether it's at the enterprise level or within particular work units, structural decisions must flow directly from a larger strategy.

Strategy sets organizational priorities and dictates which issues and concerns need to be managed most closely. For example, if markets are uncertain, competition is stiff, and customers are varied with different needs, then user groupings make the most sense. If, on the other hand, innovation in certain product niches is the priority, then it might be most effective to organize around output. If the most pressing strategic issues are cost and efficiency, then grouping by activity or function might be most appropriate. For any one strategy, management must weigh the strengths and weaknesses of the basic forms and choose the one—or the combination—that is most congruent with the company's strategy.

Consider, again, the case of Xerox in 1992. We reexamine this situation in greater detail in Chapter 7, but the general lesson is clear. The company, after operating for decades as a classic functional operation, was still falling far short of its goals of swiftly bringing to market innovative products that would meet customer needs. The traditional divisions among product development, manufacturing, marketing, and sales were making it difficult to translate technological breakthroughs into marketable products; they obscured accountability for turning new products into marketplace successes and slowed the company's response to changing market conditions and customer demands.

To implement its new strategic objectives—speed, accountability, product-based innovation, and customer focus—Xerox decided that it had to reorganize into distinct business units, each focusing on different products and services directed at different segments of the office market. It became a complex hybrid, with product development and manufacturing maintaining much of their functional focus but meshed through a series of matrix groupings with the product/user focused business units. In Chapter 7, we see exactly how this structure worked; for now, the important point is that a shift in strategy required the company to completely revamp the functional grouping that had served as its basic framework ever since the company's early days.

The same principles hold true as redesign moves down through the organization. At the subunit level, grouping forms should be driven by each unit's strategic objectives. For example, the Technicon research lab we discussed in Chapter 3 was a textbook case of activity-based specialization—so much so, in fact, that conflict among disciplines impeded the collaboration essential to successful product development. That was a critical problem, given Technicon's need to roll out a steady stream of innovative new products and testing processes. Though the lab director's reorganization process was counterproductive, his basic idea was right; he needed to move in the direction of output groupings, with an emphasis on cooperative, interdisciplinary work aimed at specific projects.

Clearly, different forms of grouping may be appropriate at various levels of the organization. Recall the pre-1992 Xerox structure described in Chapter 2 (see Figure 2-1). At the corporate level, the organization was divided by classic functional groupings—research, manufacturing, and marketing. At the next level, however, the groupings were by customer, with each unit shaped by geography. The grouping decisions made at the top of the organization are most critical because they constrain the configuration of the rest of the organization. Beyond that, the greater the strategic and competitive complexity, the more complex the organization must be to handle the different strategic contingencies.

Any single level of an organization should be focused either on activity, outputs, or users. It's entirely possible, however, that while the organization may have a strategic focus on one area—technological innovation, for instance—it may have long-time strengths in others, such as manufacturing competence or a strong sales force. Think about our opening case, SMH; despite its proliferation of competing product lines and flawed marketing strategies, the company still retained technological superiority in manufacturing quality watches at every price level. Another example: Even during Xerox's darkest days, when it suffered from unexciting products, high prices, and slow delivery times, it still enjoyed a highly skilled sales force that was in close contact with businesses and offices in every corner of the United States and in major markets around the world.

In such cases, it's important to maintain and capitalize on existing sources of competitive advantage while reorganizing to meet new strategic objectives. And that can best be achieved through mixed organizational forms. At Xerox, each of the product-based business units interfaces with customers through a combined customer operations unit that encompasses the traditionally strong sales and service staffs.

Grouping and Specialization

Once the organization has made its basic grouping decisions, managers at each succeeding level have to determine the degree of specialization they want in each of their subunits. For example, John Whitehead at the Technicon lab could divide Research and Advanced Development, or he could combine them into a single unit with more general objectives. Take a more common example: A division general manager, after selecting a functional structure for his division, has to decide whether to split Marketing from Sales or to leave them together in one department. Regardless of whether they're explicitly described in terms of specialization, those decisions go on at every level of the organization where grouping decisions are being made. Those decisions, in turn, generally dictate the number of subunits reporting to each manager.

While the overall organizational form hinges on strategic considerations, specialization is closely associated with work requirements and the degree to which they vary. Mass production, with huge numbers of people doing similar work, requires little specialization, while a medical center involving people assigned to numerous functions—and then further divided among narrowly focused disciplines involving special competencies and information needs within each function—involves proportionately greater specialization.

The challenge, of course, is finding the right mix. Less specialization simplifies management; on the other hand, it can also diminish the organization's capacity to respond adequately to specific internal or external demands. Overspecialization, on the other hand, complicates information processing requirements, increases management costs, and heightens the opportunities for conflict. Managers need to have a firm grasp on just how much specialization is enough, without becoming too much.

Grouping and Organizational Politics

It's essential to keep in mind that organizations, in the final analysis, are political systems with complex patterns of power and influence. Consequently, grouping decisions—which, by their very definition, reshape those patterns through the rearrangement of priorities and the reallocation of resources—invariably are emotionally charged. The informal organization—which we discuss in depth in Chapter 10—tends to view company politics as a zero-sum game. If new grouping patterns seem to elevate one group over another, channel increased resources to a particular activity, or substantially alter reporting relationships, some manager or group will be seen as winning at the expense of someone else. Managers involved in making these decisions need to have their eyes wide open, understanding that any grouping changes can be counted on to trigger some response from the social structure.

At Technicon, for example, any move to a project or matrix structure would be perceived as a threat to the disciplinary dominance of the laboratory. Moreover, chemists would be watching carefully to see if any of the changes diminished their perception of their own exalted status compared to the engineers in the lab. This perceived threat and loss of status can lead to resistance to change, adding an informal but nonetheless important ingredient to the mix of how effective grouping patterns will be. Successful managers always take into account the social constraints imposed by the informal culture, as well as strategic objectives, work requirements, and specialization needs, when assessing the impact of any potential grouping design.

At senior levels in the organization, grouping decisions also have a direct impact on the power, influence, and career opportunities of top executives. While few organizations launch major restructuring with the idea of completely shaking up—or replacing—the senior team, that's often what happens. Sometimes, it's because the new form of organization requires people with a combination of experience, perspectives, and skills that can be found only by recruiting outside the organization and, sometimes, outside the industry. In some cases, the reorganization implicitly involves a repudiation of the way things were run in the past, making it unlikely that the people who shaped and managed the old structure will be capable of suddenly reversing the values, beliefs, and behavioral patterns that earned them their senior positions in the first place. At Technicon, the first thing John Whitehead did in connection with his reorganization was to bring in a new second in command from the outside. At BOC, C. K. Chow made wholesale changes among his senior executives. At Xerox, one of the company's most senior officials left because of his intense opposition to the new structure. Considering how common that pattern is, it's no wonder that restructuring is viewed throughout any organization as an intensely political experience.

Swatch Revisited

Soon after taking over SMH, Nicholas Hayek was clear about his strategy: His company would combine the Swiss reputation for excellence with technologically innovative production techniques and exciting, sharply delineated product lines to compete across the entire spectrum of the global watch business.

To do that, he first had to centralize both product development and manufacturing. By combining more than 100 small, inefficient watch manufacturing and assembly operations into one, he immediately reaped enormous economies of scale. Then new, state-of-the-art technology was introduced; one of the SMH plants now turns out 35,000 Swatch watches and millions of components each day with virtually no people involved in the process. Together, mass production and new technology massively lowered production costs.

At the same time, the marketing, sales, and distribution functions were completely decentralized and reorganized along product lines with global product managers (see Figure 5-5). In addition, SMH named a country manager everywhere it sold watches to maintain and strengthen its localized customer connections.

The result, to use our grouping terms, was a functional organization (in terms of product development and manufacturing) along with a double matrix—an output grouping based on product lines and a user grouping based on geography. Making that kind of complex structure operate effectively required a cultural revolution within SMH as a hodgepodge of competing fiefdoms was fashioned into a global operation totally dependent on the willingness and the ability of its managers to negotiate and cooperate across boundaries of function, product, and geography. It's also worth noting that in the course of reshaping the company and its culture, Hayek eventually replaced every member of the original executive team.

The result was an astounding success. In 1983 SMH suffered a loss of $124 million on sales of $1.1 billion. Ten years later, it was reporting $2.1 billion in sales and $286 million in profits. The com-

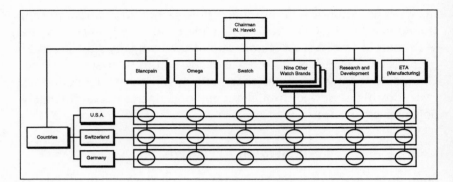

Figure 5-5 SMH (1994). (*Note:* Simplified structure)

pany Hayek rescued from bankruptcy, in ten years, had amassed a market value of $3.5 billion.

As the SMH case illustrates once again, effective decisions about organization design are invariably rooted in strategic objectives. Once the strategy is clear, then executives and managers at each level of the organization face profound decisions about how people and their jobs should be grouped to best implement the overall strategy at each level of the enterprise. Grouping decisions involve weighing the relative strengths and weaknesses of each pattern and deciding which model most closely matches the needs of the organization's strategy. The more complex the organization and the strategy, the more complex the grouping patterns that should be employed. In most cases, no single form of grouping will suffice; it is the responsibility of managers to draw on their creativity and their knowledge of their business to devise the most effective combination of grouping arrangements.

But while grouping represents a crucial design decision, it is only the first of several. No group, no matter how imaginatively it's configured, works in a vacuum. The key to transforming isolated groups into an integrated whole lies in coordination. In Chapter 6, we turn to the design of structures and mechanisms for linking the competitive forces within the organization.

Bibliography

For more detail on strategic grouping issues, see the following:

Bartlett, C., and S. Ghoshal. *Managing Across Borders*. Boston, Mass.: Harvard Business School Press, 1991.

Chandler, A. *Scale and Scope.* Cambridge, Mass.: Harvard University Press, 1980.

Duncan, R. "What Is the Right Organization Structure?" *Organization Dynamics* (Winter, 1979).

Hamel, G., and C. K. Prahalad. *Competing for the Future.* Boston, Mass.: Harvard Business School Press, 1994.

Lawrence, P., and D. Dyer. *Renewing American Industry.* New York: Free Press, 1983.

Lawrence, P., and J. Lorsch. *Organization and Environment: Managing Differentiation and Integration.* Boston: Graduate School of Business, Harvard University, 1967.

Pettigrew, A. *Continuity and Change at ICI.* London: Blackwell, 1986.

Quinn, J. B. *Intelligent Enterprise.* New York: Free Press, 1992.

Rumelt, R. *Strategy, Structure and Economic Performance.* Boston, Mass.: Graduate School of Business, Harvard University, 1974.

Taylor, W. "Message and Muscle: An Interview with Nicolas Hayek." *Harvard Business Review* (March 1993) 99–110.

Thompson, J. *Organizations in Action.* New York: McGraw-Hill, 1967.

6

Coordinating Work—
Strategic Linking

ABB (ASEA Brown Boveri)—A Global Federation of Local Businesses

ABB, the Zurich-based industrial giant that designs, produces, and sells electrical systems and equipment around the world, employs a complex organizational structure based on a series of strategic contradictions.

Formed in 1988 through the merger of Sweden's ASEA and Switzerland's Brown Boveri, ABB now does business in 140 countries. As the two companies were being merged, CEO Percy Barnevik envisioned a strategy that would exploit global economies of scale and the swift transfer of expertise while capitalizing on the deeply local roots of the hundreds of companies that made up the conglomerate. In other words, ABB wanted to be both big and small, both centralized and decentralized, both global and local.

Faced with that challenge, Barnevik assigned ten of the company's brightest people to a team he dubbed "The Manhattan Project" and gave them six weeks to design an entirely new organizational structure. The result: a complex matrix in which each of the 300 local companies is grouped within one of fifty business areas, which in turn are grouped into a dozen or so industry segments. In addition,

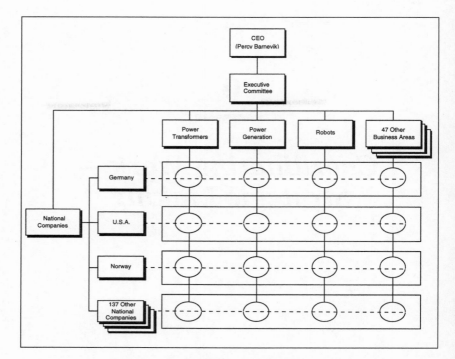

Figure 6-1 ABB (*Note:* Simplified structure)

for each country in which ABB operates, there is a manager who oversees areas such as governmental relations, labor-management issues, and staff development for all the ABB units within that country. Consequently, each company president reports to two bosses— a country manager and a business area manager. The president of ABB Combustion Engineering in Windsor, Connecticut, for example, reports both to the U.S. country manager and to the global manager of the Power Engineering Business Area (see Figure 6-1). The result is an organization that can act as a global powerhouse to amass resources, technological know-how, production innovations, and distribution networks to compete on a par with any major corporation even as it constantly emphasizes its deep connections to local markets and customers. The coordination of 210,000 employees, working in 300 companies and 5,000 profit centers in 140 countries, demonstrates the crucial role of linking mechanisms in turning a complex kaleidoscope of grouping patterns into a smoothly functioning organization. ABB also illustrates how successful such designs can be; with net income of $1.3 billion, ABB saw its stock price double between 1992 and 1996.

The Need for Coordination

Strategic grouping, as we described it in Chapter 5, by definition separates some jobs and individuals at the same time it brings others together. For example, if Percy Barnevik had decided to group ABB's companies exclusively by business area or by country, huge walls would have instantaneously gone up between operations with shared interests and responsibilities. If he'd chosen a geographic grouping, for instance, plants manufacturing similar products in Germany, Poland, and Muncie, Indiana, would have found it much more difficult to share staff and production technologies. If the grouping had been solely by business area, on the other hand, ABB companies in Norway or Portugal or any other country would have lacked the centralized leadership that has allowed them to deal efficiently with common issues such as tax policy, labor unions, and executive recruitment.

Strategic linking, in essence, involves the design of formal structures and processes to link related operations that have been separated by strategic grouping. Once the key decisions have been made about strategic grouping, the next step is to provide the necessary mechanisms to coordinate work so that the company can work as an integrated enterprise.

While grouping decisions are driven by strategy considerations, the basis for linking decisions is rooted in the concept of *task interdependence.* Different degrees of task interdependence among groups call for different kinds of formal linking mechanisms; the objective is to design mechanisms that allow each group to receive from other groups the information it needs to perform its work and achieve its objectives. Linkages that are incapable of providing the necessary flow of information inevitably result in poor coordination; those that are more extensive and elaborate than necessary prove costly and hinder the flow of information. The key is to figure out which mechanisms are essential, without going overboard. In this chapter, we discuss different variations of work interdependence, present a range of formal linking mechanisms, and offer an approach to making linking decisions. We conclude by looking at ways in which the informal organization enhances coordination throughout the organization (see Figure 6-2), supplementing the formal linking mechanisms.

Varieties of Work Interdependence

Linking, like grouping, involves several sets of considerations. For the organization designer, the problem is to select the right set of

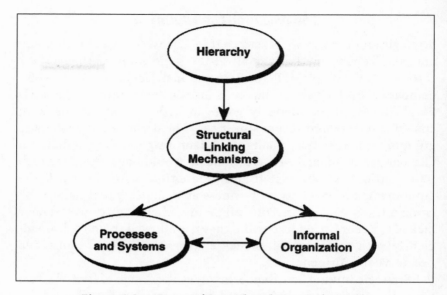

Figure 6-2 A Range of Formal Linking Mechanisms

linking mechanisms to deal with: (1) work flows between distinct yet interdependent units, (2) the need for disciplinary or staff-based professionals to have contact across the company, and (3) work flows associated with emergencies or temporary, short-term goals.

The conceptual thread running through work flow, disciplinary linkages, and work requirements under crisis conditions is *work-related interdependence.* Managers choose linking mechanisms to deal with this source of uncertainty. The greater the task interdependence, the greater the need for coordination and joint problem solving. The higher the degree of interdependence, the more complex the formal linkage devices must be to handle work-related uncertainty. On the other hand, groups that are only minimally interdependent have relatively little need for coordination and joint problem solving and therefore need fairly simple formal linking devices.

Consider branch banks located throughout a city. Each branch's operations are largely independent of the others, except to the extent that they share advertising and marketing resources. Similarly, business units within a diversified company with completely different product/market niches are also essentially independent of each other except for those corporate resources, such as staff and technology, that are shared among divisions. Both examples illustrate *pooled interdependence,* characterized by relatively independent units of the same organization that share certain scarce resources. In

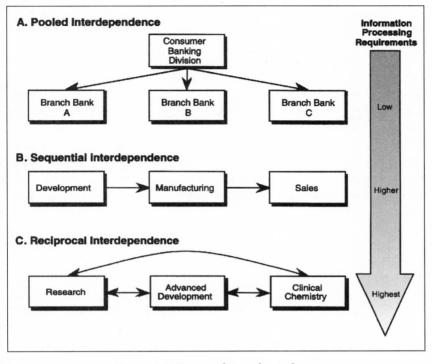

Figure 6-3 Forms of Interdependence

these situations, there is only a limited need for coordination and linking mechanisms (see Figure 6-3).

Now think about the back office operation of bank, where checks move through a progression of departments before exiting the bank. This is an example of *sequential interdependence;* each work unit must interact closely with those that immediately precede and follow it in the orderly sequence of performing a particular work process. Sequentially interdependent units must deal with a greater degree and variety of problem-solving and coordination requirements than is required for units that have pooled interdependence. Groups with sequential interdependence require close coordination and timing so that work flows remain smooth and uninterrupted; each unit in the work flow is dependent upon the units back upstream.

If you consider our Technicon case, described in Chapter 3, the marketing division was heavily reliant on both R&D and Production for the development of new laboratory testing products. Each functional area had to be in close contact with the others to ensure the synthesis of market, technological, and production considerations.

Similarly, in an advertising agency, the media, creative, and account services areas must work closely in the development of ad campaigns for their clients. These are examples of *reciprocal interdependence,* in which each group must work with all the others to create a common product or service (see Figure 6-3). Reciprocal interdependence imposes substantial coordination and problemsolving requirements between units; no single unit can accomplish its task without the active contributions of every other unit.

Pooled, sequential, and reciprocal interdependence represent progressively higher degrees of work-related interdependence. Reciprocal interdependence imposes greater coordination costs and complexity than does sequential interdependence, which, in turn, requires greater coordination than pooled interdependence.

Beyond normal work flows, organizations sometimes experience situations characterized by abnormally high degrees of task interdependence; these include emergencies, crises, short-term projects, and one-time efforts aimed at resolving important problems that require participation from throughout the organization. These are situations in which units that normally pool their resources suddenly have to work together with much closer coordination. Going back to our branch banks, for example, if a power blackout were to hit one part of town, branch banks in the unaffected areas would have to work together to deal with the emergency. Temporary alterations in interdependence frequently occur when product divisions that share similar technologies or knowledge bases are asked to join forces on a particular corporate venture that requires the combination of their resources and particular skills.

Finally, quite apart from work flow considerations, professionals must maintain contacts across organization boundaries. If grouped only with others of the same discipline, they run the risk of becoming overly specialized; if cut off from professional colleagues, they may lose touch with current developments in their respective fields. The greater the rate of change in the particular discipline, the greater the need for interdependence.

Whether driven by work flows, crises, or professionally anchored need for collaboration, these differing degrees of work-related interdependence impose different information processing requirements. Those units that have pooled interdependence (or in which the rate of change of the underlying knowledge base is low) have fewer coordination demands and information-processing requirements than do units that have reciprocal interdependence. The designer's challenge is to choose the appropriate set of linking mechanisms to deal with the information-processing requirements that arise from work-related interdependence.

Finally, just as strategic grouping is relevant at multiple levels of analysis, so too is the assessment of work-related interdependence. At Technicon, not only was there reciprocal interdependence among the functional areas, but within R&D, each discipline was reciprocally interdependent in new-product-development efforts. Just as grouping patterns may vary from one level of the organization to another, and from one division to another, so too may the patterns of work-related interdependence vary throughout the enterprise. More and more companies are developing linking patterns that extend beyond the traditional outer boundaries of the company to reflect heightened interdependence with customers, suppliers, and partners, a trend we explore in greater detail in Chapter 7.

Strategic Linking: A Range of Alternatives

Various types of formal mechanisms can be used to link and coordinate the efforts of organizational groups. Our objective is to choose those structural linking mechanisms that provide adequate information flows, procedures, and structures to deal with the information requirements imposed by work-related interdependence. The various options can be assessed in terms of their ability to handle information flows and complex problem-solving requirements.

The most obvious form of structural linking is the *hierarchy*— the formal distribution of power and authority. The hierarchy of authority follows directly from grouping decisions. In a divisional structure, for example, functional managers report to their respective divisional general managers, who, in turn, report to the company president. Coordination and linking between managers at the same level can be accomplished via their common boss, who channels information, controls the type and quantity of information that moves among groups, and adjudicates conflicts. If you think about it, that's precisely the function served by the hierarchical structure of ABB, our opening case. The combination of country managers and business area managers provides for linkages—coordination of joint projects, sharing of pooled resources, and continual flow of information—across functional and geographic boundaries.

The formal hierarchy is the simplest and one of the most pervasive formal linking mechanisms. Focused, sustained, and consistent behavior by the manager can both direct and set the stage for the effective coordination between organizational groups. And yet, hier-

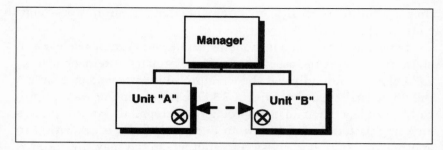

Figure 6-4 Liaison Roles

archy is a limited linking mechanism. Uncertainty about external conditions, special projects, joint operations, occasional crises—any and all of the shifting conditions that can rearrange the interdependence of units with an organization can easily overload an individual manager. When that happens, other devices must be used to complement the manager's role as a linking mechanism. These include:

- *Liaison roles.* Situations involving two or more groups in intensive problem-solving situations often require the assignment of specific people to work together in liaison roles. They serve as sources of information and expertise and as contacts and advisers on work involving their respective groups. In essence, they serve as information conduits deep within the organization. Although people in liaison roles are responsible for enhanced coordination and information flows between units, they rarely have the authority to impose their decisions on others. The liaison role is not usually a full-time responsibility but rather is done in conjunction with other activities (see Figure 6-4).

- *Cross-unit groups.* Another device used frequently to coordinate the work of multiple units is the cross-unit group. These are groups designed to focus on particular clients, products, markets, or problems. Representatives from each related work group are pulled together, either permanently or on an ad hoc basis, to pool their expertise and to coordinate their efforts. In contrast with liaison roles, cross-unit groups provide a more extensive forum for coordinating, exchanging information, and resolving conflict among work units. Although these task forces, teams, or groups may be created only when needed, it often makes sense to design them into the formal structure if it's apparent that cross-unit projects will be common. In a medical center, for example, a permanent group with representatives of each of the major divisions of

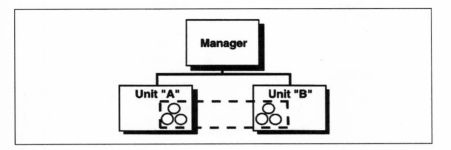

Figure 6-5 Cross-Unit Groups

the complex might be responsible for establishing and adjusting guidelines and processes that affect work flows across divisions (see Figure 6-5).

- ***Integrator roles.*** In situations that require decisions involving several groups, informal teams and liaison roles might not be sufficient. No single individual may feel accountable for collective performance. The manager responsible for the various groups may lack the time or the expertise to adjudicate differences. Faced with the need for swift problem-solving and a general management perspective, organizations sometimes assign an individual to act as an integrator. The person in this role is responsible for taking a general management point of view in helping multiple-work groups accomplish a joint task, such as a specific product or project (see Figure 6-6).

  Product, brand, geographic, and account managers all are examples of formal integrator roles; their purpose is to identify someone who will share a general management perspective with other, specialized managers who bring to the table essential expertise but relatively narrow concerns. Integrators have the formal responsibility of achieving coordination across the organization. While they report to senior management, they usually lack the formal authority to direct their functional and/or disciplinary colleagues. Because of this dotted-line relationship to members of their team, integrators must rely on expertise, interpersonal competence, and team and conflict-resolution skills to shape the efforts of sometimes recalcitrant team members.

  It's essential for integrators to acquire the functional or disciplinary resources necessary to accomplish their work. When there are several projects, accounts, or products, each is competing with the others for scarce resources. Consider the Technicon research lab we discussed in Chapter 3. Each project manager was left to his or her own devices to scavenge help from each of the

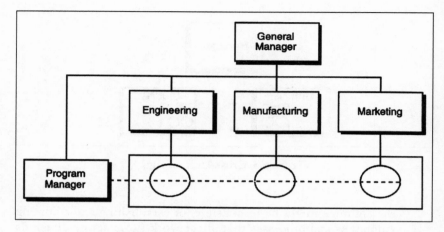

Figure 6-6 Integrators (Project, Brand, Program, Account Managers)

divisions within the lab; all were competing for some of the same people, while the division heads were reluctant to part with any staff at all. In such situations, to increase the power of the special projects integrators and to coordinate resources, organizations sometimes create departments specifically to oversee product development (see Figure 6-7).

These structures are common in functional or geographic organizations that must also focus on developing specific products. In these situations, the product side of the organization has its own senior manager, who reports along the same line as the functional managers. This senior manager formally represents the product side of the organization at senior levels and assists in resource allocation across projects. However, the functional organization still reports to its functional supervisors and has a dotted-line relationship with the project/product manager. Consider how this might have worked in the Technicon lab; the project managers, who continued to complain of their inability to deal with the resistance of lab division managers might have had more success if they had been reporting to a product development manager who reported directly to the lab director.

While we've focused on integrator roles in the realm of product development, the role is, in fact, quite common and applicable in numerous situations. Regardless of the nature of the organization in which it is used, the purpose of the role is to offset the counterproductive consequences of strategic grouping and to achieve coordination and real-time problem solving at lower levels of complex organizations.

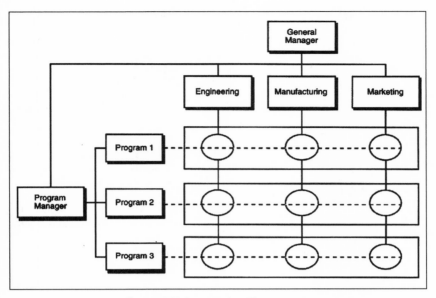

Figure 6-7 Integrating Department

- ***Matrix structures.*** As we've already seen in the cases of Xerox, SMH, and ABB, corporate strategies frequently require equal attention to multiple priorities: products and functions, for instance, or markets and technical expertise. Whenever strategy requires simultaneous emphasis on several dimensions—product, market, and geography, for example—or when numerous operations are positioned in permanent relationships involving intense degrees of interdependence, normal integrator roles lack the capacity to handle the enormous information-processing requirements. In these situations, what's called for is a matrix structure.

  A matrix organization structurally improves coordination by balancing the power between competing aspects of the organization and by installing systems and roles designed to achieve multiple objectives simultaneously. For example, an R&D facility that wants to maximize both disciplinary competence and product focus might design a matrix structure, with directors of the different laboratories reporting to both disciplinary and product managers. The dotted-line relationship (seen in the integrator role) becomes solid; key members of the laboratory have two bosses. In more concrete terms, that's exactly the way ABB is set up: The president of each operating company has two bosses, a country manager and a business area manager.

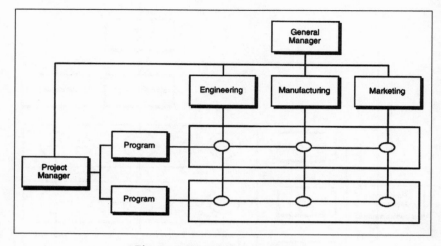

Figure 6-8 Matrix Organization

Figure 6-8 illustrates a classic matrix structure, with two chains of command. On the right side are the traditional functional departments: engineering, manufacturing, and marketing. The organization still benefits from the information exchange and control provided by the grouping of people by function. On the left is another chain of command, with a product manager for each major new product coordinating the activities of individuals across functional groups. Thus, functional managers who supervise product-related activities have two bosses—a functional boss and a product boss. In this way, information is processed both within and across functional groups at the same time that product-related activities are being coordinated.

From every perspective, matrix structures are complex. They require dual systems, roles, controls, and rewards. Systems, structures, and processes must be developed to handle both dimensions of the matrix. Furthermore, matrix managers must deal with the difficulties of sharing a common subordinate, while the common subordinate must face off against two bosses.

As shown in Figure 6-9, the general manager is the single boss, the point at which each side of the matrix comes together. This individual must ensure that each side of the matrix enjoys equal power and influence; otherwise, the organization will revert to a single-focus organization. Below the matrix manager there is also a clear hierarchy; his or her subordinates report to one boss. The matrix is most directly felt by the matrix manager and the two matrix supervisors. It is this relatively narrow slice of the organization that really sees matrix systems, roles, proce-

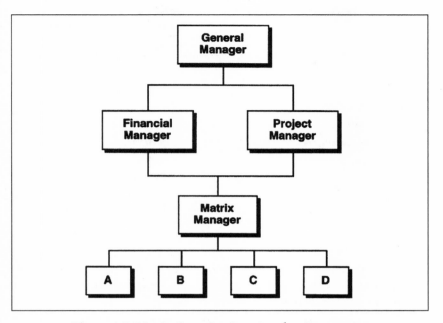

Figure 6-9 Matrix Organization: Another Perspective

dures, and processes. This set of four roles must constantly balance the pressures and conflicts in a structure that attempts to work several strategic directions at once.

In the case of ABB, only 500 or so of the 210,000 employees actually find themselves in matrix roles, with two bosses. But for each of them, the challenge of handling continuous ambiguity is considerable. Those managers, says CEO Percy Barnevik, "must have the self-confidence not to become paralyzed if they receive conflicting signals, and the integrity not to play one boss off against the other" (Taylor 1991).

While the matrix structure is the most complex and conducive to conflict of the major linking mechanisms, it is, at the same time, the only structure designed to maximize several strategically important considerations at once. Given its complexity and its inherent instability, a matrix structure should be reserved for situations in which no other linking alternative is workable.

Making Structural Linking Decisions

There are a number of basic criteria for comparing alternative linking mechanisms: cost and resource utilization; dependence on the

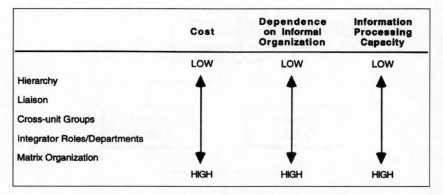

	Cost	Dependence on Informal Organization	Information Processing Capacity
	LOW	LOW	LOW
Hierarchy	↑	↑	↑
Liaison			
Cross-unit Groups			
Integrator Roles/Departments			
Matrix Organization	↓	↓	↓
	HIGH	HIGH	HIGH

Figure 6-10 Consequences of Structural Linking Mechanisms

informal organization; and inherent capacity for processing information (see Figure 6-10). The key to effective decisions about linking mechanisms is to choose the formal structures that are most consistent with the work-related interdependence of the groups to be linked. As we stated earlier, overly complex mechanisms are expensive and inefficient; arrangements that are too simple for the work at hand just won't get the job done.

In general terms, major forms of structural linking mechanisms can be assessed on the basis of these dimensions:

1. The *cost, in terms of both money and resources,* associated with each mechanism differs greatly. The formal hierarchy and liaison roles require sustained attention to coordination by only a few key individuals; matrix structures, on the other hand, require dual structures, systems, and procedures. Matrix structures also require time, energy, and effort devoted to committees and teams that attend to both axes of the matrix. The more people, systems, and procedures that are involved, the more costly the linking mechanism.

2. Formal linking mechanisms also differ in their *dependence on the informal organization.* Whereas the hierarchy and some liaison roles rest firmly on the formal organization, cross-group units, integrator roles, and matrix structures depend to a great degree on a healthy informal organization. Those more complex linking mechanisms actually create conflict within the organization; accordingly, they succeed best in situations where a resilient informal operating environment can handle the ambiguity and the conflict inherent in intense relationships of interdependence. Indeed, matrix structures work only in organizations whose values, beliefs, and practices

allow for open conflict resolution, constant collaboration, and ambiguous relationships. Thus, the more complex the formal linking mechanism, the greater the dependence on the informal system.

3. The *information-processing capacities* of the various linking mechanisms vary significantly. The hierarchy and the liaisons forms are limited by capacity of the individuals involved to collect, process, and channel information. These simple linking mechanisms deal well with simple interdependence but cannot deal with substantial uncertainty or complex work interdependence. Liaison roles, for example, can relay only limited amounts of information; while they can identify issues that require coordination, their capacity to resolve conflicts is limited. Integrator roles, task forces, cross-unit groups, and matrix structures not only can identify the issues to be handled but can also involve the right number of people from various units to coordinate and complete a job. These more complex mechanisms push decision making deep into the system and take advantage of a great many more resources and perspectives. They allow for multiple points of view and real-time problem solving and error correction.

As is the case with grouping, decisions about linking must be made at every level of the organization. Because managers at each level are dealing with different degrees of work interdependence and different information-processing requirements, each will face different choices about linking mechanisms. For example, the sequential interdependence at the corporate level can be handled by a senior team or committee; more complex linking mechanisms are required to deal with reciprocal interdependence within the division.

Structural linking is an important managerial tool. Whereas a single form of strategic grouping is selected for each level of the organization, there may be a host of structural linking mechanisms within a single unit. At Technicon's R&D facility, for example, structural linking might be accomplished via a matrix organization throughout the laboratory. Furthermore, special task forces might be set up to deal with the impact of new technologies on the organization; a top team might be convened to deal with a new competitive threat; and informal committees might be established to share expertise across disciplines within the laboratory. Linking, then, can be a powerful and flexible tool to deal with the different coordination requirements that exist within all organizations.

Finally, as work interdependence shifts over time, so too should the choice of linking mechanisms. These mechanisms need not be

permanent; indeed, one of their advantages is that they can be created to deal specifically with an immediate problem—the rapid development and introduction of a new product, the formulation of a
response to an immediate competitive threat, or the resolution of
problems involving a specific customer or supplier. At Ford, for
example, a special Skunk Works was created in 1989 for the express
purpose of redesigning—and, in truth, rescuing—the Mustang. Engineers and production specialists from throughout the Ford empire
were drafted to work exclusively on the project, which lasted until
the first new Mustang rolled off the assembly line in 1993. At that
point, the team was disbanded, although the Skunk Works concept
had proven to be so effective that Ford decided to use it again to focus
cross-unit resources intensively on other problems (Ingrassia and
White 1994).

Linking through Processes and Systems

Up to this point, we've discussed linking mechanisms largely in
terms of the formal roles and structures that constitute the hierarchy of any organization or work group. But designers of organizations have become increasingly aware in recent years that *processes*
and *systems* also play a vital role in coordinating activity and in
enabling people to link their efforts into productive work. In this
context, we use the term "processes" to describe sequences of collaborative efforts by groups and individuals, at various organizational levels and frequently across structural boundaries, performed in
the pursuit of a common objective. The term "systems" refers to
mechanisms that use human or physical technology to enable people and groups to perform the work required by a particular process.

Although processes and systems seem somewhat nebulous in
contrast with formal hierarchical structures, they are gaining growing attention as potentially powerful sources of linking in coordination. In practice, processes and systems often complement formal
hierarchical roles and structures. In some cases—and to a limited
extent—processes and systems can even take the place of traditional hierarchies.

Because the focus on processes is a relatively recent phenomenon, there is still considerable discussion and a wide range of views
on how to approach them from the perspective of organization
design. In general, however, we believe that organization processes
can be classified in three broad categories:

1. *Strategic management processes.* These are processes involved in shaping, directing, and controlling activity at the enterprise level. Strategic planning, general management, resource allocation, and operational reviews all fall into this category. These are processes that link and coordinate activities by creating overall plans, providing the resources and direction that allow units to mesh their activities in accordance with the plan, and then assessing the degree to which the units have met their goals. These are basically control processes that set direction and provide the information necessary for assessment and error correction.

2. *Business management processes.* These processes coordinate work flow—the movement of products, services, and resources through the organization and across grouping boundaries—in order to create an offering of value to the customer. More and more organizations are coming to perceive product development, for example, as a cross-unit process rather than as the exclusive domain of a single department where scientists and engineers work in a vacuum to dream up new products divorced from any timely insights into market trends or customer needs. Increasingly, product development is being seen as a continuous feedback loop, with sales, marketing, and service people working closely with the units that design, produce and distribute goods and services; it is a multidimensional process that draws on the skills, experience, and information of numerous people from a wide range of functions and disciplines. The design of product development, order fulfillment, and customer management as coordinated processes, rather than as isolated departments, represents a fundamentally new way of thinking about how organizations should be architected.

3. *Support management processes.* These include activities such as human resources, public relations, and information management, which provide the policies and practices that enable the organization to conduct its operations in an orderly way and in keeping with its articulated standards and values.

It's important to note that each set of processes has an associated set of systems—communications systems, production systems, systems for staff selection and training. Processes and systems are inherently wed; generally speaking, processes are incapable of functioning without the requisite systems. A budget-planning and control process, for example, is worthless without an appropriate business information system capable of identifying, gathering, processing, and reporting the necessary data. At each level, the smooth integration of processes and systems plays a large role in determining the organization's capacity to coordinate work.

While the emergence of business processes as an important form of linking has attracted considerable attention—and is discussed in depth in Chapter 8—design leaders should also be paying close attention to the significant linking power inherent in support processes such as human resources, quality assurance, and information systems.

Support Management Processes

Consider, for example, the strategic selection process at Xerox, first designed to identify candidates for top-management positions during the 1992 restructuring. In this process, a systematic determination of the skills and the personal characteristics required for leadership positions is made; these are then matched with profiles of prospective candidates. The employment of a company-wide process for selection and assessment, including a shared list of the most important criteria, not only links the business units through a shared understanding of leadership requirements; it also helps identify people in each unit who have the potential to take on important jobs in other parts of the company.

Reward systems, in particular, are among the most potent support processes for reinforcing linkages throughout the organization by motivating the required behavior. It's only human nature for each of us to pay close attention to the performance criteria on which we'll be evaluated and rewarded. Consequently, there has to be a high degree of consistency between linkage mechanisms and patterns of rewards; otherwise, the organization is sending conflicting signals, which can only result in confusion, frustration, and inadequate performance.

Consider, for example, an organization in which the manufacturing division is rewarded on the basis of gross margins, while the sales division is rewarded for volume. Clearly, sales will do everything possible to reduce the unit price in order to sell as much as possible. Every time it drops the price—and, as a result, the margin—the manufacturing group takes a beating. Manufacturing, on the other hand, may be cutting corners wherever possible to lower the unit cost—but in the process, it may be diminishing the product's quality or eliminating popular features that the sales force believes are important to customers. Driven by contradictory rewards systems, the two divisions end up working at cross-purposes. There is no set of structural linking mechanisms that can overcome such starkly conflicting reward patterns.

The Technicon research lab, despite its other problems, was making a creditable attempt to align its rewards systems with its linkage mechanisms. In the past, in keeping with its functional and activity-based grouping, scientists were rewarded solely on the basis of the technical quality of their research and of the recognition they'd won within the discipline. As the lab was reorganized with a team of project directors to focus attention on developing marketable products and processes, the incentive system was fundamentally changed; rewards were directly tied to product-related achievements.

Any bonus and incentive systems should incorporate these general principles:

- Incentives should clearly link performance to pay and should directly link performance to specific standards and objectives. If a team's objective is customer satisfaction, that should be the measure of performance, rather than volume or duration of service calls, which may bear little relation to whether the customer's needs were actually met.

- Rewards should relate directly to the nature of performance required at each level of the organization. At Corning, for example, in order to develop a true team perspective among top executives, the bonus plan for each member of the senior team is based largely on the entire company's success in meeting certain specific financial goals, such as stock price. But in other situations—fund managers in an investment firm, for example—it's more appropriate to base rewards on each person's individual performance.

- Rewards should be directly linked to objectives that are within the group's or individual's power to control. The manufacturing division we just mentioned had no control over margins, the basis of its incentives, as long as the sales division could unilaterally change prices to fuel volume sales.

- Incentive plans should match measurement periods for rewards to relevant performance periods; some goals can be assessed after three months, while it might not be practical to evaluate others in less than a year. Some incentive programs recognize that fact by containing both short- and long-term goals.

- Reward systems should be guided by the principle of equity, not equality.

From the standpoint of organizational architecture, designers need to step back, take a broad view, and appreciate the importance of processes at all three levels—strategic, business, and support. They need to examine these two issues:

1. To what extent will a new design affect existing processes? Some processes will continue to be valid, while others will become obsolete. Some processes may still be necessary but become unworkable in their present form.
2. In light of new grouping patterns introduced by redesign, what new processes will be needed to link those reconfigured groupings?

In short, as designers look at the new organization and the need for linkages, they need to think beyond traditional ideas of hierarchies and formal structures and fully explore the expanding role of processes in modern enterprises.

Staff Versus Line

Implicit in our discussion of processes is the obvious need for people to perform these vital management and support functions. But that's become something of a touchy subject in these times of downsizing, lean bureaucracies, and an overwhelming focus on concentrating resources in those areas that provide immediate value to the customer, and add value directly to the bottom line.

Yet, the fact remains that no complex organization can function efficiently over an extended period of time without proper management, control, and support. The issue for designers is to figure out the extent to which those processes are required and then to manage the inherent conflict between staff and line positions. To be clear about our terms, *line* positions are jobs directly involved with the organization's core business processes—designing, producing, delivering, or selling the organization's offerings. *Staff,* on the other hand, refers to people and jobs assigned to management and support processes such as human resources, finance, planning, legal, and information services. Staff positions are essentially extensions of the management function, with the purpose of aiding in control and coordination.

The design of staff jobs always raises some fundamental problems. First, because these jobs, by definition, are not directly involved with producing or selling the company's offerings, they're generally viewed as unproductive overhead. Moreover, at a time when many companies are seeking the benefits of decentralization, staff jobs are seen as extensions of centralized planning and decision making. Indeed, staff jobs are often perceived as not just unproductive but as downright counterproductive.

That's an unfair generalization, although it's easy enough to understand the ongoing friction between line and staff managers. Particularly in large organizations, staff groups serve important functions. To begin with, as we've already seen, grouping promotes focus; without some staff groups, certain functions outside the realm of the core business, such as human resources, would inevitably become after-thoughts or even drop from sight altogether. Staff groups augment the ability of senior management to gather, process, and disseminate information; in a large corporation, it's just impossible for top executives to be everywhere and see everything. Third, staff groups monitor and coordinate policies among various units, ensuring consistency throughout the organization in areas such as personnel policies and financial reporting requirements. Finally, the pooling of expert resources in staff groups ought to provide economies of scale. Corporate human resource, planning, and research staff groups, for example, develop specialized expertise in their respective areas. They serve as resources for professionals working within the divisions and coordinate, link, and update their more local colleagues.

Those are the advantages of staff groups. On the other hand, the problems they present, in practice, are considerable. Some of the major ones are these:

1. *Proliferation and growth.* The seeds of staff groups, once planted in organizational soil, take root quickly and grow like crazy. After reaching maturity, they're tough to cut back and nearly impossible to wipe out; the work they do, by its very nature, never seems to be finished.

2. *Direct costs.* On one hand, staff groups do not directly contribute to output, nor do they generate revenue. But their payrolls can be staggering.

3. *Indirect costs.* In addition to salaries, expenses, clerical support, and facilities, support staffs impose substantial indirect costs. The most important are the time and effort line managers spend responding to requests, demands, and requirements imposed by staff. There's also the additional time required for making decisions whenever staff people get involved.

4. *Competition for power.* The often adversarial relationship between line and staff creates dysfunctional conflicts and power plays. The costs to the organization, both direct and indirect, can be immense.

5. *Internal management and motivation.* Staff groups frequently are hard to manage, difficult to motivate, and impossible to satisfy. Their work rarely lends itself to easy measurement or assessment, so rewards are tricky. Moreover, because of their role outside the core functions, they see their career opportunities as severely limited.

6. *Bureaucratization.* Staff groups, focused by definition on processes rather than outputs, can encourage bureaucratic cultures marked by increased costs, slower response times, and widespread frustration.

7. *Building defensive staffs.* The staff problem becomes truly critical when line managers create their own "defensive" staffs to ward off the attacks of the invading central staff. Like other staffs groups, the new ones contribute nothing to output or revenue, drive up costs, and immediately begin proliferating, thus continuing the perpetual life cycle of staff groups.

Given both the need for certain staff functions, plus the serious problems often associated with staff groups, the organization designer faces a delicate balancing act. The trick is to create staff groups capable of control and coordination without creating a bureaucratic monster that can reshape the very nature of the organization it was supposed to assist.

There are some specific techniques that effective organizations have used to prevent staff groups from manifesting some of their more dysfunctional characteristics. These include:

1. *Layering*—limiting the number of layers of staff groups by prohibiting redundant staffs at successive levels. Layering prevents excessive staff-to-staff interaction and speeds the movement of information through the hierarchy.

2. *Rotating*—limiting the number of career staff people and rotating line employees into staff assignments. This combines technical expertise with practical knowledge of the core business. It also alleviates internal management problems, minimizes conflict, and builds greater appreciation of various perspectives within the organization.

3. *Pruning*—periodically "pruning" staff groups by reassigning as many people as possible to line positions.

4. *Clarifying*—wherever possible, stipulating management processes and individual roles. The laws of organizational physics state that staff groups will expand to fill vacuums left by ambiguous processes (such as those for goal setting, decision making, and allocating resources). Clear boundaries limit their expansion and decrease opportunities for conflict.

5. *Managing*—articulating and demonstrating what you believe to be the proper role of staff groups. How managers spend their time—and who they spend it with—clearly conveys their true feelings about the respective roles of line and staff groups.

Informal Linking Processes

Before leaving the topic of strategic linking, it's important to note that within most organizations there are powerful linking forces that lie beyond the scope of formal structures and processes. Although they are not an obvious element of the formal design process, they nevertheless are significant factors that managers need to take into consideration as they think about redesigning existing organizations. At the very least, managers should be looking for ways to provide for designs and roles that are consistent with—and that capitalize on—these informal processes.

The first informal process can be described as *socialization.* Each organization's culture—its values, beliefs, and behavioral norms—helps people understand how they're expected to act, even in the absence of formal structures and processes. Particularly in professional service firms—law firms, medical practices, accounting firms, for example—people tend to behave in accordance with a commonly shared code of conduct. That code is an integral part of the training people receive when they first enter the profession, and it is reinforced over the years through everyday practice.

Particularly in organizations with strong cultures, these universal codes of behavioral expectations play a powerful coordinating role that cuts across physical distances and jurisdictional boundaries. They provide a common language that facilitates collaboration, a frame of reference that helps guide decision making in ambiguous situations, and a set of expectations about how to deal with employees, peers, customers, and competitors.

A second source of linking lies in *informal relationships.* Particularly in large organizations with operating sites spread all over the country or around the globe, collaboration and decision making are infinitely easier if people have some relationship with the colleagues with whom they're dealing, rather than simply respond to a detached voice on the phone or an impersonal e-mail from a virtual stranger. That's why organizations such as ABB, among many others, go out of their way to provide periodic opportunities for managers from different countries and business groups to spend time together at training sessions and management conferences and in other settings where they can spend some time building the informal relationships that can prove invaluable down the road.

At the same time, informal relationships play an important linking role in practically every organization. In a classic situation we describe in much greater detail in Chapter 10, General Motors found out just how vital those relationships were in 1984 when it embarked on a massive restructuring that almost overnight disrupted thousands of relationships that had been built up over the years. Managers who would have in the past normally performed a certain job on the basis of a phone call from a colleague suddenly reverted to formal procedures and demanded half a dozen sign-offs from higher-ups before agreeing to the same request from a stranger (Keller 1989).

The third source of informal linking relates to what we call *emergent roles.* Over time, certain people, without being asked, tend to take on certain roles that serve important coordination functions. These roles, though nearly always informal, provide crucial linkages between various formal groups. They generally fall into four categories.

The first group can be described as *idea generators.* These are the people who, regardless of their job descriptions, have the inclination and the ability to synthesize creatively ideas and insights from different groups and disciplines. The second group includes the *champions,* those who take creative ideas—their own or someone else's—and bring them to fruition by selling the ideas, taking risks, and finding the necessary resources to pursue the "cause." The third group can be described as *gatekeepers* or *boundary spanners.* These are the people with an unusually global view of their industry or profession who effectively link their colleagues to important information outside the organization or business unit. Finally, there are the *sponsors,* the senior people within the organization who provide informal support, resources, and protection for unusual projects or ideas.

These critical linking functions can't be formalized; they can't be made part of the organization's official structure or systems. Indeed, turning them into formal jobs generally renders them ineffective. Their success relies on the skills and the interests of a small number of essential people; research suggests that no more than 15 percent of the employees within an organization actually perform these key functions.

While these informal roles can't be formalized, they can be encouraged and expanded. For example, one R&D director tried unsuccessfully to appoint gatekeepers. Having failed, she then identified people who were informally filling that role, gave them access to databases and an increased travel budget, and then found new ways to involve them in task forces with people throughout the organization. And she explicitly rewarded them for their successful efforts.

These informal roles can be critical. Without idea generators, the quality of interunit collaboration suffers. Without champions, joint efforts tend to fizzle on the launch pad. Without gatekeepers, both in-house and external expertise go to waste. And without senior sponsors, parochial resistance stymies collaborative projects.

These informal roles tend to evolve in organizations with particularly clear core values; their clarity and consistency give people both the guidance and the confidence to take on responsibilities beyond their specific job descriptions. When core values are murky, the informal organization tends to be chaotic, people hesitate to take on informal roles, and those who do assume them often become embroiled in conflict.

ABB Revisited

ABB, as it has emerged over the years, illustrates practically every major form of structural linking mechanism. To begin with, its very structure—a complex matrix system—is, in essence, an organization-wide linking device. In that sense, ABB provides linkage through its hierarchy. Indeed, the linking extends even within the senior team; each of the dozen executive vice presidents has a variety of responsibilities; a single executive may supervise a corporate functional area, such as finance, oversee a large geographic area, and manage an industry segment involving four or five of the fifty business areas. It is a structure designed to maintain the close integration of 5,000 far-flung profit centers in a tight corporate office consisting of only 150 people.

Moreover, ABB links its operations at every opportunity—while still maintaining the essentially local nature of each operating company—by sharing technology, expertise, marketing strategies, and distribution networks. ABB companies around the world speak the same language, both literally and in terms of performance standards and strategic objectives. It is a constant balancing act—as Barnevik said—between big and small, global and local, centralized and decentralized. It is an amazingly complex pattern of linkages, a worldwide confederation of local companies.

While grouping decisions set the groundwork for organization design, the ensuing decisions about linking mechanisms are no less vital. They are essential to achieving the effective coordination of the various disparate units created by the grouping process.

Linking mechanisms can range from simple devices, such as liaison roles, to much more complex approaches, such as the matrix system we've described at ABB. Whatever their form, their function remains essentially the same: to provide whatever channels are necessary to let information flow freely among people and units separated by grouping. Those information-processing requirements will vary according to the information-sharing requirements that exist between each group. The challenge to managers is to design the appropriate pattern of linkages that will create the clearest channels of information with the minimum commitment of people, time, money, and other organizational resources.

In Chapters 5 and 6, we've laid out the basic building blocks of design—grouping and linking. Now it's time to begin applying these theoretical concepts to the actual work of design organizations and work units. We turn first, in Chapter 7, to enterprise-level design and explore some of the new architectural forms that are being developed to unlock an organization's untapped competitive strengths.

Bibliography

Our work on linking, managerial systems, and informal organizations builds on many others, including the following:

Brown, S., and K. Eisenhardt. "Product Development: Past Research and Present Findings." *Academy of Management Review* 20 (1995): 343–378.

Clark, K., and S. Wheelwright. "Organizing and Leading Heavyweight Development Teams." *California Management Review* (Spring 1992): 9–26.

Davis, S., and P. Lawrence. *Matrix.* Reading, Mass.: Addison-Wesley, 1977.

Eccles, R., and D. Crane. *Doing Deals: Investment Banks at Work.* Boston: Harvard Business School Press, 1988.

Galbraith, J. *Designing Complex Organizations.* Reading, Mass.: Addison-Wesley, 1973.

Hammer, M., and J. Champy. *Reengineering the Corporation.* New York: Harper, 1993.

Iansiti, M., and K. Clark. "Integration and Dynamic Capability." *Industry and Corporate Change* 5 (1994): 24–36.

Ingrassia, P., and White, J. B. *Comeback: The Fall and Rise of the American Automobile Industry.* New York: Simon & Schuster, 1994.

Katz, R. "Organizational Socialization." In R. Katz, ed., *Managing Professionals in Innovative Organizations.* New York: Harper, 1988.

Katz, R., M. Tushman, and T. Allen. "Dual Ladder Promotion in R & D." *Management Science* 41 (1995): 848–862.

Keller, M. *Rude Awakening: The Rise, Fall and Struggle for Recovery of General Motors.* New York: Harper/Collins, 1989.

Kerr, S. "On the Folly of Rewarding A, While Hoping for B." *Academy of Management Executive* 9 (1995): 7–14.

Lawler, E. *Pay and Organization Development.* Reading, Mass.: Addison-Wesley, 1981.

Lucas, H. The *T-Form Organization.* San Francisco: Jossey-Bass, 1996.

Nohria, N., and R. Eccles. *Networks and Organizations: Structure, Form and Action.* Boston, Mass.: Harvard Business School Press, 1992.

Roberts, E., and A. Fusfeld. "Staffing the Innovative Technology-Based Organization." *Sloan Management Review* (1981): 19–34.

Sayles, L., and M. Chandler. *Managing Large Systems.* New York: Harper, 1971.

Taylor, W. "The Logic of Global Business: An Interview with ABB's Percy Barnevik." *Harvard Business Review* (March 1991): 91–104.

Van de Ven, A., A. Delbecq, and R. Koenig. "Determinants of Coordination Modes within Organizations." *American Sociological Review* 41 (1976): 322–337.

Wageman, R. "Interdependence and Group Effectiveness." *Administrative Science Quarterly* 40 (1995): 145–180.

7

Designing at the Enterprise Level

Xerox 1992—A New Architecture for the Enterprise

In 1991, as we discussed in Chapter 2, the Xerox Corporation launched a year-long redesign process aimed at meeting its strategic objectives as "The Document Company." The design intent was clear: Xerox had to become more customer focused; it had to do everything faster, from product development to customer service; it had to make people more accountable for the development and delivery of products and services; and it had to increase productivity by unleashing the creativity and the entrepreneurial instincts of its people.

Early in the process, one thing became clear: Another of Xerox's periodic, incremental restructurings wouldn't get the job done. No amount of tinkering would help the old organization fulfill the new strategy. What Xerox needed was an entirely new architecture—a dramatic new design built on new structures, new processes, new patterns of groupings and linkages, new ways of managing and performing. In the end, Xerox transformed a traditional functional structure (see Figure 2-1) into an organization of independent, end-to-end business units linked by three sets of shared processes (see Figure 7-1). The basis of the structure was the formation of nine business divisions—for example, Personal Document Products,

117

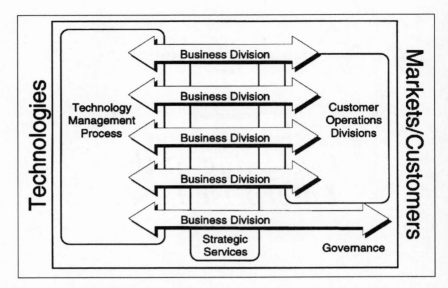

Figure 7-1 Xerox 1992 Organization Chart (*Note:* There were 9 Business Divisions which included: Personal Document Products, Xerox Engineering Systems, X-Soft, Office Document Products, Office Document Systems, Document Production Systems, Printing Systems, Xerox Business Services, and Document Solutions)

Printing Systems, and Advanced Document Services—segmented on the basis of products and users. Each was to be headed by an executive with front-to-back responsibility, from product development all the way to sales and service. At the same time, Xerox looked for ways to capitalize on its traditional areas of strength, with the independent business units sharing pooled resources where it made sense. A set of processes—technology, manufacturing, strategic planning, and customer operations (sales and service)—was therefore designed to provide benefits of scale and to avoid duplication of resources by contracting the services of these areas to each of the business units. The corporate staff was significantly reduced, as much of the heavily centralized decision-making apparatus was dismantled and executives running the business units were empowered to make most decisions on their own. In effect, the corporate office shifted its emphasis from tight control of functional operations to strategic coordination of integrated, semiautonomous units.

In many ways, the change was a wrenching one for Xerox and its people. One of the most senior executives, absolutely convinced that the shifting of immense power and responsibility from the central office to the chiefs of each business division would make the company totally unmanageable, ended up leaving. Managers who in the past might have been obvious candidates for some of the most desirable new jobs were passed over in favor of less senior people who had demonstrated greater potential to handle the entrepreneurial roles required of business unit presidents. But Xerox understood that a radical new architecture—including radically altered managerial roles—was essential if it was to successfully exploit its full competitive advantage.

Patterns of Enterprise Architecture

The design of organizations at the enterprise level—in essence, the overall architectural framework for the organization—used to be a relatively simple exercise. As we've already seen, traditional organizations consisted of configurations of functional units engaged in product development, manufacturing, and marketing. Depending on the degree of interdependence required for each group to mesh its work with the activities of others, management would create a series of linking mechanisms to coordinate their work.

Moreover, there was an underlying assumption that "big is beautiful" and "more is better." Until fairly recently, the implicit imperative was to grow—to add new divisions, bring outside functions inside the corporate tent (as General Motors did with engineering, manufacturing, and, more recently and unsuccessfully, data processing), to acquire more subsidiaries, to branch out into more and more businesses.

The 1990s have witnessed a marked reversal of that trend. More and more holding companies found they had gobbled more new and unrelated businesses than they could digest. It became increasingly obvious that corporations could test the waters of new markets and new technologies through strategic alliances that didn't require risky, expensive, and energy-sapping acquisitions. And numerous companies, including Xerox, came to understand the untapped competitive forces that could be unleashed by rethinking the way they organized their internal operations.

In the late 1990s, there's a growing recognition that in many situations, "smaller is better." In the mid-1990s, this trend became a major driving force in corporate America, with companies such as AT&T, Corning, Melville and Dial voluntarily spinning off key operations into separate businesses. Less dramatic but more common were restructurings of the sort illustrated by our Xerox case—the reorganization of the enterprise into smaller, sharply focused units freed from centralized decision making and sluggish bureaucracies.

In this chapter, we want to focus on this emerging approach to enterprise-level design and how it is giving rise to new architectures that not only significantly alter internal structures but also create new designs that extend beyond the corporation's traditional outer walls. We're not suggesting by any means that these are the only forms of enterprise-level design or that they're equally appropriate for every company. But the truth is that most managers already operate, either consciously or unconsciously, with their own conceptual models based on the traditional functional organization and the old ITT-style conglomerate. Our purpose here is to explain some of the newer, more complex notions of enterprise architecture with the hope that managers, armed with that new perspective, will be better equipped to recognize the untapped opportunities for competitive advantage that lie within their own organizations.

Let's begin by envisioning a range of architectures at the enterprise level (see Figure 7-2). At one end of the scale is the *integrated enterprise*—another name for the traditional organization—the structure that characterized Xerox through 1991. It is, in essence, a single business composed of different functional groups—one developing products, another producing them, a third selling and servicing them. This structure involves the coordination and control problems we've discussed in earlier chapters—basically, how to link a series of processes that are inherently interdependent.

At the other end of the scale is the *organizational network*, an enterprise made up of a federation of independent business units. General Electric is the classic example. It is a conglomeration of companies with little in common, producing everything from light bulbs and household appliances to jet engines. It is a tent large enough to hold the broadcast giant NBC and the financial powerhouse GE Capital. GE's companies operate in different markets with unique technologies and separate infrastructures.

Organizational networks typically are characterized by combinations of loose and tight linkages. Generally, the various businesses are loosely coupled, except at those few points where resources can be shared and leveraged: management talent, access to capital, common technology. ABB, as we saw in Chapter 6, clearly operates as an organizational network. Each of its 300 companies operates largely as an independent entity, linked to the central office and the other companies primarily through management and support processes and informal sharing of technology.

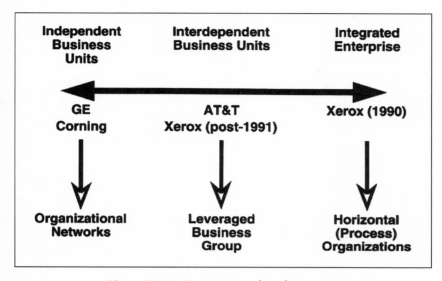

***Figure* 7-2** A Continuum of Architectures

The developing area of design lies somewhere between the integrated enterprise and the organizational network. It is the architecture adopted by Xerox in 1992—the alignment of *interdependent business groups.* As we saw with Xerox, these are collections of business units that independently pursue different market segments while enjoying the economies of scale they derive from pooled resources, shared processes, and centralized coordination. Underlying these new designs is a growing appreciation of two fundamental concepts of organization architecture: focus and leverage.

Focus and Leverage

Let's begin by considering the concept of *focus.* In this context, it relates directly to the notion that any business consists of a basic sequence of processes that transform basic technologies and materials into offerings that are brought to market (Porter 1985). Moving from the "back" of the organization to the "front," these processes typically include conceiving, designing, developing, manufacturing, selling, distributing, and supporting an offering. Each step along the value chain either contributes to the chain, takes from it, or, in most cases, both. As illustrated by Figure 7-3, the process of moving technologies to markets moves from left to right or from back to front. The far right side of the chain represents the interaction with the customer; we label that the "front" because it is the portion of the

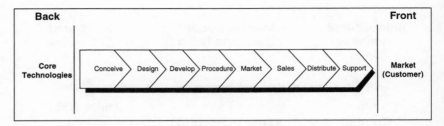

Figure 7-3 Value Chain (*Adapted from:* Porter, Michael E. *Competitive Advantage.* N.Y.: The Free Press, 1985)

chain that provides the source of most innovation. In traditional integrated organizations, each process within the value chain was relegated to a clearly definable and rigidly structured functional "silo." Each group's focus was immediate and internal—taking output from the preceding unit in the value chain, transforming it into input for the next. Each unit focused on its piece of the action; what happened once the product moved down the line was someone else's responsibility.

The new architectures, such as the interdependent business units adopted by Xerox, give each business unit within the company end-to-end, or back-to-front, responsibility for the entire value chain. The business unit that handled desktop copiers, for instance, had responsibility for everything from working with R&D on new innovations in copiers to devising marketing strategies that would open the doors to new customers. And that's what we mean by "focus"—the benefits that accrue from giving a set of people effective responsibility for each element in the value chain.

The experience of companies like Xerox, among others, is demonstrating some of the advantages that can be derived from breaking up a monolithic corporation into smaller, interdependent, and sharply focused units. To begin with, smaller, focused units allow businesses to get closer to their customers, providing people with the incentive to zero in on particular customers and market segments. Decentralization typically translates into greater speed, because decisions can be made by the people directly involved in the action. Similarly, the units benefit from being freed from the bureaucratized constraints of centralized planning. And accountability, often obscured by functional operations in which processes are handed off by one group to the next, comes into sharp focus.

Focused units hold benefits for the people who work in them, as well as for the organization as a whole. The responsibility for running an operation is stimulating for many people, who are eager to be rewarded for their initiative, creativity, and aggressiveness. In most situations, greater emphasis is placed on the role of teams, rather than a single boss, to solve problems and seek out opportunities. In general, greater independence results in more challenging, enriching jobs.

The second architectural concept driving the new designs is *leverage*—the capacity to derive advantages of scale from the common resources shared by the organization. These can be in the areas of common design, basic technologies, production capabilities, distribution networks, or customer operations, for example.

Consider the Minnesota Mining and Manufacturing Company (3M), a proven master at finding ways to leverage its core technology for an assortment of uses by its various business units. Its basic technology in the area of microreplication—covering surfaces with millions of tiny structures that lend different properties to the surfaces to which they're attached—began with the development, in 1964, of the lens for overhead projectors; since then, it has led to products as diverse as fasteners, specialty films, adhesives, CD-ROMs, lighted highway lane markers, and X-ray scans. The list goes on and on and includes products that in 1995 alone produced $1 billion in sales for 3M (Fortune 1996).

Or look at Dow Jones & Company, which led the news business in finding creative ways to repackage and resell the same news and advertisements. Pooling the news-gathering, advertising sales, and, in some cases, production capabilities of its various operations, it leverages those resources to recycle editorial and advertising output for a range of products: *The Wall Street Journal,* the *AP-Dow Jones* news service, the *Asian Wall Street Journal, The Wall Street Journal-Europe, The National Business Employment Weekly,* a weekly business report for Asia, syndicated radio reports, faxed news products, and a customized on-line news and stock report. The company relentlessly searches for new ways to leverage its basic technology—the ability to gather and process business-related news and advertising.

Designing for Focus and Leverage

Let's take our analysis a step further by combining the two concepts, focus and leverage. In organizations that successfully achieve this mix, the result is a series of business units, focused on particular market segments, that combine the entrepreneurial speed, efficiency, and customer focus of a small company with the economies of scale normally available only to large corporations. The issue for designers of organizational architectures, therefore, becomes one of identifying where potential sources of leverage can be successfully combined with a focused independent unit to gain competitive advantage. In general, using the "back-to-front" perspective of the value chain, there are three places in the organization that should be considered possible sources of leverage (see Figure 7-4).

One potential source of leverage is the "front," the organizational processes involved in bringing the offering to market and dealing face to face with the customer. This can involve marketing, customer service, and sales, for example. Xerox has traditionally fielded one of the most effective sales forces in the United States and Europe; as Xerox reorganized in 1992, it wouldn't have made much sense to create an independent sales team for each of the nine business units, with sales reps from each unit bumping into each other as they sought business from the same clients. The same was true of customer service; a single service team could take care of customer's problems, no matter which of the nine Xerox business units happened to design and produce any given piece of equipment.

Second, there is potential leverage in the "back" of the organization, the creation of products and services, through shared technologies and standardized production "platforms." Xerox, at one point, had more than half a dozen different groups working simultaneously—but in total isolation—on the same expensive job: designing keyboards. By the same token, General Motors during the 1980s, when it was stamping out five lines of practically identical cars that consumers could barely tell apart, still allowed nearly invisible design variations between comparable Chevrolets and Pontiacs that cost millions of dollars. In both cases, the companies squandered what should have been leveraged technology, expertise, and production capacity. Honda, on the other hand, demonstrated how to leverage the "back" when it launched its upscale Acura using the same chassis, the same technology, and many of the same parts as it used in its mid-priced Accord. With relatively minimal investment, Honda was able to introduce an entirely new product that allowed it to compete, for the first time, in the luxury auto market.

Third, some organizations have discovered opportunities for leverage in the "middle," the processes and mechanisms the organization uses to deliver products and services to its customers. Xerox moves literally tens of thousands of machines, components, and parts around the world at any given time; having each of the nine business units separately handle purchasing, inventory, and the movement of

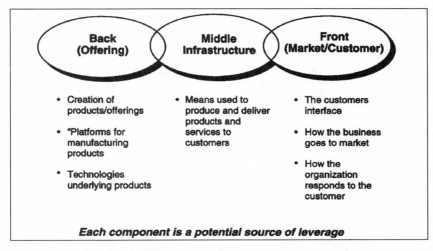

Figure 7-4 Three Potential Sources of Leverage in Leveraged Business Groups

supplies and equipment would be an expensive duplication of effort and would lose potential savings from volume discounts. So Xerox leverages its centralized services through a system called the integrated supply chain, providing each of the nine units with pooled services and resources unavailable to smaller competitors.

Each of these leverage points, taken individually or in combination with others, provides a variety of design options. Let's consider some examples:

- *Leveraged front.* Eli Lilly, the Indianapolis-based pharmaceutical company, underwent a major restructuring in the early 1990s in which it abandoned some of the peripheral operations it had maintained for years in order to focus its resources on areas where it believed it could be a world-class player. In order to focus its business units on specific segments of the marketplace, Lilly reorganized into five disease category groups, each specializing in developing drugs for a particular medical area such as oncology or central nervous system disorders (see Figure 7-5). While the focus of Lilly's business groups is clearly on producing offerings for specific segments of the medical market, it gains leverage by combining all the sales efforts of the five groups in a single sales force, with experience and contacts throughout the entire medical community.

- *Leveraged back.* Several years before it was spun off as Lucent Technologies, AT&T's Network Systems group reassessed its strategic objectives and determined that its traditional product-

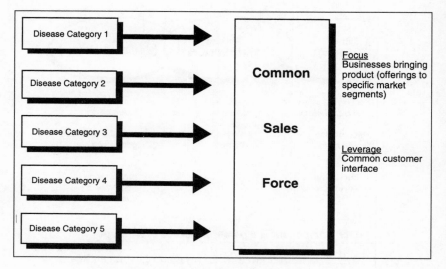

***Figure* 7-5** Leveraged Front (Eli Lilly Example)

based structure was no longer meeting the needs of many of its customers. In the past, each division had focused on producing specific components of telecommunications networks—switching and transmission equipment, cable, computer operating systems, and software. But as time went on, it became clear that the greatest growth potential lay with customers—foreign governments and telecommunications providers other than AT&T—who wanted a supplier who would design, install, service, and, in some cases, even operate complete systems for them. So Network Systems leveraged its "back" by reorganizing into a set of OBUs—Offerings Business Units—that provided technology platforms for components that could then be customized to meet specific customer needs (see Figure 7-6). At the "front" of the organization, the focus was on users; a group of customer business units, targeted at various geographic regions and segments of the telecommunications industry, would essentially pick the right parts—provided by the OBUs—off the shelf and design a system to meet each customer's specific requirements. The objective was to become a systems provider throughout the telecommunications industry. The irony of its success was that, due to continuing deregulation, it became inevitable that its customers for communications systems (such as the Bell regional companies) would also be AT&T's competitors in terms of delivering telecommunications services to customers. That internal strategic conflict helped fuel AT&T's decision to spin off Network Systems, along with several smaller

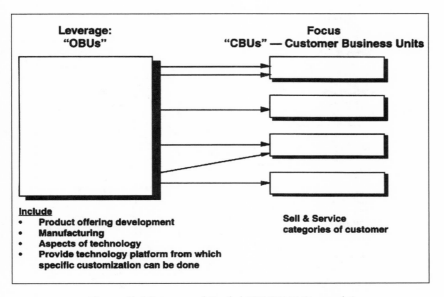

Figure 7-6 Leveraged Back (AT&T NS Example)

units and much of Bell Labs, as an independent company—Lucent Technologies.

- *Leveraged middle.* This design is increasingly common among companies in the financial services industry. Focus is maintained both at the front, through attention to products and customers, and at the back, with specialized core services, such as currency trading and portfolio management (see Figure 7-7). Leverage comes from the particular strengths of the infrastructure—a superior network, an outstanding distribution system, or a unique technology, for example. These designs require special vigilance to ensure that the "middle" remains a flexible and viable asset, rather than a rigid, bureaucratic quagmire that detracts from the focus of the core services and front-office customer relations.

- *Leveraged front and back.* This is the Xerox architecture. Xerox maintained its product focus through the nine independent business units but leveraged both its common technology and its worldwide sales force by pooling those resources at the front and the back (see Figure 7-8). The creation of independent business units resulted in entirely new ways of doing business. For example, a new unit focusing exclusively on simple, low-end business products became enormously successful by reaching out to new customers through discount office supply chains, rather than sell-

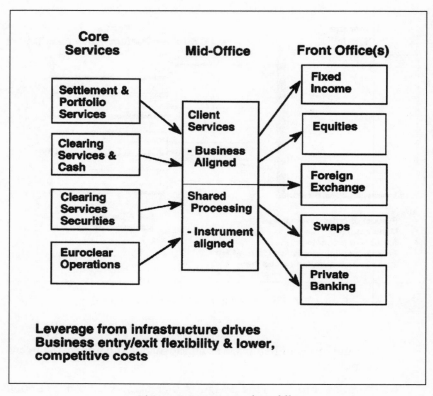

Figure 7-7 Leveraged Middle

ing exclusively through the Xerox sales force. The new Business Services unit prospered by offering to install, operate, and service entire document systems—essentially, a chance for companies to outsource their document-processing operations. In the past, that service would have been viewed as competition by the sales forces that were trying to sell as much hardware as possible; in the new Xerox, the service was correctly perceived as creating and capitalizing on entirely new markets.

- *Microenterprise units.* Sun Microsystems, a producer of computer network hardware and software, illustrates the most radical form of leveraged units, in which each and every element of the value chain is pulled out and analyzed in terms of its potential value, both within the larger enterprise and as a stand-alone operation (see Figure 7-9). The result is a group of business units structured as independent enterprises, all seeking out new customers and markets while drawing on the scale advantages of broad customer and supplier relationships.

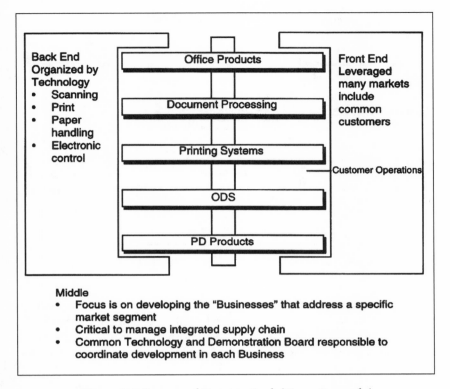

Figure 7-8 Leveraged Front to Back (Xerox Example)

The value chain begins with SPARC Technology Business, which designs and manufactures the microprocessors that are the core of the Sun system. But producing and providing chips to a single user—Sun—would make it difficult for SPARC to enjoy the scale economies and lower production costs of mass producers, such as Intel. So SPARC, in addition to supplying Sun, is out in the marketplace selling chips to a wide range of customers. Similarly, SunSoft, Inc., the creator of software products like Java and Solaris, now sells to other companies. (In fact, Sun has been giving away Java and Javascript in massive quantities in order to establish Sun's software as a standard for designers of Web sites on the Internet.)

The Sun chips and software are combined and packaged as computers by the Sun Microsystems Computer Company. The SunService division provides a full range of system support, systems integration, and information technology consulting. And SunExpress, Inc., Sun's after-marketing company, sells hardware and software produced by Sun, as well as other companies, through direct marketing.

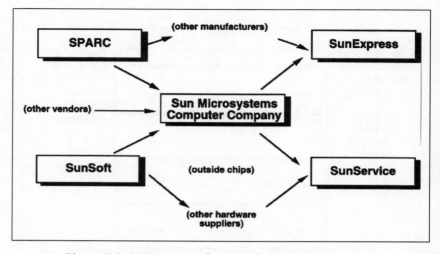

Figure 7-9 Organizational Network (Sun Microsystems)

The risk involved in these loose affiliations of market-driven enterprises is that the structural models are inherently unstable. In Sun's case, for example, the combination of five independent, aggressive units all seeking new suppliers and customers in related businesses raises the likelihood of conflicting relationships with other companies—sometimes partners, sometimes suppliers, sometimes customers, sometimes competitors. Our earlier example of AT&T Network Systems clearly illustrates the problem; while one arm of AT&T was trying earnestly to bid aggressively for a piece of business with a former Baby Bell, another arm, AT&T's communications services operations, saw that customer as a competitor and discouraged the deal. As disaggregation erodes traditional organizational boundaries, strategic dilemmas are certain to proliferate.

While the advantages of independent leveraged business groups are compelling, they present several important challenges to organizations considering them as an architectural option. The first challenge is to come up with the right definition of business units—to determine the logical combinations of products, processes, and core technologies. Once the underlying architecture is in place, the organization still faces all the design issues of grouping and linking that we discussed in Chapters 5 and 6.

Finally, the biggest design challenge facing the organization is how to link the business units without impairing their capacity to act independently. In other words, how do you maintain the necessary degree of alignment among all the different groups without controlling them so tightly that you lose the intended benefits—customer focus, speed, and the rest? As this new form of architecture develops, this issue of "tight alignment and loose control" will become increasingly crucial.

Strategic Alliances: Designing Beyond the Organizational Boundaries

In recent years, there has been a clear movement on the part of many organizations to focus their efforts on those elements of the value chain where they have some distinctive capability of competence. Conversely, they are less interested in spending time, energy and resources on those processes and activities where they have no unusual strengths.

One obvious outcome has been the huge growth in outsourcing, particularly in areas that simply aren't essential to the company's core offerings. Frequently, to use the value chain perspective, outsourcing involves the middle of the organization, the infrastructure. In 1994, for example, Xerox outsourced all its internal data processing work to EDS. But at the same time, Xerox benefited from the outsourcing trend by winning the business of numerous companies that were looking for someone else to handle their document production.

At the front and the back of the organization—those processes involving customers and basic technologies—there's been increasing interest in reinforcing and expanding the organization's competitive efforts through joint ventures and strategic alliances. Particularly in industries and professional sectors that are going through fundamental change—telecommunications, health care, and financial services, for example—companies are searching for ways to limit their exposure while testing the waters of new markets and technologies.

It's important to understand up front that most strategic alliances don't work; experience suggests that more than half run into trouble within the first two years and that the majority don't survive more than three years. There are lots of reasons for that, which we'll get to shortly. But the truth is that they are risky, often short-lived, and fraught with pitfalls. The reason they are so attractive, however, is that when they work, strategic alliances can be enormously powerful, providing the organization with the means to enter new markets and to access new technologies that might otherwise be out of reach.

The initial question, of course, is whether or not a strategic alliance makes sense and which form is most appropriate. One way to look at the problem is to consider the relationship between a venture's potential strategic importance and the organization's core competencies—in shorthand terms to think of the opportunities and the obstacles in terms of markets and technologies.

Consider the situation faced by General Electric and Microsoft in late 1995. GE and its broadcast network, NBC, had been searching in vain for ways to get involved with the Internet; but it was clear that Genie, GE's online service, was going nowhere. At the same time, the computing giant Microsoft was desperately searching for news and information content to carry on its own online service, the Microsoft Network. In December 1995, the two announced a joint venture through which they would operate both an all-news cable channel and an interactive online news service. If the new venture, called MSNBC, proves successful, the advantages to both are obvious: GE, with core competencies in producing news and entertainment programming, will gain entree to a potentially critical new market and, potentially, access to important new technologies, while Microsoft, with unparalleled access to the online market, will instantly obtain a product it couldn't possibly create on its own.

In other words, if the strategic objective is important and can be achieved with the organization's internal competencies, then by all means the venture should be kept inside. But if the objective requires skills, technologies, production capabilities, distribution systems, or other critical competencies in which the organization is weak, then it might be time to look for a partner.

There are three basic alternatives to consider when thinking about the value of strategic alliances in capitalizing upon new markets or technologies:

Scenario 1: You're considering a business venture that looks interesting. It involves a product or service aimed at a market that would be entirely new for your company; it would also require underlying technologies—skills and experience—that your company lacks. The most sensible way to dip your toes into that business with minimal risk is through a venture capital play, maintained at arm's length from your core business. If it flops, you've lost nothing but your initial investment; you haven't bulked up the payroll, built new plants, or disrupted your normal flow of business. At the same time, you've gained valuable information about new markets and technologies that will help you decide if a more serious venture is warranted.

Scenario 2: You're considering a venture aimed at your existing markets using your core technologies. You don't need a partner. Find a way to launch the venture within the organization. Companies like Xerox, for instance, have designed flexible organization structures that allow them quickly to create or disband their independent business units on the basis of changing opportunities in the marketplace.

Scenario 3: You're considering a venture that would use your core technology to go after market segments where you have no experience. Or, conversely, the markets you know intimately could be served by an offering based on technology you lack. These are the situations that offer the greatest potential for strategic alliances—each party brings something valuable to the table, but neither can be a real player without the help of the other.

Designing Effective Alliances

The problems involved in designing and structuring strategic alliances are incredibly complex. Think of all the issues involved in meshing the components of a single organization—the strategy, work, people, structures, and culture—and then multiply them geometrically.

Consider the problem in terms of our analogy with physical architecture. Imagine two companies that do business in separate but nearby office buildings. Our assignment is to design a new, small building connected to both, where both will jointly do business. One company is housed in a soaring, glass-and-steel skyscraper; the other occupies a squat structure of preformed concrete. Should the exterior design resemble one or the other, somehow combine both designs, or be something completely different? We need to tap into the heating and cooling system of one building or the other—but one runs on electricity, the other on natural gas; which do we choose? One company favors row after row of small, private offices and work areas; the other likes wide open workspaces with few offices or walls. Which floor plan do we adopt? As we start figuring out where to lay cable, and what kind, we discover that one company makes minimal use of computers and favors Macs, while the other is totally digitized and relies heavily on a complex PC-based network. How will we configure the information system in the middle building so that all three can easily communicate with one another?

It's easy to see why investing in a venture capitalist can be more attractive than a joint venture; in essence, you're just paying someone to go off somewhere and rent some space and report back to you on how things are going. The requirements for interdependence are minimal, almost nonexistent, from a design standpoint.

Given these complex issues, experience shows that potential partners in any joint venture have to reach some basic understanding about their respective organizations and about the mutual benefits they expect from the alliance before sealing the deal:

- The partners should have shared objectives and similar processes and cultures. Partnerships can tolerate only so many conflicts in values, beliefs, and ways of doing business before they tear apart. The truth is that while the partnership might make strategic sense, the companies involved might simply be too different to operate for long in close quarters.

- The strategy and objectives of the partnership need to be explicitly articulated and agreed to up front.

- The senior managers of the partnership need to have both the skills and the commitment essential to teamwork and collaboration. They need to design jointly the structures, processes, and guidelines for the operating environment of the new venture.

- Senior managers from each of the partner organizations should be given clear roles, with strict accountability, for supervising the project. That requires reward systems that give them the incentive to collaborate with their new partners.

- Partnerships should be entered into only with a clear understanding that the undertaking will be difficult and has only limited chances of long-term success. The partners should commit to giving the venture a reasonable period of time in which to succeed, understanding that during that time they'll have the opportunity to learn from both their triumphs and their failures.

The design of management structures for partnerships involves some special problems. Joint ventures are, by their very definition, matrix organizations, further complicated by the legal issues that dictate shared responsibility. The normal complexity involved in a matrix—the basic question of who's the boss—becomes even trickier.

Charles S. Raben, a colleague at Delta Consulting Group, Inc., has suggested two alternative designs for structuring the senior reporting relationships in a joint venture (Raben 1992). The first is what he calls a "collaborative structure," in which the manager of the joint venture reports to a board of directors made up of executives from each of the partner companies. On one hand, this allows both partners to be involved in strategic decisions while freeing the venture manager to act with relative independence in operational matters. But if it is to work, this structure requires a high degree of compatibility and cooperation between the partners at the board level; otherwise, decisions can get bogged down while conflict remains unresolved at the board level.

There are some essential conditions that must be met if the "collaborative structure" is to have much chance of success. Many of them overlap with our earlier list of prerequisites for successful ventures: compatible cultures, clear objectives, a commitment to giving the venture a predetermined amount of time, an understanding of the mutual benefits to be received by the partners. In addition, Raben suggests that the parties need to agree on a process for resolving differences, the need for minimal direct involvement by either party, and the basic autonomy of the venture.

If many of those ingredients are missing, Raben suggests, the partnership would fare better with an "instrumental structure." Rather than trying continually to balance control, one company becomes the dominant partner in the venture while the other assumes a passive role. The board of directors still includes executives from both partners, but its role is limited to general oversight. The manager of the venture reports directly to the dominant partner.

From an operational standpoint, the instrumental structure is cleaner, simpler, and easier to implement than the collaborative structure. The primary problem, however, is that passive partners often have a difficult time getting used to that role, particularly when they've had little experience with their new partner. There's a natural desire to be fully apprised of the venture's progress, even if they're not actively involved in running it. In theory, their participation on the board of directors should satisfy that need. But the fact remains that even in the best of situations, partnerships are complex, fragile, and fraught with danger.

Corning's Blueprint for Success

No major company has had more success with joint ventures than Corning. The company has entered into nearly fifty joint ventures since the 1920s; only six have failed. So it's instructive to consider briefly why Corning enters into these alliances and how it structures them so effectively.

Jamie Houghton, before retiring in 1996 as Corning's chairman, gave five major reasons why Corning allies itself with other companies (Houghton 1990):

1. *Gaining market access*—gaining access to new markets or to those where Corning's entry on its own would take too long. Corning's fiberglass technology, together with Owens-Illinois's production and distribution presence in the building products industry, resulted in the enormously successful Owens-Corning venture, which eventually became an independent company.

2. *"Leaping downstream"*—Forming an alliance that allows Corning to use a material or system component of its own to provide a full system. After Corning developed optical fiber, it joined forces in the 1970s with Siemens of Germany to form Siecor Optical Cable, which provides optical communications systems around the world.

3. *Applying technology*—Until it encountered its well-publicized problems with breast implants, the Dow Corning alliance converted Corning's silicon technology into literally thousands of products ranging from shampoo to sealing compounds.

4. *Accessing new technology*—In 1982, Corning and Genentech, the biotechnology company, formed Genencor, a joint venture that is primarily a research and development operation. The alliance gave Corning access to Genentech's recombinant DNA technology, while Genentech gained access to Corning's knowledge about enzyme and protein immobilization.

5. *Penetrating national markets*—Corning brings technology and product lines to the alliances, while its overseas partners provide plant sites, sales and labor forces, presence, and influence in their home countries. For example, Corning provided its picture-tube bulb technology to a joint television venture with Samsung, the Korean maker of consumer electronics.

Given its long record of effective alliances and joint ventures, Corning has developed some basic principles over the years for increasing the chances for success. Most echo the general criteria we've already discussed. This is how Corning describes those criteria:

1. Compatibility between the parent companies in terms of strategy and culture
2. Comparable contributions by each partner, in terms other than the financial investment
3. No initial conflicts of interest in respective fields of interest
4. Trust between key senior people at each parent company

5. Separation of the operating team from the parent companies, with the venture's management given a free hand to pursue its own entrepreneurial instincts

Xerox Revisited

The Xerox restructuring of 1992 illustrates a trend that is capturing the imagination of organizational designers. As we saw, the company looked for—and found—a creative new architecture that provided its major business operations with both focus and leverage. Each unit within Xerox was given end-to-end responsibility, starting with development and proceeding with a clear line of vision directly to the customer. Disaggregation freed each unit to unleash the ingenuity and the competitive spirit of its people on sharply focused markets. At the same time, the company leveraged its common technology and pooled sales force to gain scale economies that provide each business unit with important competitive advantages.

We also saw in this chapter how the traditional boundaries of the organization are eroding, with creative organizations seeking new forms of strategic alliances and new patterns of extraorganizational architecture. For now, many of those new designs remain risky and unlikely to succeed—but powerfully attractive, nonetheless, given the potential benefits.

Next, in Chapter 8, we explore the use of new designs to fundamentally change the way work is done within the organization.

Bibliography

See the following for more detail on network alliances, joint ventures, and enterprise architectures:

Bartlett, C., and S. Ghoshal. *Managing Across Borders.* Boston, Mass.: Harvard Business School Press, 1991.

Doz, Y., and G. Hamel. "Use of Alliances in Implementing Technology Strategies." In Y. Doz, ed., *Managing Technology for Corporate Renewal.* New York: Oxford University Press, 1997.

Hamel, G., and C. K. Prahalad. *Competing for the Future.* Boston, Mass.: Harvard Business School Press, 1994.

Harrigan, K. *Strategies for Joint Ventures.* Lexington, Mass.: Lexington Books, 1985.

Houghton, Jamie. Speech to Jonathan Club, Los Angeles, Calif., January 23, 1990.

Nohria, N., and R. Eccles. *Networks and Organizations.* Boston, Mass.: Harvard Business School Press, 1992.

Porter, M. E. *Competitive Advantage*. New York: Free Press, 1985.

Quinn, J. *The Intelligent Enterprise*. New York: Free Press, 1992.

Quinn, J., P. Anderson, and S. Finkelstein. "Forms of Organizing for Hypercompetition." In M. Tushman and P. Anderson, eds., *Readings in the Management of Innovation*. New York: Oxford University Press, 1997.

Raben, C. S. "Building Strategic Partnerships: Creating and Managing Effective Joint Ventures." In D. A. Nadler, M. S. Gerstein, and R. B. Shaw, *Organizational Architecture: Designs for Changing Organizations*. San Francisco: Jossey-Bass, 1992.

Roberts, E., and C. Berry. "Entering New Business: Selecting Strategies for Success." *Sloan Management Review* (Spring 1985): 2–17.

Teece, D. "Profiting from Technological Innovation." In D. Teece, ed., *The Competitive Challenge: Strategies for Renewal*. Cambridge, Mass.: Ballinger, 1987.

"3M Fights Back." *Fortune*, February 5, 1996.

8

Designing at the Operational Level

Corning, Inc.—A Design for High Performance

Set back from a commercial strip that winds through the hills outside Blacksburg, Virginia, is one of the United States's most innovative manufacturing plants. There, in Corning, Inc.'s 250-person factory, self-managed teams of workers and a small group of managers and technicians produce CELCOR—honeycombed ceramic pieces that, when coated with precious metals, absorb the noxious fumes in automotive catalytic converters.

The unionized plant operates twenty-four hours a day, seven days a week. But if you go there at night or on a weekend, chances are you won't find a single manager anywhere in the plant. Even during peak production times, you'll rarely see any supervisors on the plant floor. A single worker—an "operations associate," in Blacksburg's terminology—oversees the warehousing operation; another makes the final decision on which finished goods have met quality standards and are ready to leave the plant.

You might run into an hourly worker independently tackling a special project—for example, increasing the capacity of the automated cars that carry the ceramic pieces on their lengthy journey through the giant kilns, a project that could yield considerable sav-

139

ings each year. Another worker is completing an eighteen-month
stint as the overseer of all the dies used in molding the ceramic into
dozens of different shapes and sizes for various Japanese, Korean, and
U. S. autos. On the plant floor, one of the workers packing finished
"ware" into boxes for shipment may be working next week in the
physical properties lab, using sophisticated equipment to test the
strength and durability of finished samples.

And yet, despite Blacksburg's emphasis on trained teams of
highly motivated, minimally supervised workers, the plant could
hardly be mistaken for some ephemeral social experiment. This is
no "Operations Associates' Paradise"; the unconventional design of
jobs and work processes is firmly rooted in thoroughly conventional, hard-nosed goals of superior performance, productivity, and profitability.

What the Blacksburg plant illustrates is a manufacturing operation based on an emerging design known as High-Performance Work
Systems (HPWS). Specific elements of the design can vary radically
from one organization to another and even among various units
within the same company. But the general principles remain constant: the meshing of formal structures and social processes to provide self-managed teams of people with the information, skills,
accountability, and incentives to achieve universally understood
performance goals that will provide value to the customer.

The design is complicated and difficult to manage. It can be both
unusually stressful and highly rewarding for workers and managers.
People at Blacksburg are the first to acknowledge that HPWS offers
no panacea for every problem in the workplace, no easy formula that
can be universally applied to every business. But when it's done
right, it can be a tremendously powerful tool for increasing productive capacity. By just about every standard of measurement, the
Blacksburg plant has become one of the most productive and most
profitable of the more than forty Corning plants around the world.

Introduction

The quest for innovative architectures at the enterprise level, which
we explored in Chapter 7, has been paralleled by the emergence of
new operational designs within the office and the factory. Just as
enterprise-level design has focused on flexible designs that blur traditional boundaries within the organization and with outside partners, new microlevel designs have seized on new ways of configuring

work and business process to overcome traditional grouping patterns and formal structures. What these designs share is a focus on achieving quantum leaps, rather than incremental improvements, in productivity and customer satisfaction.

Just as most managers have grown up with a traditional model of design at the organizational level, they tend to operate with a similarly static notion of operational design—one that has lasted so long because it has produced adequate, if unremarkable, results in so many organizations for so long. It is a model based primarily on structures—formal patterns of departments and work units—with a strong bias toward activity-based groupings.

In recent years, however, the focus in operational design has shifted from structures to a fascination with process-based design, which offers a sharply increased emphasis on output and users. The parallel with enterprise-level design is clear. As we observed in Chapter 7, the new enterprise architectures center around interdependent business groups that have back-to-front responsibility for a particular business segment. At the operational level, where work actually takes place, the new designs deal with ways to gain focus by organizing around complete business processes, rather than continuing to isolate and separate the activities that make up each process. And some forms of design, as we'll see shortly, go one step further and incorporate innovative ideas in the use of empowered teams to leverage human resources that reside in the work force.

It is our firm belief that the traditional operational designs—the decades-old patterns of structures and groupings that form the basis of most organizations—are revealing some serious limitations, stemming from changes in both the workforce and the overall nature of modern competition. So in this chapter, as we did in the last, we want to focus on the newer and, to some degree, still emerging designs that have been drawing particular interest. We devote much of this chapter to a discussion of High-Performance Work Systems (HPWS), which provides the underlying design of the Blacksburg plant. We'll also explore process reengineering, a relatively new concept that experienced a period of fanatical popularity in the early 1990s. Both concepts contain approaches that, in the proper context, can be of significant help to managers looking for dramatically new designs (see Figure 8-1).

There are important differences between the two approaches. HPWS, in its fullest form, is a coherent, comprehensive approach to design. In terms of our architectural metaphor, HPWS represents a

Figure 8-1 Comparing Designs

Traditional	Process Design	HPWS
1. Internally driven design	Design focused on customers and environment	
2. Ambiguous requirements	Clear direction and goals	
3. Inspection of errors	Control of variance at the source	
4. Static designs dependent on senior management redesign	Capacity to reconfigure	
5. Highly controlled and rigidly separated units	Self-contained units	Empowered and autonomous units
6. Limited information flow	Varying information flow	Broad access to information
7. Narrowly defined jobs	Broadened but not necessarily enriched jobs	Shared, enriched jobs
8.	Technical system dominance	Integration of social and technical systems
9.	Control-oriented management structures, systems and culture	Empowering structures, systems and culture
10.	Controlling and restrictive human resources practices	Empowering human resources practices

total concept of a complete building. Reengineering, on the other hand, is merely one technique for making specific design changes; in our analogy, it's a useful way to design an innovative ventilation system. Unfortunately, reengineering ran aground when it fell short of inflated expectations that the air conditioning schematics could somehow be used as a blueprint for the entire building. As a design concept, reengineering was simply too narrowly focused to address the full range of complexities implicit in human organizations.

There are other profound differences between HPWS and reengineering that will become evident as we go on. But first, it's essential to place both approaches in the historical context of the fundamental changes that are reshaping today's organizational architectures.

The Roots of Change

The conventional approach to organization design—and the approach still used by most U.S. companies—was developed in the early years of the twentieth century and was heavily influenced by the ideas of two men, in particular. In the United States, F. W. Taylor developed a "scientific" model of organizations patterned on the machines of the Industrial Revolution. His approach, labeled "scientific management," was based on the design principles that characterized the assembly lines of heavy industry: specialization of work into narrow jobs, specification of jobs down to the smallest tasks, constant repetition of the same tasks, and the removal of any judgment or discretion on the part of workers.

At the same time, the German sociologist Max Weber was advancing the then radical idea of "bureaucracy," a management design based on formalized procedures, clear chains of command, and staffing decisions based on merit and technical expertise. As embodied in the German civil and military bureaucracies of that time, the concept represented a remarkable advance over traditional hierarchies, which were rooted in nepotism, politics, and institutionalized corruption.

The two ideas, taken together, emerged as a new organizational architecture: the "machine bureaucracy." It brought about such enormous gains in productivity that it soon became the dominant design of industrial enterprises and large corporations, and it remains so today. It has become so prevalent, in fact, that most managers have grown up with that model firmly embedded in their minds as *the* way to design organizations and work.

But as time went on, it became evident that the machine bureaucracy's success came at a high cost. Employees became alienated by the lack of variety, creativity, and motivation involved in their narrow, rigidly defined, and repetitious tasks. Groupings were so strictly enforced that coordination proved difficult. Layers of bureaucracy robbed managers of the information and the authority to make decisions, creating bottlenecks and organizational paralysis.

By the middle of the twentieth century, it was clear that the machine bureaucracy suffered from several inherent shortcomings. To begin with, the design was intended for the management of stable situations. But as the pace of change quickened, conventional bureaucracies became dysfunctional. When engulfed by instability, they were incapable of swift course corrections; the people on the front lines of change lacked the power, information, and cultural support they needed to take risks and to make bold decisions.

The second problem was that the design was based on the assumption of an uneducated, captive labor force driven exclusively by economic need. It failed to motivate employees who were searching for growth, challenge, and a sense of accomplishment—and who were willing to go elsewhere if their current employer couldn't meet their needs.

Third, the machine bureaucracies, over time, tended to become more insular, complex, and unresponsive. Seduced by their own success, they became complacent about the marketplace and shifted their focus to internal matters, inevitably feeding the growth of their powerful bureaucracies.

New Approaches to Design

Beginning in the 1940s, those inherent limitations prompted managers and academics to begin thinking in new directions. Underlying their efforts was a belief in two key principles: first, that most people fundamentally wanted to produce quality products, and, second, that there was enormous potential in the ability of teams to work together in collaboration. Over the next several decades, there were attempts to superimpose elements of job enrichment, team building, and participative management on the frame of the machine bureaucracy; in general, they failed to produce significant, long-lasting results. There were simply too many structural and cultural forces embedded in the old design to allow the innovative experiments to take root and flourish.

At approximately the same time, researchers from England's Tavistock Institute were doing groundbreaking work on the role of new technology in improving performance. Their work in the late 1940s and 1950s demonstrated that the introduction of new technology produced dramatic results only when the design of the technical system was consistent with the organization's social system. Their research laid the groundwork for an approach that came to be known as "socio-technical systems" (Cherns 1976), a dramatic departure from the notion of constructing work systems based on "one man, one job."

Through the 1960s and into the 1970s, experience with socio-technical systems—much of it outside the United States—led theorists to articulate five principles that were key to their approach (Hanna 1988; Cherns 1976). Three decades later, those principles remain crucial:

1. *Minimal rules.* Only those rules and work processes essential to success should be specified.
2. *Variance control.* Deviations from required work should be monitored, identified, and corrected at the point where they take place.
3. *Multiskills.* Each worker should be skilled in several functions to provide both variety and flexibility.
4. *Boundary location.* Interdependent roles should be grouped within common structural boundaries.
5. *Information flow.* Information systems should channel information to the point where people are working and solving problems.

Over time, two insights emerged from growing experience with socio-technical designs. First, there was tremendous potential power in the deployment of self-managed teams that determined their own procedures and work flows. That approach, known as "autonomous work teams," grew increasingly common in Europe in the 1970s. Second, designers came to realize in the 1960s and 1970s that much of the previous socio-technical work had been done with an internal focus. They suggested that the most effective designs flowed from an external or "open systems" perspective that focused on customers, suppliers, and competitors. They believed that truly effective design, rather than focusing exclusively on internal efficiency, started with an assessment of the demands and opportunities presented by the external environment (Lawrence & Lorsch 1967).

As time went on, designers began experimenting with the concepts of socio-technical design in larger arenas, such as entire manufacturing operations. By far the greatest successes came in "greenfield" situations where new plants or office operations incorporating those concepts could be designed from the ground up. Moreover, there was a growing recognition that these concepts required changes in the overall organizational architecture—the configuration of both formal and informal structures and processes that shaped the organization and the way its people performed their work. The essential concepts of that new design involved these characteristics (Lawler 1986):

- *Employee selection*—employee involvement in decisions about who would participate in the work and on what basis
- *Design of physical layout*—employee participation in the layout of the physical work setting
- *Job design*—within teams, the design of individual jobs with the specific intent of promoting autonomy, variety, feedback, and a sense of accomplishment

- *Pay systems*—the clear linking of rewards to the acquisition of multiple skills by individuals, collective performance by teams, and the attainment of overall organizational goals
- *Organizational structure*—flattened hierarchies, self-contained autonomous units, and self-managed teams
- *Training*—a heavy investment in training employees, both in technical skills and in social techniques such as teamwork and conflict resolution
- *Management philosophy*—an explicit partnership and shared commitment by management and its employees

In the 1980s, various threads of design thought came together—socio-technical systems, autonomous work teams, open systems, participative management, even some of the basic concepts of quality management. The result was the emergence of a fundamentally new organizational architecture.

The new purpose driving the architecture was the growing competitive demand on companies to increase their productivity, quality, and customer focus. The new structural materials were the emergence of self-managed teams as a proven technique and the explosion in information technology that made it possible, for the first time, truly to empower employees at all levels by providing them with the information they needed to make decisions and to exercise judgment. The collateral technologies were the new management practices and human resource processes that made it possible to select, train, motivate, and reward people in ways consistent with the new design. The blending of those critical factors—purpose, structural materials, and collateral technologies—fueled the development of the new organizational architecture: High-Performance Work Systems (HPWS). In its most basic form, HPWS is a design approach that combines work, people, technology, and information in configurations that maximize good "fit" in order to produce high performance. It emphasizes internal fit as a key to meeting external demands and opportunities. It involves both a design and the process through which an organization develops its own particular version of that design.

Blacksburg: HPWS in Practice

Perhaps the best way to explain the concept of HPWS is to describe how it actually works. It's important to understand that HPWS doesn't consist of a specific set of structures and processes that are always present in identical form. Rather, it is a conceptual approach to design. But it does involve some basic principles; as we present that list, we describe how they apply, in practice, to the Corning Blacksburg plant. Keep in mind this is simply for purposes of illustration; one of the keys to HPWS is that each organization must design its own version consistent with its own work and culture.

These, then, are what we consider to be the ten fundamental principles of High-Performance Work Systems:

1. *The design begins with an outward focus on customer requirements and works back from there to develop appropriate organizational forms and work processes.* The power of the HPWS approach lies not in patching up existing problems but in looking for entirely new ways of organizing people and their work to provide substantial benefit to the customer. In Corning's case, the company determined in the late 1980s that it needed a third CELCOR plant to meet growing demand and that the new plant had to be capable of continually incorporating leading-edge technology. They decided to place the operation in the Blacksburg plant, which had shut down four years earlier after ceasing production of stove tops and windows for wood-burning stoves. As they thought about new ways to configure the plant, Corning officials began looking at other factories and thinking about the use of socio-technical systems to enhance productivity. The incorporation of HPWS in the plant design was a response to competitive demands for innovation and productivity.

Now, in its eighth year as a CELCOR plant, customer focus remains an important part of the Blacksburg operation. It's not unusual for operations associates—the hourly workers—to meet directly with customers to discuss quality issues, sometimes visiting the plants to which CELCOR products are shipped. Indeed, the last associate to inspect each box of "ware" leaving Blacksburg marks it with his or her personalized "Quapple" stamp. (The Quapple is a stylized "Q," standing for "quality," drawn to resemble an apple as a reminder of Corning's roots in upstate New York.) If a customer complains about any shipments from Blacksburg, the associate who stamped the box must respond personally.

2. *Work is designed around loosely coupled, self-managed units that are responsible for producing complete products or processes.* Teams of workers form the heart of Blacksburg's design. They handle many of the supervisory responsibilities normally reserved for front-line and lower-level managers. The plant has only three levels of management, including the plant manager, compared with five or six at levels at comparable plants.

The operations associates at Blacksburg are divided, for the most part, into teams of twelve to fourteen people, and each team is responsible for one of the three production lines during its twelve-hour shift. The CELCOR process basically involves six steps: blending and extruding the raw materials, using powerful saws to shape the ceramic parts, firing them in a kiln, final inspection and packing, testing of samples in the physical properties lab, and shipping and receiving. In other words, the team is responsible for every process the product undergoes from the time it enters the plant until it leaves.

Each team is responsible for organizing and directing its own work to achieve specific performance objectives. The team does its own scheduling, assignments, and performance reviews. Depending on the technical training they've received, team members are assigned on a rotating basis to several functions—in general, each is certified to work at two or three of the six different jobs. Within each team, various members who have volunteered for special training serve as "coordinators" in charge of scheduling, safety, and other administrative matters. There are no foremen or supervisors on the line, just three management "line leaders" who have general oversight and final authority over what goes on. But on a day-to-day basis, they and the various technicians and specialists are there as "resources" for the teams, which do their work with a minimum of supervision.

3. *The work must be guided by clear direction, explicit goals, and a full understanding of output requirements and measures of performance.* Blacksburg's employees are awash in information. Workers on the line are acutely aware of what's expected of them, of how many pieces they need to process during their shift, of how well the plant as a whole is performing at any given time on a wide range of performance indicators. Because performance incentives can provide bonuses equaling up to 13 percent of a worker's base pay, teams are sharply attuned not only to the performance of their own members but to other teams as well. Between each shift there is a brief "hand-off" meeting between the team that's leaving and the one that's coming on.

Interestingly, despite the plant-wide emphasis on information and goal setting, the prominent scoreboards that keep a running tally on production in some plants have largely vanished from Blacksburg. As the teams grew increasingly comfortable with the notion of their own empowerment, they also became more territorial. Many of the workers, who were well aware of the production numbers on the floor, came to believe that the signs were useful primarily to managers who made occasional visits to the floor to see how things were going. There was a sense that the information was theirs, and they became reluctant to share it.

The situation represents an interesting switch in the normal flow of information. In this case, the workers are the ones who have it, and, in their own way, they are as protective of it as any traditional bureaucrat. Moreover, the situation clearly illustrates the perpetual tension that inherently lies in that gray area where management prerogatives and employee empowerment rub against each other. The tensions are milder than in most plants—but they exist, nonetheless.

4. *Variances should be detected and controlled at the source, rather than being inspected outside the work unit.* This essential element of quality management is evident throughout the Blacksburg plant. Quality inspections take place at several stages on the line, combining visual inspections with sophisticated lasers and electronic scales. In addition, team members are at work in the physical properties lab running a range of tests on samples taken from the cars leaving the kilns. When defects are found, team members can quickly identify where in their own process the problems originated. The essential concept is that each team is responsible for regularly monitoring and maintaining the consistent quality of its work.

5. *The social and technical systems are closely linked, each designed with the other in mind to produce optimal performance.* This is truly the core of the design, and the primary challenge for the designer. Experience has shown time and time again that when isolated elements of HPWS are somehow worked into conventional settings, they invariably run into trouble. That's because the formal structures, work processes, and social systems all have to fit. Some plants have tried creating one or two Blacksburg-style teams in conventional operations, with extremely limited success. Without the right work processes, incentive and reward systems, selection, training, information flows, and whole-hearted management support, these unsupported beachheads rarely make much headway.

At Blacksburg, there's been a concerted effort to integrate the entire operation. Starting with the selection process, in which employees play a key role in identifying and choosing new hires who are well suited to the plant's unique environment, all the human resource systems are geared toward training and rewarding people to work in effective teams. Managers are committed to the concept and actively support it.

Moreover, the very nature of the basic work is well suited to the team design. The work can be organized into one continuous process, requiring relatively little coordination among teams. Everyone in the plant is involved in producing and shipping several versions of the same product. It's not a huge assembly plant where thousands of pieces are shaped, joined, and finished in dozens of configurations involving hundreds of processes. Blacksburg makes one essential product in a process that allows the same people to handle it from start to finish.

The physical design of the plant, which was laid out at the same time the team design was being developed, also plays an important role. In a normal plant—even at Corning's conventional CELCOR plants—the product moves down one long, continuous assembly line, making it impossible for workers to see what happens to the product after it leaves their hands. At Blacksburg, each line is shaped generally like a comma; from the time the unformed ceramic logs ooze down from the blender to the final inspection and packing, practically the entire process takes place within full view of the entire production team.

That physical layout is tremendously important. First, it gives everyone on the team a clear perspective and sense of accomplishment; they always are within view of the finished product rolling off the line. Second, people can easily see when a team member is having problems or is getting backed up; when that happens, team members voluntarily leave their jobs to help out until the problem is solved. Finally, that visibility enables team members to gain a clear idea of the energy and work habits of their colleagues. For some, that can be difficult.

"Instead of having one supervisor," one Blacksburg worker told us, "you've got twelve sets of eyes that are counting how many times you go to the bathroom and watching how long you took for your lunch break. After a while, some people find that very stressful." The truth is that's just one of several ways in which peers often tend to be tougher bosses than traditional supervisors.

6. *The unimpeded flow of all relevant information to the people who need it is critical to the HPWS design.* As already mentioned, workers at Blacksburg are privy to all kinds of confidential, competitive information. In fact, any of them can log onto the plant's computers and gain instant access to virtually any piece of operational information. Beyond numbers, the employees are exposed to a wealth of information involving the state of the company, developments within the auto industry that will affect Blacksburg as a supplier, and even general training in business finance.

The flow of information takes place at several levels. As we mentioned, teams meet briefly at the end of each shift as one takes over from another. Each team also meets by itself after each shift to discuss how things went that day. Generally, the meetings are quite brief; other times, there may be lengthy discussions of particular problems or of unusual projects or rush jobs that are in the offing. Beyond that, the plant manager meets regularly with all the teams to discuss Blacksburg operations and general business conditions.

As a result, the teams understand enough about the overall operation to make a wide range of decisions. In some cases, the breadth of knowledge is remarkable; two managers, describing one of the most knowledgeable hourly workers who has served in special assignments throughout the plant, suggested that if the plant manager were called away on emergency, "she could probably run the place while he was gone."

7. *Enriched and shared jobs increase the motivation of individuals and enhance the organization's flexibility in assigning work and solving problems.* One of the essential elements of the Blacksburg operation is the cross-training of operations associates. At one level, each is encouraged to learn at least a dozen of the basic jobs each team performs. After achieving a required level of proficiency, the worker receives a permanent boost in base pay. With additional training, associates can qualify for eighteen-month assignments as technicians, a level that carries even higher pay—but only for the duration of the assignment. During these rotations, the specialists leave their teams (and their twelve-hour shifts) and work at particular jobs—such as overseeing the dies or conducting specialized lab tests—where they're available to work with any and all of the teams, as needed. Finally, trained associates can qualify for temporary assignments as special project associates, rotations that can last anywhere from a few weeks to several months, depending on how long it takes to complete the assignment. The arrangement provides some clear benefits. Most workers enjoy the variety. And the fact that everyone knows how to do the most basic jobs, and that everyone is capable of doing twelve or fourteen of them, lends tremendous flexibility to scheduling.

Moreover, the cross-training means that the teams generally have the information either to solve problems as they occur or to understand the problem fully enough to know who to call for help. Quite often, the team includes associates who have previously worked as project technicians or special projects associates and who have specialized knowledge and skills typically available only from outside technicians. Managers at the plant believe this in-house knowledge provides significant cost savings over time; without it, says one of the top managers, other plants end up spending "two or three times more than you need to" in order to fix one-time problems.

8. *Human resource practices must complement and strengthen the empowerment of teams and individuals.* It's difficult to imagine an operation in which human resource processes play a more integral role than at Blacksburg. The process begins with selection, a comprehensive, two-month ordeal in which applicants are carefully screened by a joint group including plant leadership, operations associates, and maintenance engineers (a small but separate category of hourly workers). Beyond the basic requirements, applicants are probed for their ability to work with teams, their compatibility with the working environment, and their acceptance of Blacksburg's core values and beliefs. At one point, their families are brought in to view a video about the plant and talk with other workers about the realities of twelve-hour shifts, overtime, and the unique pressures of the plant—a stage at which some applicants decide to look elsewhere.

The reward systems—pay for skills, bonuses for individual, team and plant performance—all are structured to reinforce the plant's operational design. In addition to technical skill training, there's coaching in supervisory and team-building skills, as human resource professionals help workers who serve in team coordinator roles learn to handle sticky social issues. One of the most difficult of these involves annual performance evaluations, which are performed by team members, not by managers. Teams, like managers, vary widely in their ability to give frank assessments to likable individuals who are marginal performers. Management is looking for ways to make the evaluation process more consistent without limiting the empowerment of the teams.

Similarly, the hourly workers are deeply involved in the assignment and promotion of their fellow workers. Those interested in becoming project technicians must apply for the eighteen-month positions and are selected by their peers through a process most describe as much more rigorous than the initial selection procedure; in addition to lengthy interviews, they're often required to take tests or perform certain projects. There are cases of associates who have applied five or six times for a project technician rotation before finally succeeding.

9. *The management structure, culture, and processes all must embrace and support the HPWS design.* Blacksburg enjoyed a distinct advantage over many plants. Its HPWS design was championed

from the outset by top corporate and plant officials, and the entire plant and all its operations were redesigned in 1988 with that in mind. Corning has found it much more difficult to superimpose individual elements of the design on existing conventional plants; continuing efforts along those lines have met with only limited success.

After eight years, most of the original senior managers had moved on to other jobs. But they were carefully replaced by others who shared the commitment to Blacksburg's unique design. They, in turn, carefully look for other managers who have the combination of self-confidence, flexibility, and strong leadership skills required to succeed there. "This is not touchy-feely management," says one top manager. "You have to know when to tighten up on the reins and when to loosen them."

10. *The organization and its work units must have the capacity to reconfigure themselves to meet changing competitive conditions.* Since it opened in the late 1980s, Blacksburg has been through a process of continuous change—expanding the number and the makeup of teams, modifying the relationship between teams and management, and redesigning work processes to achieve dramatic improvements in productivity. In 1995, for example, as the automotive market flattened out, the plant let go about sixty temporary workers—the equivalent of nearly 20 percent of the hourly work force. By that point, so many processes had been streamlined and redesigned that "you hardly noticed the temps were gone," according to several associates. A market downturn—or, more precisely, the absence of a projected upturn—also halted the installation of a fourth line. Because of the plant's configuration, the partially completed line was installed without causing any disruption to the existing operation and is maintained in a state of readiness so that construction can resume at any time.

HPWS and Performance

Although the HPWS design has been in use at Blacksburg only since the late 1980s, it has been employed in various forms in both plants and offices for well over two decades. In that time, it has demonstrated consistent results:

- Using comparable technology, HPWS operations produce the same products as conventional work units, but at 40 to 50 percent lower cost.
- HPWS units consistently demonstrate higher quality and lower error rates in the services and products they offer.

- Employees in HPWS organizations display higher than normal levels of motivation, commitment, and pride in their work.
- HPWS organizations experience lower than normal turnover and rates of absenteeism.
- The emphasis on training and multiple skills, along with team responsibility for entire processes, leads to greater openness to new ideas and a heightened emphasis on the value of learning at HPWS organizations.
- The empowerment of employees who are closest to the customer increases the capacity of HPWS organizations to respond more quickly than conventional operations to changes in customer demands.

Blacksburg is no different. By almost every measure—and despite the fact that it is heavily unionized—Blacksburg has emerged as one of Corning's most productive and profitable plants. One example: All Corning plants are rated on the basis of material utilization. The norm for Corning plants is 60 percent, after waste and substandard products are recycled back through the process. When Blacksburg opened, its material utilization was at 40 percent; by 1995, it led the company with 73 percent.

But the true value of the HPWS shows up in other, important ways. Employees are quick to recount stories describing difficult nights when teams voluntarily stayed on after their shifts, without being asked and without being paid, to fix problems and get a job done. Those stories are told proudly and often; they are embedded in Blacksburg's culture. It's hard to put a price tag on that kind of collective commitment. Yet, no system is perfect, not even a model operation such as Blacksburg, which was designed under absolutely ideal conditions. The plant continues to struggle with issues that may well confront others who design their own versions of HPWS. Some of these are:

- *Unrealistic expectations.* The sheer uniqueness of the system creates a sense, particularly among new employees, that they're embarking on an exciting, new adventure. Sooner or later comes the realization, as one manager puts it, that "this isn't Utopia. It's still a job. It's work." For some managers, that creates a sense of frustration, as one put it, that "you can only take upskilling so far. No matter how hard we try to design interesting, motivating jobs, somebody's got to stand there putting pieces in a box." Some workers feel that same frustration—probably more so. Beyond that, the heightened expectations became evident during contract talks in the early 1990s. Twice the union voted down the company's contract offer, expressing the workers' belief that "if we're so special, we should be paid like we're special." The contract was ultimately ratified, but not without some hardening of the battle lines.

- *Unclear career tracks.* A related problem of expectations involves workers who gain special skills and enjoy considerable responsibility—and then, at the end of their special assignment rotations, find themselves back on the line doing the most basic jobs and working unappealing shifts. So far, Blacksburg managers concede they haven't figured out a way to balance one of the great pluses of HPWS—the integration of highly skilled, responsible workers into the teams—with the desire of ambitious workers to advance their careers. While the problem hasn't reached critical proportions, a handful of top workers have gone on to better jobs with other companies rather than return to their former jobs on the floor.

- *Social dynamics.* The personal interactions within teams assume tremendous importance, given the unprecedented power people hold over their peers. On some teams, the pressure to perform—the sense of always being watched and judged by coworkers—can be tremendously stressful. On other teams, people who are popular with their coworkers can get away with poor performance for years. Performance appraisals, as mentioned earlier, are terribly uneven. And normal working relationships can become highly uncomfortable when peers are making crucial decisions—not only about who works which jobs, who works on holidays, and who works overtime—but concerning the selection of applicants for project technician slots. "It's kind of tough to come in and work along side those people, day after day, after a bunch of them have put you through the grinder and then decided you weren't up to the job," says one worker. The social pressures have grown to the point where some qualified workers are refusing to volunteer for choice assignments.

- *The "gray area."* Both managers and workers talk about the "gray area," the disputed turf that lies between management rights and team empowerment. Each team, for example, sets its own rules on overtime and tardiness—and at times, they've varied widely from one team to another. But management's attempts to impose uniform rules have drawn considerable resistance. Similarly, managers were initially involved in the performance appraisal process but gradually ceded the entire responsibility to the teams. Now that there are some glaring problems and managers want to reassert themselves, the teams don't want them back. The result is a tricky situation in which managers have to know when to leave the teams alone and when to assert their authority. "Some people make the mistake of thinking this is a place for laid-back managers," says a human resource official. "It's not. Our managers have to be very strong, very forthright."

In short, the HPWS design has some clear benefits—increased productivity, higher quality, sharper customer focus, greater motivation and commitment among workers, greater flexibility in operations, and, in general, a less hostile, confrontational work environment. But precisely because it is a system built on the recognition of employees as thinking, responsible individuals rather than as human machine parts, it confronts managers with a new and infinitely more complex range of issues on a daily basis.

Reengineering: The Revolution that Wasn't

It is a somewhat disheartening commentary on the state of U.S. management that throughout the 1980s and 1990s, while the elements of High-Performance Work Systems were quietly being developed—and achieving substantive results—many managers and much of the business press were fixated on the phenomenon of reengineering. If the concept hadn't been mass-marketed with such hyperinflated fanfare, it might have survived the unrealistic claims made on its behalf. The fact that it's now discredited with the same vigor with which it was praised is unfortunate, because beneath all the glitz and hype lay some valuable substance.

Reengineering—though it wasn't called that in the beginning—had its roots in the convergence of the quality movement and its emphasis on the design of business processes, with massive advances in information technology and growing pressure on companies to achieve dramatic gains in productivity. More and more organizations began looking for ways to redesign completely the business processes involved in delivering a product or service to the customer, rather than looking for incrementally better ways to keep doing the same thing.

The idea took on the trappings of a movement in 1990 when the *Harvard Business Review* published Michael Hammer and James Champy's article "Reengineering Work: Don't Automate, Obliterate." The movement evolved into a full-blown fad in 1993 when Hammer and James Champy published their remarkably successful book, "Reengineering the Corporation." By 1995, when Hammer published "The Reengineering Revolution," the wave had already crested; reengineering per se was already heading toward the final resting place that awaits each of the magical solutions that periodically promise, and then fail, to transform U.S. business. Yet, despite its fall from popular grace, reengineering continues to offer some concepts that smart managers can use to their benefit in microlevel design.

Hammer and Champy's work was founded on a relatively simple notion. Reengineering, by their definition, was "the fundamental rethinking and radical redesign of business processes to achieve dramatic improvements . . . in performance." Their work rested on a few attractive ideas.

The first idea was that managers should focus on business processes—the combination of tasks and activities that together create a product or service of value to the customer, rather than on specific jobs, functions, or operations. Taking a page from the quality movement, reengineering started with an external focus on the customer and then looked at new and different ways of performing a given process—order fulfillment, for example—rather than on starting with an examination of the existing warehousing, distribution, and billing operations.

Second, while the quality movement incorporated the Japanese notion of *kaizen*, or continuous improvement, reengineering viewed incremental change as slow suicide. In emphatic—often dogmatic—terms, reengineering stressed the necessity of wiping out existing procedures and starting with a blank page. In some cases, that radical approach was entirely appropriate—but not always.

Third, reengineering focused on fundamentally new ways of designing processes to achieve dramatic improvements. It had no patience with managers looking for 10 percent increases in productivity or savings; this was a process, its supporters claimed, for the tough, hard-nosed managers who were willing to do whatever had to be done to produce radical results.

Fourth, reengineering was deeply rooted in the use of new information technology to fundamentally recreate business processes. Its advocates were quick to explain that they weren't talking about traditional automation, which could lead to the more efficient use of computers to perform irrelevant or unnecessary activities. Instead, they believed, information technology was the solution to problems that the manager probably didn't even know existed. The key was to search for places to apply the solution.

In theory, many aspects of reengineering had tremendous appeal, promising a short cut to efficiency and profitability. It swiftly drew an army of enthusiastic advocates. Consultants and suppliers of information technology quickly saw the potential for marketing new products and services. The business press, as usual, was eager to proclaim "the next big thing." And executives, who had recently emerged from a round of drastic cost cutting in the early and mid-1980s only to find that the pressure for profits hadn't let up, were attracted by a concept that promised massive savings. As increasing numbers of companies launched their own reengineering efforts, their competitors felt compelled to do their own reengineering or risk being left behind.

The results? According to the "State of Reengineering Report" published in 1994 by CSC Index, the Boston consulting firm that, more than any other, spawned the reengineering movement, 67 percent of the completed reengineering efforts they tracked produced results that were either unremarkable or were outright failures. (Davenport 1995). Moreover, reengineering efforts had proved to be disruptive, time-consuming, and downright expensive. In retrospect, there are two reasons that reengineering failed to live up to the grand expectations created by its proponents. First, regardless of what its early advocates might have had in mind, reengineering quickly became a euphemism for downsizing. The purveyors of reengineering in the consulting and information technology firms were essentially telling managers, "Look. Forget about laying off a few people here and there. Reengineering will eliminate the need for entire departments." Indeed, the 1994 CSC Index report showed that 73 percent of the companies surveyed had used reengineering to eliminate, on the average, 21 percent of their jobs (Davenport 1995). As reengineering gained a reputation as a management weapon of mass destruction, more and more companies encountered stubborn resistance from fearful employees—at all levels—as soon as reengineering was even mentioned.

Moreover, reengineering ignored the general move toward sociotechnical systems by focusing exclusively on the technical aspects of work and ignoring the social implications. Reengineering, in practice, became an authoritarian, top-down approach to redesigning work and jobs, an anachronistic throwback to the old "scientific management" principles of a bygone era. People resented—and resisted—the notion that they could simply be rearranged and thrust into different jobs like so many machine parts.

Reengineering, in essence, ignored the principle understood by so many managers today: "The soft stuff is the hard stuff." No long-lasting, fundamental redesign can be implemented without considering its impact on people, both individually and collectively—their motivation, commitment, social relationships, and organizational culture. Redesign failed because, in practice, it proved to be too mechanistic, dehumanizing, and downright scary to win the support of the people in each organization who were being counted on to make it work. It came to represent an impersonal, almost "macho" approach to hard-nosed management—and it crashed and burned.

Finally, reengineering couldn't hope to live up to its advocates' claims that it represented a dynamic new way of redesigning organizations. The reengineering of business processes is important—in some cases, perhaps, even critical. But as we've seen, true organizational design is a complex process that flows directly from strategic considerations and then carefully weighs the impact and the implications for the work, structures, people, and culture of the organization. The focus of reengineering is considerably narrower. It's an interesting—and sometimes useful—way of looking at how an organization performs a given process; it's of little use when it comes to conceptualizing and planning the shape, contours, and texture of a dynamic organization.

Summary

In their own ways, our discussions of High-Performance Work Systems and reengineering both illustrate the same lesson: There are no simple, prepackaged, guaranteed solutions to the complex problems of organization design. The achievements of HPWS far exceed those of reengineering. In part that's because HPWS proponents have correctly viewed it as a general framework and a set of guiding principles, not as an off-the-shelf product that any manager can simply plug in and watch the profits roll in. It is a conceptual approach to design work, not a mass-marketed, one-size-fits-all design kit. It involves hard work, lots of frustration, massive participation, a deep understanding of the organization and its people, and enormous patience. That doesn't make for a sexy hard sell. But the plain truth is that there are no shortcuts to effective design.

So far, we've been talking about the fundamental concepts and alternative patterns of organization design. In Chapter 9, our discussion turns to the design process, as we lay out a specific sequence of events for shaping a new design, fleshing out its operational details, and laying the groundwork for implementation.

Bibliography

Abrahamson, E. "Managerial Fads and Fashions: The Disfusion and Rejection of Innovation." *Academy of Management Review* 16, no. 3 (1991): 586–612.

Argyris, C. *Personality and Organization.* New York: Harper, 1957.

Cherns, A. "The Principles of Socio-Technical Design." *Human Relations* 29 (1976): 783–792.

Davenport, T. "The Fad that Forgot People." *Fast Company,* November 1995, 70–74.

———. *Process Innovation: Reengineering Work Through Information Technology.* Boston, Mass.: Harvard Business School Press, 1993.

Hackman, R., and G. Oldham. *Work Redesign.* Reading, Mass.: Addison-Wesley, 1980.

Hammer, M., and J. Champy. *Reengineering the Corporation.* New York: Harper, 1993.

Hammer, M., and J. Champy. "Reengineering Work: Don't Automate, Obliterate." *Harvard Business Review* (1990): 104–112.

Hanna, D. *Designing Organizations for High Performance.* Reading, Mass.: Addison-Wesley, 1988.

Lawler, E. *High-Involvement Management Participative Strategies for Improving Organization Performance.* San Francisco: Jossey-Bass, 1986.

Lawrence, P., and J. Lorsch. *Organization and Environment.* Cambridge, Mass.: Harvard University Press, 1967.

Lucas, H. *The T-Form Organization.* San Francisco: Jossey-Bass, 1996.

Nonaka, I. "Redundant, Overlapping Organizations: A Japanese Approach to Managing the Innovation Process." *California Management Review* (Spring 1990): 27–38.

Trist, E., and R. Bamforth. "Some Social and Psychological Consequences of Long Wall Goal-Getting." *Human Relations* 4 (1951): 3–38.

Tyre, M., and W. Orlikowski. "Exploiting Opportunities for Technological Improvement in Organizations." *Sloan Management Review* 35, no. 1 (1993): 13–26.

Walton, R. "The Diffusion of New Work Structures: Explaining Why Success Didn't Take." In P. Mirvis and D. Berg, eds., *Failures in Organization Development and Change.* New York: Wiley, 1977.

9

A Process for Design

Kaiser Permanente Northern California—
A Broad-Based Redesign

The early 1990s were a period of major upheaval in the health care industry, with growing resistance to rising costs, rapid expansion of managed care, and political pressure to overhaul the entire health insurance industry. At Kaiser Permanente's Northern California Region, managers of the Hospitals and Health Plan (H/HP) operation were becoming increasingly concerned, not only about how to deal with new competition and market forces but also about their ability to seek out new markets and successfully meet changing customer needs. In the course of analyzing both its markets and its organizational capabilities, H/HP's leaders came to the conclusion that their new customer-focused approach would require a fundamentally new organizational design.

Kaiser Permanente, headquartered in Oakland, California, is the nation's largest not-for-profit HMO, and Northern California is its biggest region, accounting for $4.5 billion of the company's $12 billion in total revenue in 1993. With fifteen medical centers (primarily hospitals) and thirty-one satellite medical offices, its 35,000 employees served nearly 2.4 million members. As in Kaiser's other regions, Northern California had two components: the Hospitals and Health Plan, which included the medical facilities owned outright by the HMO and staffed by Kaiser employees, and the Permanente Medical Group (TPMG), the physicians who provided their services to the HMO on a contractual basis.

In early 1992, David Pockell, executive vice president and Northern California's regional manager, initiated a strategic planning process aimed at helping H/HP understand the competitive forces reshaping its market and identify the barriers that stood in the way of H/HP's successful response. The results of that work—soon confirmed by an independent assessment by outside consultants—led to the realization that in order to focus on customers and adapt quickly to the changing marketplace, H/HP would require a major redesign (see Figure 9-1).

Pockell and a few senior leaders, assisted by the consultants, worked closely for several months to clarify the change objectives, define a new culture to match those objectives, and develop an overall plan for moving the change process forward. In the summer of 1993, Pockell and his team decided to go public with the process and started actively involving people from throughout H/HP in designing and implementing the necessary changes.

In the first of a series of video-conferenced meetings with all H/HP's employees, Pockell explained that the organization faced two crucial strategic imperatives. First and foremost was a glaring need for customer focus. The second, which Pockell described as the "capacity to act," flowed directly from the first. He explained that it would be impossible for H/HP to focus on its customers until it had developed a new operating environment and organizational structure. The new design would enhance the employee's ability to make well-informed, timely decisions at levels closer to the customers, freed from bureaucracy, archaic structures, and internal barriers to cooperation.

Looking around the organization, Pockell explained, he saw "departments and functions that live in narrow silos and don't see out to the other silos. We have to take down the walls and allow for freer flows of information and freer cooperation among all the departments and functions and locations in the areas we serve."

As first steps in this major change, Pockell announced that he had installed a three-member interim leadership team, including himself, to run H/HP. At the same time, he appointed a new seven-member strategic design team to fully assess the company's needs and to recommend a full-scale plan for reorganization.

Pockell made it clear to the employees that the design team had been chartered to examine every aspect of the organization—not only

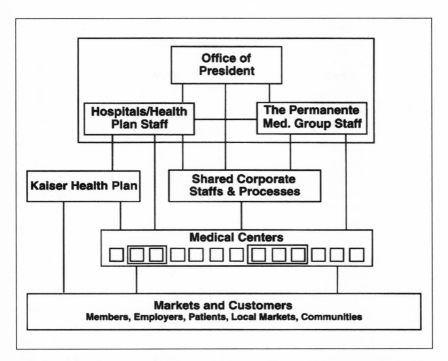

Figure 9-1 Kaiser Foundation Hospitals/Health Plan Northern California Region—Span of Support Model

its structures and processes but, even more important, the ways in which people worked with each other, with customers, with suppliers, and with the community at large. The team, he said, "will help us determine what kind of organization we want to be in the future."

Pockell then introduced Bernard Tyson, an outstanding young administrator working in Santa Rosa, who, over the course of the coming year, would lead a succession of teams whose recommendations would guide the dramatic redesign of the Northern California HMO.

Introduction

Most of us have either witnessed or felt the direct effects of slipshod, haphazard reorganizations—what we've come to think of as the "cocktail napkin school of design." Now that we've explored the complexity of the issues involved in design—complexities that are real and important even when the designers neglect to address them—it's time to lay out a step-by-step process for dealing in a rational, fully informed way with the full range of design decisions. As we detail the process, we'll use the Northern California H/HP as a point of reference, illustrating the way this process can and should be done.

The opening case illustrates part of what made the Kaiser process so effective—and, to a certain extent, so unusual. From the very outset, the senior executive acknowledged that any effective redesign had to involve every component of the organization. There was explicit attention to groupings, linkages, information flows, and interdependence. Beyond that concern with formal structures and processes, however, there was a clear understanding that much of what had to be done would fly in the face of the existing culture. At one point in the process, as the full design was unfolding, Pockell told employees that the formal structures constituted perhaps 20 percent of the change involved in the redesign; the rest of the change, he explained, would involve the values, beliefs, and behavioral patterns that shaped the way people worked.

Moreover, to an unusual extent, the design *process* was perceived as being nearly as important as the design itself. The leadership was committed to a broad-based, participative process—one that would simultaneously elicit ideas from some of the organization's best minds and, at the same time, lay the groundwork for implementation even as the design was still being developed.

In this chapter, we present a step-by-step process for strategic design that deals with the overall architecture of the organization. We then describe the close relationship between strategic design and the operational design process that flowed directly from it. And we pay particular attention to one of the key design issues: who should be involved. Before moving on, we want to acknowledge the assistance of our Delta Consulting Group colleagues—Michael Kitson, Marilyn Showers, and Sam Davis—who worked closely with H/HP throughout the design and helped shape the process.

The Sequence of Design Decisions

In general, the full sequence of activities involved in organization design can be divided into four major phases.

Phase 1: Preliminary Analysis. The first step in strategic design is a full-scale organizational assessment. As we saw in our earlier discussions of organizational models, problem solving begins with an understanding of how the organization is functioning, where there are performance gaps, and, in particular, how performance relates to strategy. The formulation of strategy is a complex issue in its own right, and one that merits separate treatment in other works. In short, the purpose of an organizational assessment is to determine exactly what it is about the organization that isn't working. The need for strategic design is not necessarily a foregone conclusion. In some instances, the real problem might be a totally inadequate strategy. Or it might be a problem involving top leadership or human resource practices. Redesign is only one of several possible outcomes of the organizational assessment process.

The process begins with data collection and analysis. Three kinds of information are absolutely critical: data concerning the strategy and specific strategic objectives; data about how the organization actually operates—how information flows, what information is required by whom and how quickly, and the structural, social, and technological obstacles to information processing; and specific identification of current problems that the redesign should correct.

In the Kaiser case, the initial diagnostic work was accomplished in two stages: first by Kaiser's own strategic planning process and then by outside consultants, Michael Kitson and Sam Davis, who worked closely with Pockell's leadership team. Both studies analyzed H/HP's problems and its ability to handle new challenges and opportunities. Both processes arrived at the same conclusion: A major reorganization design was in order.

Phase 2: Strategic Design. The second stage, assuming the organizational assessment concludes that a redesign is called for, is the formulation of a strategic organizational design—an "umbrella structure," as Marilyn Showers describes it, that gives overall shape to the organization. This entails the enterprise-level design decisions we discussed in Chapter 7. It involves an analysis of broad information-processing requirements and the selection of general patterns for grouping and structural linking.

Strategic design also focuses on the top layers of the organization, with particular emphasis on the roles and the structures of corporate governance. It deals with the processes that should be used—and who should be involved—in making top-level decisions about strategies, markets, external relationships, and internal policies. In the Kaiser process, the members of the strategic design team initially wanted to wade into operational details. In time, they came to understand that those decisions couldn't be tackled until an overarching design for the top of the organization had been developed.

Strategic design generally focuses on the top two to four levels of the organization and takes into consideration formal structures and processes, as well as the informal operating environment, which we deal with in more detail in Chapter 10. The central point is that effective design starts at the strategic level, creating a framework that guides operational design.

Phase 3: Operational Design. Some strategic designs simply reposition groups and change a few reporting relationships; in those cases, the operational design work is fairly simply. More typically, strategic redesign profoundly reshapes the organization. That requires extensive operational design, the detailed attention to work flows, resources, reporting relationships, business processes, and human resource practices that is required to turn the new pattern of boxes and lines into a fully functioning organization. At Kaiser, the strategic design team was given three months to come up with a new organizational plan; then the core design team overseeing the operational design worked nearly twice that long to flesh out their plan.

Phase 4: Implementation. One of the most common reasons that redesigns fail is the all too common assumption that the job essentially ends with the announcement of the new design. In reality, that's where much of the toughest work begins. Implementation requires careful planning, close monitoring, and constant management. It is an enormous task, one that we explore in considerable detail in Chapter 10.

A Framework for Strategic Design

While each step in the design sequence is important, the strategic design step is particularly critical because it provides the overarching framework for all the decisions that follow. Before going through the specific steps of strategic design, it's important to understand the logic that underlies the process (see Figure 9-2).

The design process itself involves four stages, each of which we'll explore shortly in much more detail. The first objective is to identify the requirements for the design and then to generate a broad number of design alternatives. These alternatives are then tested, evaluated, modified, and refined. At each step, some designs are discarded, so at the end of the process, the designers have one design (and perhaps some backup designs). The four stages are:

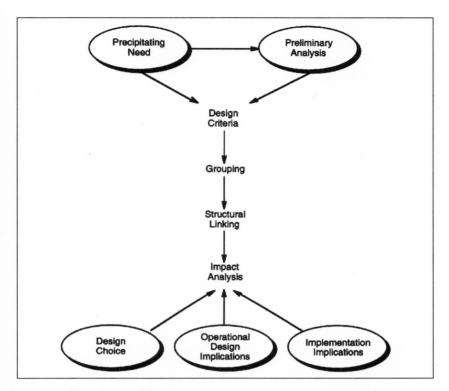

Figure 9-2 The Strategic Organization Design Process

1. *Development of design criteria.* On the basis of the underlying need for change and the preliminary analysis, the designers write a series of statements that describe what the new design should accomplish. These statements then become benchmarks for potential designs.

2. *Grouping decisions.* Designers develop and evaluate several options for general grouping.

3. *Linking decisions.* For each set of grouping alternatives that survive the evaluation stage, the designers devise a series of linking mechanisms. Some alternatives are combined, and some are dropped.

4. *Impact analysis.* The grouping and linking designs are assessed from the standpoint of their potential fit with the other formal and informal components of the organization. Again, assessments, changes, and modifications are made. The impact analysis will contribute to the recommendation and selection of a final design. The impact assessment should also provide information useful in the subsequent operational design and planning for implementation.

One of the important keys to making this process a success is the consideration of a wide range of alternatives. Unfortunately, far too many redesigns amount to little more than incremental tinkering with the first reasonable proposal that lands on the table—very often, the one the senior executive already had in mind at the outset of the process. The real value in this process lies in the full discussion of as many alternatives as possible, including, one hopes, some that require the designers to step back and look at the organization and its work in entirely new ways.

A closely linked issue is the question of who should be involved. The makeup of both the strategic and the operational design teams at Kaiser, as we'll see shortly, was fundamental to the entire process. Pockell could easily have closeted himself with a few senior executives and consultants and hammered out an acceptable design. Instead, there was a conscious decision to expand the process and use it to identify, educate, and develop lower-level managers who would go on to play major roles in implementing the design they'd helped to create.

The Ten Steps of Strategic Design

Using Kaiser as our case study, let's now walk through the ten specific steps involved in the process of strategic organization design. Some require considerably more elaboration than others, and it's not our intention to exhaustively document each step in Kaiser's yearlong process. Also, as is often the case in practice, some steps tend to blend into others. But as a general process, with differing degrees of emphasis depending on particular circumstances at any given organization, this framework describes the sequence of decisions that ought to be confronted and resolved (see Figure 9-3).

So, we rejoin Kaiser late in the summer of 1993. As we noted earlier, Pockell and his senior colleagues had already been working on a whole range of organizational change issues for several months. In July they appointed a strategic design team that consisted of seven second-level through fourth-level managers from different disciplines and geographic areas. They were selected for their knowledge, credibility within the organization, and proven ability to think creatively.

"We didn't just go out and round up the usual suspects," Pockell explained when he announced the appointments. The team's members were seen as people "who would challenge us to think about things differently." Beyond that, they were seen as future leaders;

Figure 9-3 Strategic Organization Design Process:
Specific Decision-Making Steps

Step	Objective
1. Generate design criteria	Create a series of statements that can serve as criteria for assessing different designs.
2. Generate grouping alternatives	Create a large number of different grouping alternatives designed to meet the design criteria.
3. Evaluate grouping alternatives	Assess grouping alternatives in terms of design criteria; eliminate, modify, and refine alternatives.
4. Identify coordination requirements	For each grouping alternative, identify the information-processing needs, working from the design criteria.
5. Generate structural linking mechanisms	For each grouping alternative, create a set of structural linking mechanisms that will be responsive to the coordination requirements and will enhance the extent to which the design meets the design criteria.
6. Evaluate structural linking mechanisms	Assess each alternative in terms of the design criteria; eliminate, modify, and refine alternatives. Combine alternatives if necessary.
7. Conduct impact analysis	Assess each surviving design alternative in terms of predicted impact on or fit with other organizational components.
8. Refine and eliminate designs	Based on the impact analysis, eliminate designs, resulting in a first choice design recommendation, and refine designs as appropriate.
9. Identify issues for operational design	Based on impact analysis, identify where operational design needs to be done and issues to be addressed by the design.
10. Identify issues for implementation	Based on impact analysis, identify key issues to be considered in planning implementation of the design.

the question being put to them, Pockell said, was "What do you want the organization to look like when you're leading it?"

In reality, the assignment turned out to be a unique training ground for potential senior leaders. They were being asked to consider problems and perspectives they'd never personally encountered in their careers. Given their experience, they tended early on to focus on operational details; gradually, they understood that their new assignment was to "wear the big hat"—to think about issues more globally, from an enterprise perspective.

They also had the opportunity to dig deep into the organization and learn about its operations, people, and culture in tremendous depth. Early on, the team pursued its own data collection to supplement the initial analysis done months earlier by the consultants. They held one-on-one interviews with dozens of managers, focus group sessions with front-line employees, and face-to-face sessions with major customers and suppliers

Finally, the assignment provided the team members with an unusual degree of interaction with the people at the top of their organization. The design process involved continual discussions between the leadership team and the design team as they worked through a whole series of complex issues. The design that emerged— and the operational plans that came later—were the result of the ongoing collaborative efforts between the top leaders and the teams they'd created.

The strategic design team, led by Bernard Tyson, was given ninety days—from August 1 to November 1—to come up with recommendations for an overall strategic design. Pockell and the other top leaders had shared with the team members the results of the initial assessment made by outside consultants, the change objectives, and a description of the new culture and then had charged them to come up with a design that would enhance both customer focus and the capacity to act. Now it was time for them to pursue the 10 steps of the strategic design process. Throughout the process, there was constant interchange between the Senior Leadership Team and the Strategic Design Team. At regular-scheduled meetings, both groups shared and tested ideas, assumptions, and work in progress.

1. Generate design criteria. The first step is to develop a set of specific criteria for directing and assessing the design efforts. Design criteria are statements that describe precisely what it is that the redesign ought to achieve. Each statement should begin, "The organization design should . . ." That statement should be followed by an action verb, followed in turn by a very specific goal. In Kaiser's case, Pockell and his two colleagues on the leadership team worked through a set of guidelines with the newly appointed Strategic Design Team. After adding two criteria (numbers 12 and 13 below) to the list they'd initially worked out with the leadership team, their list of design criteria was complete. The following summarizes the statement of design criteria they used in shaping and evaluating alternative designs:

The organizational design alternatives should:

1. Drive the organization toward customer focus.
2. Reduce the hierarchy to ensure those serving the customer have information, resources, and freedom to act.
3. Allow flexibility for changes in enrollment and customer requirements.
4. Enhance partnerships with patients, members, suppliers, purchasers, communities, labor unions (and others, including the parent Kaiser Permanente organization).
5. Cut "Kaiser time"—the time required to make decisions and get things done.
6. Maximize capacity for organizational learning.
7. Simplify work and reduce bureaucracy.
8. Support individual and team accountability for results.
9. Support fundamental process improvement and redesign.
10. Minimize organizational boundaries.
11. Achieve deep change throughout the organization.
12. Reduce the cost structure.
13. Make (the organization) the health care employer of choice.

Of course, useful lists of design criteria don't come out of thin air; they shouldn't simply reflect one or two executives' personal notions of what might be attractive objectives. Instead, they emerge from analysis of information from four sources. First is the organization's business strategy, particularly its perspectives on markets, offerings, and the company's own competitive strengths. The second source involves the basic characteristics of the work flows required to execute the strategy. Third, the criteria should reflect the diagnosis of the obstacles the organization faces. Finally, the criteria should include any other relevant information about constraints or demands that may be placed on the emerging design.

We can't overemphasize the importance of well-founded, carefully delineated, and clearly articulated design criteria. They drive the entire process, ensuring that the design remains grounded in the strategy. They also provide a concrete framework for assessing all the alternatives that will surface during the course of the process.

2. Generate grouping alternatives. The next step is for the design team to develop a range of substantially different grouping alternatives on the basis of the options and combinations we described in Chapter 5. The emphasis at this stage is on creativity;

this early in the process, the team shouldn't feel constrained by questions of implementation, feasibility, or practicality. One frequent danger at this stage is that all the alternatives may amount to little more than variations on the existing design theme. Some design leaders confront this problem head-on by instructing the team to come up with a specific number of options, only one of which can bear any resemblance to the current design. Depending on the complexity of the organization and the amount of organizational change required by the design criteria, teams may come up with anywhere from three or four to a dozen alternatives at this point.

3. Evaluate grouping alternatives. Having developed the widest possible list of grouping alternatives, the team then rates each on the basis of how well it fulfills the design criteria. Occasionally, teams do this quite formally, rating each option on a numerical scale. The main objective is for the team to get a good sense of the relative strengths and weaknesses of each design and of the trade-offs involved in each. It's common at this point for designs to be combined and reconfigured and, sometimes, for entirely new designs to emerge. The goal is to rethink, refine, and reject various designs. However, it's preferable at this stage to keep several designs on the table; it's still too early to settle on just one.

The Kaiser team, at this point, had boiled down its realistic alternatives to two general categories, both markedly different from the existing functional structure, in which administrators of various health care facilities and operations reported straight up through a centralized hierarchy. One was a geographic structure, grouping all the facilities and operations in specific communities and clusters of communities into a collection of subregions. The other grouped facilities on the basis of services, with a reach that transcended geographic boundaries.

4. Identify coordination requirements. Up to this point, the grouping alternatives may have included some basic reporting relationships and a structural hierarchy, but that's just the beginning of design. Now, for each alternative grouping pattern, the team has to start thinking about how work and the flow of information would be coordinated among the various groups. In particular, it needs to consider those information-processing requirements and capabilities in the context of the design criteria; clearly, different objectives might well require different information flows.

5. Develop structural linking alternatives. For each grouping alternative still on the table, the team must design structural linking mechanisms that address the coordination requirements identi-

fied in Step 4. While a range of alternatives is theoretically preferable, in practice most designers settle on just one set of structural
linkages for each of the grouping alternatives. This is a crucial step;
this is the point at which teams sometimes come to the realization
that there is just no feasible way to coordinate work and information
requirements in some of their grouping options, which end up falling
by the wayside.

In Kaiser's case, as the focus narrowed to spotlight the importance of geographical groupings, the team realized that operational
services, such as geriatric or obstetric care, as well as management
and business processes, such as human resources and purchasing,
had to be linked and coordinated throughout the entire organization.
As time went on, much of its work—and the work of the operational
design teams that succeeded it—centered on the role of systemwide
services and processes as essential mechanisms for linking and coordination.

6. Evaluate structural linking mechanisms. Now the team has
a collection of alternatives on the table, each including a pattern of
groupings and linkages. The next step is to assess those alternatives
in light of the basic design criteria and any additional coordination
requirements that were identified in Step 4. The assessment process
is similar to the earlier one; each alternative is given a rating, and,
very often, features of various alternatives are combined and modified. At the end of this step, the team should be considering somewhere between two and four design alternatives.

7. Conduct impact analysis. Through Step 6, the design decisions have been driven largely by strategic objectives and work
requirements. At this point the feasible set of alternatives under
consideration is subjected to an impact analysis, a list of questions
focusing on the potential consequences associated with each alternative (see Figure 9-4).

The questions run the full gamut of organizational concerns,
ranging from the staffing and capital costs involved in implementing
each option to the impact on leadership styles and career opportunities and on changing skill requirements. In terms of the congruence
model, the team is taking each design alternative, plugging it into
the "formal organizational arrangements" slot in the model, and
then examining how that change would affect each of the other components—work, people, and informal arrangements. The goal, again,
is an assessment of each alternative's impact—either positive or neg-
ative—with specific written comments on the design's implications
for operational design and implementation.

Figure 9-4 Key Impact Analysis Questions

Individuals

To what extent does the design decrease the quality of fit between the requirements of the work and capacities of individuals?

To what extent does the design require managerial skills, talents, or experience that is not currently present?

To what extent does the design limit or decrease opportunities to meet individual needs?

To what extent does the design limit or decrease the ability to motivate needed behavior?

Informal Organization

To what extent does the design conflict with the following factors:
   current leadership?
   current organizational culture (values and beliefs)?
   current communications and influence patterns?
   other informal arrangements or aspects of the informal organization?

Formal Organization

To what extent does the design pose problems in relation with the outside environment?

To what extent will the design require significant additions to or reallocations of human, capital, plant, technological, or other resources?

To what extent will the design create problems because of past practices?

Cost

To what extent will the implementation of the design require incurring additional costs (direct or indirect)?

---

8. Refine and eliminate designs. The team examines the designs, makes refinements or modifications to address issues surfaced by the impact analysis, and eliminates those designs that clearly raise too many problems. Typically, this process leaves one design as the obvious first choice, although it's preferable to identify a backup. Each remaining design should be accompanied by a written description of its major features, its relative strengths and weaknesses, and its potential impact on the rest of the organization.

9. Identify issues for operational design. Next, the team needs to consider what kinds of operational design work will be necessary to make the new strategic design function effectively. The operational impact may be minor; at other times, the magnitude of the strategic design may require a nearly complete overhaul of the operational design. The important thing is for the design team to consider carefully two concerns: the operational issues raised by the impact analysis and any of the original design criteria that might not be fully met by the strategic design and that ought to be addressed through operational design. Finally, as a kind of doublecheck, the team should spend some time tracing how essential work would flow through the new organization and try to determine where the current operational structures or processes might break down.

In practice, operational design and planning for implementation, rather than being separate processes, are sometimes assigned to the same group. That's fine, as long as that decision is made deliberately and the appropriate people are given the resources they need to complete an adequate operational design.

10. Identify issues for implementation. Finally, the design team needs to gather information about problems likely to be encountered during implementation. Again, the primary source of this information is the data collected during the impact analysis. This information could be vitally important for those facing the enormous challenges of implementing a major change, as we see in Chapter 10.

While not an explicit step in strategic organizational design, it's useful for the team to compile its completed analysis in a design document. Particularly during major redesign projects, this information can prove invaluable; the people involved in operational design and implementation may not have been involved in the strategic design process and may therefore have never seen the data underlying the design team's decisions. If the design team has been diligent throughout the process, all that remains is for it to prepare a brief narrative to accompany the documents produced during the course of its work.

At Kaiser, the initial stage of the design process ended in November when the strategic design team delivered its design options to David Pockell and the other senior executives. The options included dismantling the existing functional organization and replacing it with eight geographically based customer service areas plus a ninth unit, Regional Health Plan Services.

One of the team's findings was that HMO customers tended to use a relatively small number of Kaiser facilities, all clustered around their communities. In order to get closer to customers and to understand their health care needs, the team felt that it made sense to group the facilities geographically, the way the customer used them, rather than by traditional functional groupings. Each customer service area would, in effect, become a miniregion within the Northern California region, with responsibility for patient care, membership services, local area group accounts, local business planning, and community relations. Responsibility for membership growth, capital planning, and, most important, the P&L all were shifted from the central offices to each of the service areas. The areas, in turn, would be linked through a customer service council, which would include the manager of each area, and through the regional unit, which would continue to coordinate both overall governance issues, such as region-wide human resource policies and relations with the parent company, and "commodity" management, such as bulk purchasing and telecommunications.

At the same time, the team recommended replacing the traditional structures for administering facilities and departments, citing what David Pockell described as serious problems with fragmentation and insufficiently integrated services. Instead, the team proposed a collection of "service lines" more closely aligned with patient care requirements. For example, the manager responsible for the geriatric service line would coordinate the provision of all the necessary services—home care, outpatient physical therapy, and pharmaceuticals, for example—regardless of where in the service area those facilities might be located. In turn, the geriatric service line leaders from each of the eight customer service areas would serve together on a council of their own, to coordinate services, share innovative ideas and new developments, and focus on quality management.

Pockell and his senior team reviewed the options and made some important modifications. In particular, they looked for ways to balance a structure based on geography with the need to deliver health care and support services on an enterprise-wide basis. Continuing to reshape the proposals with the strategic design team, they ultimately arrived at a design that integrated horizontally driven health care delivery and business processes with vertically driven geographically based customer service areas (see Figure 9-5).

Over the next two months, top management began implementing the basic outline of the strategic design. At this point, Pockell and his team used a collaborative staffing process to appoint the leaders for each of the new eight customer service areas and began readying them for leading the new structure. Pockell also assigned Bernard Tyson to coordinate the change implementation process.

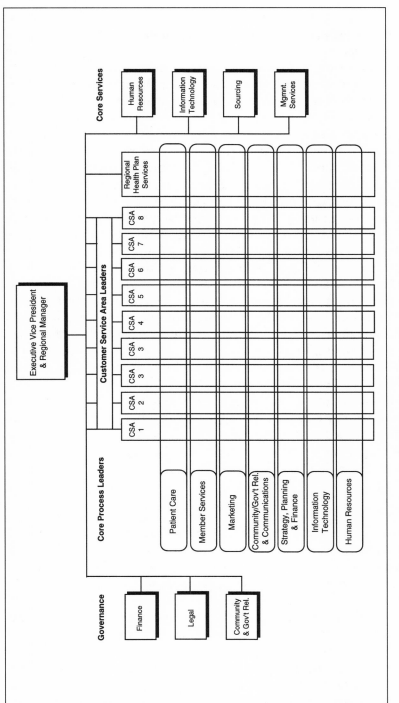

Figure 9-5 Kaiser Permanante Health Plan & Hospitals (Post-restructuring, 1995)

It was clear that there was an important next step: operational design. As we discussed in Chapter 8, operational design involves the development of the structures, processes, and systems that are required to turn translate the strategic design into a functioning organization. Clearly, a wide variety of approaches can be used, so long as the design at the operational level continues to address the initial design criteria that guided the process from its inception.

In Kaiser's case, the process employed for strategic design was extended through operational design. A core design team was appointed in January 1994, with appointments based on the same criteria as were used in selecting the strategic design team. As it set about its work, the core design team created twelve subteams—eight assigned to business processes and four to specific structures—to do the data collection, analysis, and development of recommendations for filling in the important blanks. Those teams focused on resource allocations, staffing needs, reporting relationships, coordinating roles and mechanisms, and, in some cases, specific staff selections. Their recommendations—2,500 pages of recommendations and backup material—went back through the core design team and top leadership for assessment, debate, modification, and final decisions. In July 1994, almost a year to the day since the appointment of the first design team, David Pockell addressed his employees and unveiled the new strategic and operational design for the Northern California region. In the terms we've been using, they produced a matrix structure based on both geography and customer-oriented services, linked by formal structures—the various councils—and by both management and business processes involving joint strategies, region-wide policies, and pooled resources.

Summary

Throughout this chapter, we've constantly referred to "the team" when discussing who develops the strategic design. We've used that terminology as a matter of convenience, because the Kaiser redesign used teams. But that shouldn't imply that there's only one way to do the job.

Depending on the size, complexity, history, politics, and leadership style of the particular organization, there are any number of ways to handle the process. In some cases, the owner of a small business or the operating head of a specific unit can do this work alone, or with the help of one or two advisers. Often, the design team consists of the senior team, assisted by staff or outside consultants. And in successful large-scale projects such as the one we just reviewed at Kaiser and in the similar ones at Xerox, Corning, and ABB, specific design teams consisting of high-potential managers from several levels throughout the organization, were appointed which then worked closely with the CEO throughout the process.

However the design process is staffed or structured, experience—with both successful and failed redesigns—suggests some basic ground rules. First, the best designs are those that emerge from consideration of the widest possible range of alternatives. Second, the best design processes involve people who fully understand the organization and its work; in large corporations, third- and fourth-level managers are positioned better than either the senior team or outside consultants to understand the way the organization works, both formally and informally. Third, the best designs are developed with implementation in mind. And design—like any organizational change—will have significantly better chance of success if the people responsible for making it work feel they were a part of shaping the change. That's why it's valuable for both the senior team and a widely respected, influential nucleus of lower-level managers to be involved in the process, as we see in more detail in Chapter 10.

The most important factor, regardless of who is involved, is the thought process that goes into the design. If one person sitting alone in a room can fully assess the data, diagnose the problems, formulate a design intent, devise a concrete list of design criteria, and then construct, assess, and refine a full range of grouping and linking alternatives, then that one person can theoretically produce a viable strategic design. In a reasonably large organization, the chances that a design secretly developed by one or two people behind closed doors will be cheerfully embraced and implemented by the organization are almost nonexistent. In Chapter 10, we consider the complexities involved in successfully implementing a major strategic redesign.

Bibliography

Bliss, David R. "Strategic Choice: Engaging the Senior Team in Collaborative Strategy Planning." In D. A. Nadler, M. S. Gerstein, and R. B. Shaw, *Organization Architecture: Designs for Changing Organizations.* San Francisco: Jossey-Bass, 1992.

10

Implementing New Designs

General Motors—Designing for Disaster

In the early 1980s, General Motors embarked upon a desperate program. Known within the company as GM-10, its objective was to design and introduce an entirely new line of mid-size cars to fend off growing competition from both Japanese automakers and Ford.

Embattled GM executives, seriously concerned for the first time about squeezing the product cycle and slashing development costs, seized on a radical idea: to pool resources from around the corporation in one unit with start-to-finish responsibility for designing, engineering, and producing the new cars. In fact, the concept wasn't radical at all; the Japanese had been producing cars that way for years. But as the GM-10 project bogged down, executives were confronted by a chilling reality: General Motors was structurally incapable of that kind of cooperation and joint effort. Although the rest of the world saw it as a tightly controlled monolith, GM was actually a loosely run hodgepodge of warring fiefdoms, each fiercely protective of its own resources and boundaries.

On one hand were the five car divisions—Cadillac, Oldsmobile, Buick, Pontiac, and Chevrolet—each of which would develop the concept and design for a particular car. The Fisher Body unit would take the design, tell the designers that the car they had in mind couldn't possible be engineered, and then send its own version of the engineering specs to the manufacturing unit, General Motors Assembly Division (GMAD). There, the assembly people would protest that the car engineered by Fisher Body couldn't possibly be built, and then they'd produce their own version of the car.

The only formal link among the various operations was at the very top, through the senior executives in charge of each division, who all reported to the president of General Motors. Throughout the decades when speed and efficiency weren't matters of particular concern to GM, the structure wasn't seen as a problem; it flowed directly from GM's early history of growth through acquisitions. Many of the companies it had swallowed up—like Fisher Body, which had been acquired in 1926—still considered themselves to be independent operations with no particular sense of partnership with the rest of the corporation. In particular, the towering walls surrounding Fisher Body and GMAD came to be seen as the most impenetrable barriers to internal cooperation.

As the GM-10 program stumbled toward disaster, interminably stalled by the inability of the disparate divisions to collaborate, GM's top executives gradually concluded that there was no way to retain the traditional structure and meet their newly articulated strategic objectives, including significant improvements in product quality, employee relations, asset utilization, market share, and management effectiveness. Then, in early 1984, GM stunned not only the business world but its own employees with the announcement of a truly radical restructuring: The five car companies, Fisher Body, and GMAD all were being disbanded. Instead, GM's North American operation would be divided into two groups—Chevrolet-Pontiac-Chevrolet Canada (CPC) and Buick-Oldsmobile-Cadillac (BOC). Each would have its own design, engineering, and manufacturing components, all reporting to the same group executive.

As Maryann Keller explains in *Rude Awakening*, her penetrating chronicle of GM's turbulent era, it was as if everyone in the company had unexpectedly been told to pack up and be ready to move to a new office where he or she would be doing a new job, working for a new boss, and putting out a new product—all starting tomorrow (Keller 1989). The result was chaos.

Introduction

In the annals of contemporary business, the GM restructuring of 1984 has emerged as the classic example of what not to do.

But that judgment may be unfair. GM's disaster became so well known because it happened at a company that had become the symbol of corporate America. The truth is that other companies, big and small, in one industry after another, have botched their restructurings as badly as GM; they were just fortunate enough not to unravel under the spotlight of worldwide attention. In many ways, the Technicon lab restructuring was GM 1984 in microcosm. As we've already seen, Technicon executives—like their counterparts in numerous other businesses—thought that the hard work of restructuring was drawing the new boxes and lines; once you'd done that, they figured, you just made the announcement and watched the changes. Their second problem was their failure to understand the crucial role played by culture and the amount of work it would take to create the collaborative environment essential to making their new structure function as planned.

GM made those same mistakes—and more. It's hard to pinpoint the most serious flaw in the GM process. Certainly, it was doomed from the outset by the peremptory way the restructuring was announced and implemented. Changes happened so suddenly, and with so little preparation, that people literally walked around for months not knowing what their jobs were. In one situation after another, people simply didn't know whom to call to get a job done. Inattention to internal politics fostered widespread pockets of passive resistance. And while thousands of people were being reassigned and thousands more were being given separation packages, the determination to completely staff up every department in the two new groups and to keep the old corporation running in the meantime resulted in a hiring spree in which literally tens of thousands of new employees were recruited (Keller 1989).

The second crucial mistake was that the executives and the consultants who designed the restructuring completely overlooked the importance of culture, or, in the terminology of our model, the informal organizational arrangements. They simply didn't understand that the formal structures and processes they were rearranging were often obsolete and irrelevant; throughout the company, the vital processes and the key relationships were rooted in the informal culture. Because the designers failed to accommodate culture in their design, their restructuring inadvertently obliterated many of the essential, informal work flows. The result, in many cases, was outright paralysis.

Strike three, which we mention here just in passing, was that the new design was fundamentally flawed. In effect, GM replaced one huge, unwieldy, and dysfunctional functional design with two smaller versions of the same thing. There was nothing inherently different about the two new divisions that would promote team-work, speed, efficiency, and accountability, prompting the BOC executives to start redesigning their group even while the initial restructuring was still under way.

Managing major change within an organization is always diffi-cult. Implementing a redesign is particularly risky; more reorganiza-tions fail because of poor implementation than because of faulty design. A mediocre design, if implemented well, can be made reason-ably workable over time. But even the most sophisticated and elegant designs are doomed if management fumbles the implementation.

This chapter is devoted to the implementation of organization designs and to the closely associated issue of managing organiza-tional culture. As David Pockell told the employees of the Kaiser Permanente Northern California Region during their design process, "If we just move boxes around without dealing with culture, then all we're doing is moving boxes around." In other words, redesign that ignores culture is merely an intellectual exercise that has little to do with truly reshaping an organization and the way it works.

This chapter is intended to serve as an overview of two related topics, both of which merit deeper consideration by managers who are likely to find themselves personally involved in periods of major organizational change. There are numerous works that focus specif-ically on these issues; as a starting point, we suggest *Discontinuous Change: Leading Organizational Transformation*, by Nadler, Shaw, and Walton (1995).

Fundamentals of Organizational Change

Not surprisingly, the past two decades have seen a surge of interest in the subject of organizational change. One of the more useful approaches was originally proposed by Richard Beckhard and Reuben Harris. They saw the implementation of change—including new organizational design—in terms of transitions (see Figure 10-1).

At any given time, they suggested, the prevailing conditions within an organization can be described as the *current state*. In terms of our congruence model, the current state is the existing con-figuration of strategy, work, people, formal structure, and informal culture. The objective of major change, then, is the successful move toward a *future state*, a vision of how the organization ought to func-tion. The critical in-between stage—the condition of the organiza-

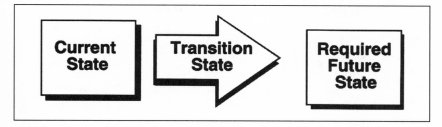

Figure 10-1 Organization Change as Transition

tion after it has disengaged from the current state but before it has arrived at the future state—is the *transition state.*

In the most general terms, then, effective change management involves: 1. developing an understanding of the current state; 2. articulating a clear vision of the future state; and 3. guiding the organization through a delicate transition period. The design of the transition state is as important as the future state; both are critical.

Using this change framework—the movement from the current state through the transition state to the future state—we can say that a major change, including a redesign, has been successful if it meets these criteria:

1. The organization truly moves from the current state to the future state—in other words, the new design is actually implemented.
2. The organization, after reaching the future state, actually functions in ways that meet expectations; that is, the new design works in practice the way it was drawn on paper.
3. The transition is accomplished without undue cost to the organization. This means that the design is implemented without significant disruptions to the business or damage to relationships with customers, suppliers, or regulators.
4. The transition is accomplished without undue cost to individual organization members.

Of course, not every implementation of a new design can be expected to meet all of these criteria, but they provide a reasonable goal. The question for managers, then, is how to implement a design change in ways that increase the chances of hitting those targets.

The Problems Inherent in Change

Our experience in change management situations make it clear that three general problems nearly always surface whenever an organization undergoes significant change.

Problem 1: Power

Every organization is inherently a political system made up of various individuals, groups, and coalitions that compete for power. In the transition state, the political dynamics leap to a new level of intensity as the status quo is dismantled and a new design takes shape. People, both individually and collectively, are likely to engage in political activity if they believe that the impending change will produce a major shift—for either better or worse—in their relative positions of power within the organization. In addition, individuals and groups sometimes engage in political resistance because the new design, strategy, or approach conflicts with their personal values or their image of the organization. At GM, for instance, the restructuring ran headlong into the fierce loyalty and intense identification many employees felt for their particular divisions, whether Buick, Fisher Body, or GMAD. To these people, as Maryann Keller points out, the restructuring took on the overtones of a hostile takeover.

Problem 2: Anxiety

For those involved, the transition from the current state to the future state represents a frightening journey from the familiar to the unknown. It's only natural that people will have a host of concerns. Will I still be needed? Will I have a new boss? How will my job change? Will I maintain my current status? Will I need to learn new skills? Will the career path I've been following still make sense? All those concerns boil down to the same question, the one that every person worries about as soon as he or she hears of an impending organizational change: "What does this mean for me?" The longer that question is left unanswered—and the less complete the answer—the greater the stress and the anxiety people will experience. Before long, behavior and job performance start to suffer. At the very least, stress impedes people's ability to hear and to integrate information about the impending change. They may engage in irrational and even self-destructive acts. More typically, they find subtle, passive ways to derail the new processes and procedures.

Problem 3: Organizational Control

A major redesign disrupts normal activity and undermines routine management control systems, particularly those embedded in the formal organization. Managers begin to feel that they're losing control. As goals, structures, and people enter the transition state, it becomes increasingly difficult to monitor and correct performance. Moreover, because most management and control systems are designed to maintain stability, they're inherently ill suited to managing periods of change.

Our experience makes it clear that there are specific things managers can do to counteract each of these change-related problems. These tactics don't necessarily guarantee success; rather, they represent common actions taken by many of the organizations that manage effective change.

Shaping the Political Dynamics

Problems related to the reapportionment of power require managers to understand—and to manage—the organization as a political system. The first credible hint of impending change instantly unleashes furious political activity—particularly among those opposed to the change—and diverts energy and attention from normal work. Consequently, it's crucial for managers to act before the change is announced and to continue working throughout the implementation process to shape and manage the political dynamics. There are four ways this is often done:

1. *Build a critical mass of support for change by winning over the key power groups.* The organization, as a political system, is filled with groups, cliques, coalitions, and special interests, each competing for power, position, status, and resources. Some will favor the impending change, some will oppose it, and some won't care one way or the other. The political challenge facing managers is to build a critical mass of support for change—not necessarily a numerical majority, but an influential group whose support can ultimately be leveraged to win widespread acceptance.

The first step is to identify the crucial power relationships within the organization and to determine which groups and individuals have the most to gain or lose from the impending change. One method we strongly recommend is to actually construct a stakeholder map, illustrating not only who is likely to take which position but also people's relationships to one another and their patterns of influence. These diagrams can be extremely useful in anticipating successive waves of reaction to change beyond the obvious initial responses.

The next step is to think about specific approaches to building support. The first—and, by far, the most crucial—is *participation.* The single most common flaw we see in failed change efforts is an absence of appropriate participation by people who are expected to become major stakeholders in the future state. All too often, managers develop a new design behind closed doors, either alone or with the assistance of one or two consultants or trusted advisers, and then present their executive teams and the organization with a complete, finalized package. The predictable responses are skepticism, resentment, and resistance.

On the other hand, companies that have successfully managed dramatic change—Kaiser Permanente, Xerox, and Corning, for example—have gone out of their way to involve literally hundreds of people in successive waves moving out through the organization in planning both the substance and the implementation of the design change. Those who have been brought into the process not only feel a sense of ownership toward the impending change; they typically form the nucleus of the critical mass necessary for building support.

Realistically, there are some people whose involvement is likely to be disruptive; their participation might simply enhance their ability to block change. In those cases, the right strategy may be *negotiation*—cutting deals to win their support or neutralize their opposition. A third step is *isolation,* reassigning change opponents to far-flung positions outside the mainstream of the organization. And in extreme cases, when individuals persist in active opposition, managers must weigh the possibility of outright *removal.*

2. *Build political momentum through the actions and behavior of leaders.* Leaders have enormous power to mold perceptions and to create a sense of political momentum by sending focused signals, providing crucial support, and dispensing rewards.

First, leaders can articulate a clear vision of the future state. Second, they can serve as models, demonstrating through their own actions the kind of behavior they expect of others. Third, leaders can play a crucial role by rewarding key individuals and specific types of behavior. Fourth, leaders can employ resources and use their political influence to eliminate roadblocks and to create momentum.

Finally, leaders can send important signals through their personal actions. During periods of change, their routine words and deeds take on disproportionate importance; attendance at certain meetings, the use of key phrases, subtle nuances of body language—each can send powerful messages rippling through the informal organization. The deliberate use of informal signals plays an enormous role in shaping the attitudes of others.

3. *Use symbols creatively to build the perception of momentum in support of change.* Symbols, so important in political and social movements, play a similar role in the politically charged atmosphere that surrounds organizational change. Symbolic words, acts, and physical representations all create focal points for identification and the sense that change is not only inevitable but already well under way.

For example, immediately after being named CEO of GM in 1992, Jack Smith began streamlining and modernizing GM; after only three weeks, in fact, he had dismantled the ineffective CPC-BOC structure instituted in 1984. Amid the flurry of activity, Smith moved his base of operations from the executive suite on the fourteenth floor of the GM headquarters building to a working office at the GM Technical Center in nearby Warren, where the new North American Operations group was headquartered. It was a powerful symbolic act in a company so accustomed to the elitist traditions of its top executives (Ingrassia and White 1994).

Because symbolism can become such an emotional force, managers must constantly keep it in mind. Keller describes a particularly poignant scene that occurred one night during the 1984 GM reorganization, as fourth-generation Buick workers and their families gathered in Flint, Michigan, for a formal recognition dinner. GM officials had somehow chosen that same day to remove the Buick sign from the plant and replace with a new BOC sign. The employees—all of them children, grandchildren, and great-grandchildren of Buick workers—were predictably enraged (Keller 1989).

4. *Reduce anxiety-induced political activity by building and maintaining a sense of stability.* Pervasive uncertainty can easily raise political conflict to destructive levels. The organization must provide certain "anchors" to create a sense of stability in the midst of transition.

First, managers should provide people with as much information as possible about the change before implementation actually begins. Second, some stability can be preserved—even in the face of change—if managers are careful to maintain the consistency of their messages throughout the transition period. Conversely, any perception of discord or confusion within management ranks fuels instability and strengthens the resolve of those still hoping there's a chance to block the change.

Third, it may be essential to the overall sense of stability to preserve certain highly visible aspects of the business—organizational names, management processes, or specific job assignments. Finally, it's important during the midst of change to make sure people under-

stand what's not changing. From a cultural standpoint, senior executives at Corning, Xerox, and AT&T felt that it was important to
continually underscore those time-honored values and beliefs that
would remain constant despite widespread restructuring. At a more
basic level, it makes sense to give people all possible information
about what's changing and what isn't; however unsettling the truth
might be, it's rarely as scary as the scenario being discussed around
the water cooler.

Motivating Constructive Behavior

As mentioned earlier, the question foremost in everyone's mind as
soon as change is announced is "What does this mean for me?" It's
not surprising; we each play the starring role in our own personal
dramas, and it's frightening to suddenly have the script ripped from
our hands.

Anxiety leads to a number of predictable reactions, ranging from
panic to withdrawal to active resistance. The role of management is
somehow to relieve that anxiety and to motivate constructive
behavior by providing information and by rewarding those who
earnestly try to exhibit the behavior required in the future state. The
four action steps are:

1. *Prepare people for change by creating—or surfacing—dissat-
isfaction with the current state.* People are essentially creatures of
habit; we grow comfortable with what we know, and we fear what
we don't know. Few among us are adventurous enough to step over
the precipice without a fairly good reason. A critical step in managing change is therefore to help people understand why it's in their
best interests to "let go." Managers must show people how unrealistic it is to believe that the current state is wonderful, has always
been wonderful, and will remain just as wonderful in the years
ahead. The goal is to "unfreeze" people from their inertia and to per-
suade them at least to consider the necessity of change and the possibilities that lie ahead.

It's important at this stage to present specific information about
the shifts in the business environment that led management to
decide that change was essential. It's useful to emphasize the dis-
crepancies between people's perceptions and the realities of the current situation. And it's particularly persuasive to point out the
consequences of not changing, including the prospects for full-scale
disaster. Sometimes, rather than having managers present this scenario, it's more effective to involve lower-level employees in col-

lecting information and presenting their own perceptions. People often attach more credibility to arguments from their peers than to pronouncements by management.

It's absolutely essential, during this period, for managers to over-communicate. Extreme anxiety impairs normal functioning; most people become literally incapable of accurately hearing and fully integrating messages the first time around. It's therefore necessary to communicate key messages two, three, four, and even five times through various media. During the Kaiser Permanente redesign discussed in Chapter 9, for example, David Pockell and the managers involved in the redesign effort held regular monthly teleconferences with the entire workforce, followed by opportunities at each site for people to talk personally with executives and members of the design team. Indeed, from the earliest days of the redesign, employee communications played a key part in Kaiser's implementation strategy.

2. *Motivate people through widespread participation in planning and implementing change.* We can't overemphasize the importance of employee participation in the change process. It captures people's excitement, enhances communications, and results in better decisions. To be fair, participation also entails some costs: It takes time, involves giving up some control, and may create conflict and increase ambiguity. The question, then, is to choose where, how, and when to build in participation.

People might participate in the early diagnosis of problems, in the design or development of solutions, in planning the implementation, or in the actual execution. Participation can be direct and widespread or indirect through representatives. The options are varied. Regardless of the details, experience shows that some form of participation almost always outweighs the costs certain to arise later on if there's no employee involvement at all.

3. *Be sure to visibly reward desired behaviors during both the transition state and the future state.* The transition state is typically a time when the old reward system has lost its relevance to new objectives but hasn't yet been replaced. Consequently, people sometimes find that they're asked to start performing in new ways but that they can be rewarded only by continuing in their old ways. In effect, the anachronistic reward system penalizes them for doing precisely those things required to make the change successful. As a result, it's crucial during transition periods for managers to pay special attention to performance, pay, and promotions. In addition, there are informal rewards—recognition, praise, and special assignments, for instance—that should be carefully managed to ensure

that they consistently support the desired new behaviors. And one of the priorities should be the earliest possible creation of an appropriate reward system for the future state.

4. *Provide people with adequate time and opportunity to disengage emotionally from the current state.* People associate organizational change with a personal sense of loss. Inevitably, they go through the equivalent of a mourning process as they let go of the old structure. Managers need to understand and assist in this process, providing people with adequate time and appropriate opportunities to work through their institutional grieving.

Managing the Transition

The serious control problems common during periods of organizational change often flow from the inherently unstable characteristics of the transition state. The current state has been dismantled, but the future state is still taking shape. The only way to maintain control is through skillful management and attention to detail. Again, we propose four specific areas where managers can have an impact:

1. *Focus attention and activity by developing and communicating a clear image of the future state.* Change without focus creates huge problems. It's hard to manage people in a certain direction if they don't know where they'll be once they get there. In the absence of a clear direction, the organization suffers "transition paralysis." Activity grinds to a halt, because people are no longer sure what is considered appropriate behavior.

The first thing managers must do is develop as complete a design as possible for the future state; at the very least, they should articulate a vision ahead of time. Second, and again to the extent possible, managers should draw up a statement that identifies the impact of the change on each part of the organization. Third, it's important to avoid unnecessary changes, extreme modification, or conflicting views of that vision during the transition.

Finally, there is a critical need to communicate. As we have said, it's important for managers to communicate repeatedly, using a range of media—video, small group discussions, written memos, newsletters, electronic bulletin board postings, letters sent to homes, large group meetings—to deliver consistent messages. Think of this communication as both "a telling and a selling" activity. This may necessitate repeated explanations of the rationale for the change and the advantages of the future state. Finally, the new organization must be made real, visible, and concrete, with as much detailed information as possible about structures, procedures, and reporting relationships.

2. *Use multiple and consistent leverage points for changing behavior.* This relates to our earlier discussion of the congruence model of organizations and its role in managing change. During transition periods, chances are much greater than normal that "fit" among components of the organization will be knocked out of sync. Managers should consistently think about change in terms of the fit among work, people, formal structures, and informal arrangements, and they should closely monitor those relationships throughout the course of the transition.

3. *Maintain control through the use of special transition management devices.* Because the transition state differs in so many ways from the current and the future states, it's often necessary to create formal organizational arrangements specifically designed for managing transitions. These might include: 1. a transition manager; 2. specific transition resources, including budget, time, and staff; 3. specific transition structures, such as dual management systems and backup support; and 4. a transition plan. All of these can help focus management attention on the difficult issues that inevitably crop up during transitions.

4. *Actively seek feedback and obtain assessments on the condition of the transition state.* During the transition it's particularly essential for managers to know what's going on within the organization. But upheaval usually disrupts the normal feedback channels; heightened anxiety discourages people from sharing bad news with their bosses.

It's therefore critical during transitions for managers to construct new and focused feedback mechanisms. Formal methods may include individual interviews, focus groups, surveys, or feedback gathered during normal business meetings. Informal channels, particularly face-to-face encounters between senior managers and employees far removed from the corporate offices, are particularly useful. Finally, management can promote regular feedback by having representatives of key groups participate directly in planning, monitoring, and implementing the design change.

Transition management, in short, requires an initial emphasis on communicating a clear image of the future state. Next, there's a need to pay close attention to the changing configuration of the organization and, where necessary, to develop special mechanisms for managing the transition period. Finally, it's essential to maintain a steady flow of feedback, even when the normal course of events is disrupting all the normal information channels (see Figure 10-2). All of these are important elements in managing transitions.

Implementation and Culture

If you think about it, most of our discussion of implementation has revolved around aspects of the organization that don't show up on any formal charts. Ideologies, political alliances, collective self-image, webs of influence, career expectations, patterns of behavior, informal feedback channels—many of the problems and related solutions involve culture, or what's come to be known in recent years as "the soft stuff" of organizational management and design.

There's a distinct parallel here between the architectures of technology and of organizations. The concepts of hardware and software apply to both. In organizations, the formal structures and processes are the equivalent of hardware—the boxes, chips, and operating systems that provide the computer's information processing capabilities. But it is the people and the culture—the software—that bring the boxes and lines to life and dictate the form and content of the information that's processed. Hardware and software are useless without each other and ineffective if mismatched. The same is true of formal structures and informal cultures.

It's not our intention here to provide an in-depth exploration of culture, a subject dissected in great detail in numerous other works (Nadler, Shaw, and Walton 1995; also Kotter and Heskett 1992). But in the context of implementation, it's essential for managers to have a rudimentary understanding of this crucial aspect of organizational architecture.

In terms of strategic design, the truth is that strategic linking is an essential—but not sufficient—element in coordinating the work of people and units separated by grouping. Formal linkages must be supported by an informal operating environment that encourages the work flows and the performance patterns called for by the design intent. At GM, decades of hostility and mistrust among designers, engineers, and production people, buttressed by workers' deeply embedded loyalties to their divisions rather than to the overall corporation, couldn't be erased simply because executives decreed that literally overnight General Motors would become a model of efficiency and teamwork. Organizations just don't work that way.

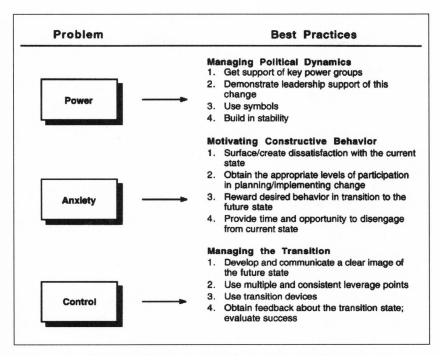

Figure 10-2 Managing Organizational Change

As patterns of interdependence among various work groups become more complex, the role of the informal organization becomes increasingly crucial in providing the social "glue" that reinforces the structural linking. In addition, just as decisions about grouping and linking have to take place at various levels throughout the organization, so too must managers be keenly attuned to variations in subunit cultures within the larger enterprise.

The fact is that culture—the informal organizational arrangements, to use the language of our model—is the single most difficult aspect of organizational architecture to reshape in a lasting way. That's why experienced executives and managers—Xerox chairman Paul Allaire, for example—repeatedly remind their people, "The soft stuff is the hard stuff."

Values, Beliefs, and Norms

The basic building blocks of any organizational culture are *values* and *beliefs.* Core values are expressions of what the organization believes is good (or bad, for that matter). Either you agree or you don't; values can't be proved or disproved. Corning, for example, has a list of seven "Big Vs"—values the company holds in high regard, such as "Integrity," "Quality," "Performance," and "Technology." These are essentially articles of faith, statements of collective priorities.

Beliefs, on the other hand, embody particular views about how the world works. They imply cause-and-effect relationships and are open to debate. Technological innovation leads to market leadership; a passion for customer service builds business; superior quality provides a strong source of competitive advantage—all are statements of widely held beliefs. They might or might not be valid, given particular industries or competitive situations.

Norms, the third element of culture, are the behavioral manifestation of values and beliefs. They are the set of expectations about how people will conduct themselves in ways that are consistent with the organization's core values and beliefs.

A second aspect of culture is the sharing of values and beliefs. Culture involves *a set of values, beliefs, and norms* (i.e., expected behaviors) *that are held in common by people in a group*. Thus, culture is defined by the values that people hold jointly and the beliefs they develop together over time.

Third, culture provides organization members with an *integrated image* of their organization. Core values, beliefs, and norms are not random. Rather, they fit together to form a larger picture of the organization and of how it should work. They provide a conceptual framework that helps individuals define their own roles and helps focus individual and group behavior.

Finally, cultures grow stronger over time. Once they take hold, they become fiercely resistant to change, as people cling to the values and beliefs that nurtured their careers and molded their professional relationships. This characteristic inertia is both the major strength and the potentially fatal weakness of the phenomenon we call culture. Think about AT&T; for its first seventy years, the values and beliefs embodied in the corporate mantra of low-cost, universal service virtually became a religion for Ma Bell's minions, who viewed their work not as a business but as an ennobling form of public service—which, in some ways, it was. During AT&T's decades as a benevolent monopoly, that culture served the company and its customers with great distinction. But in the years immediately following the court-ordered breakup, the service-oriented culture stymied AT&T in its initial efforts to become a tough, aggressive, and innovative competitor in the cutthroat world of telecommunications.

Values and beliefs are present, to one extent or another, in every organization. At Xerox, for example, customer service has been a guiding value since the company's earliest days. At 3M, where a sizable percentage of sales is expected to come from new products each year, the core value is innovation. At ABB, as Percy Barnevik went about building his loose network of companies around the world, the overused phrase "think globally, act locally" became more than a cliché—it emerged as a core value.

While values may be largely ephemeral, they find their overt expression in norms, or clearly specified forms of behavior. Norms provide the guidelines for acceptable behavior; the clearer the core values, the more consistent the behavioral norms.

Norms guide all aspects of organizational life. They define broad issues, such as "how things get done here," "what it takes to get ahead," and "how we treat our employees," to more mundane matters, such as appropriate dress, humor, and language; how decisions really get made; who gets what parking space; who eats with whom; how many hours of work to put in each week; and how to deal with conflict. Groups enforce their norms and punish those who violate them. Furthermore, groups recruit, socialize, and train new members of the organization who perpetuate the traditions, bolstered by an overarching set of core values.

Driven by contrasting core values, similar organizations can display dramatically different norms. In some companies, for example, managers wouldn't dream of attending a meeting with the president without first tightening their ties and buttoning their suit jackets. At other businesses—many high-tech outfits, for instance—wearing a suit and tie to see the president would constitute a serious gaffe, a visible violation of the organization's anticorporate values. The norms embodied in these informal dress codes clearly reflect core values ranging from buttoned-down, high-level customer contact to "let's get down to work and dispense with formalities." Nobody hands out memos explaining how to dress when you see the boss—it's just something everyone knows.

Culture and Performance

Clearly, culture is an important component of organizational architecture. What's less clear is the relationship between culture and performance.

Successful companies tend to have highly focused and widely shared values, and they work hard at keeping these values intact, even during periods of radical change. At Xerox, during a period of tremendous upheaval in the 1980s as the company essentially redesigned itself to regain its market leadership, management took great pains to remind employees of the core values, such as customer service, that *weren't* changing.

At the other end of the scale are organizations with ambiguous or inconsistent values. In general, they tend to be consistently mediocre performers. At Technicon, for example, the absence of clear values—the gradual shift from being a hotbed of innovation to being a company that imported new processes from the outside— produced an R&D facility where product development ground to a halt as each lab department headed off in its own direction.

But before you leap to the conclusion that sharply focused and strongly held values and beliefs are the secret ingredient of corporate success, remember GM, U.S. Steel, and Penn Central. Each suffered disastrous setbacks precisely because it clung so desperately to values and beliefs that no longer served it well.

In other words, strong culture seems to be a prerequisite for— but not a guarantee—of success. Strong culture leads to focused behavior, but it's entirely possible for people to join forces in dysfunctional behavior that's not in the organization's long-term best interest. In the case of GM, for example, the culture—and even stronger subunit cultures—simply reinforced the widespread adherence to the traditional values, beliefs, and practices, reinforcing the company's sense of infallibility and blinding it to the historic changes that were transforming the competitive landscape.

Truly focused cultures become deeply entrenched because with the passage of time, the values and beliefs they embrace become indistinguishable from those of the individuals within the organization. In a very real sense, the culture and its members reinforce each other. In many instances it is the culture of the organization that attracts certain kinds of individuals. The more in tune employees are with the culture, the more likely it is that they will succeed and progress to senior positions where they can influence—and sustain—the culture. In time, culture takes on a self-perpetuating life of its own.

Consequently, culture is a double-edged sword. Culture can be the cornerstone of the informal organization that influences behavior and drives performance in the desired direction. A clear, coherent, and intense culture can infuse enormous energy into an organization and provide essential support to the formal organization. In some cases where the formal organization has become obsolete—as was the case at GM—the informal organization can actually supersede it with processes that are less costly and more efficient. Moreover, strong culture can keep an organization generally on course even during intermittent periods of poor leadership.

On the other hand, organization cultures can become obsolete. If the work or strategy changes, previously effective cultures can become seriously dysfunctional. In our opening case, the British conglomerate BOC, the tradition of absolute autonomy among the various gas companies in different countries became a potentially critical obstacle to success in an era of global customers and swift technological innovation. If C. K. Chow had not worked to instill a new culture based on collaboration and shared technology, it's hard to imagine how BOC could have remained a major international competitor much longer.

The problem is that, unlike strategy, work, or formal structures, which can be changed with relative speed, cultural change is difficult and takes time. While strategy, structures, and specific people may change, culture remains rooted in the organization's past, sowing the seeds of conflict and trauma.

Organization cultures have got to adapt to changing strategies and objectives. The challenge in managing cultural change is to reinforce as many of the core values as possible, bolstering links to the past even while pruning obsolete values and adding new ones that reflect current strategic demands.

Key Implementation Tasks

Throughout this chapter, we've used a fairly broad brush to illustrate the two broad concepts involved in the implementation of new organizational designs. The first is change management. Progress toward the future state always requires movement through a transition state, and that requires strong leadership and deliberate management. The second concept is culture and the need to manage and shape the informal organization in ways that are appropriate to the new strategic design.

Before we leave the subject, there are two additional points that deserve some mention. The first is the vital importance of putting the right people in the right jobs as an integral part of implementation. That might seem self-evident, but the fact is that too many organizations based their staffing selections—and in some cases, the operational designs themselves—on the perceived need to make sure there are no "losers" among the current cast of characters. While looking out for current employees is certainly a laudable goal, the fact is that the people currently holding senior or key managerial jobs may be too emotionally devoted to the old structure and culture, too limited in their experience, and too unsuited by temperament or personality to fill the kinds of roles demanded by the new design.

In most situations, the very success or failure of the design implementation depends on identifying the right people and placing them in the right jobs. Elsewhere, we have laid out a specific process, called "strategic selection," that has been successfully employed by major organizations in finding appropriate managers for brand-new positions created by redesigns (Nadler and Gerstein 1992). It is a fairly formalized process for objectively matching job requirements with detailed assessments of the strengths of weaknesses of a large field of potential candidates for each available job. Whatever process is used, it's crucial for managers to understand that they can easily destroy the most brilliantly conceived design by filling key positions solely on the basis of sentiment, loyalty, and, even more frequently, the desire to avoid highly unpleasant personal confrontations.

The second point, which should be clear by now, is that the line between design and implementation is awfully fuzzy. The truth is that the two processes are inseparable, and the earlier implementation becomes a design concern, the better. As we've already seen, decisions about who's involved in initially planning the design, who participates in the later stages of the process, and how the design process can be used to build political support all have a direct bearing on the success of implementation. Similarly, there's a tremendous amount of operational design that goes on even after the process has theoretically entered the implementation stage.

Figure 10-3 offers a way to visualize the process. It illustrates the relationship between design and implementation as they relate to the organizational hardware, software, and people.

General Motors Revisited

In retrospect, the most remarkable failure of the GM restructuring of 1984 may well have been the underlying assumption that an unwieldy collection of proud, independent, and uncooperative divisions and their hundreds of thousands of employees spread across a continent could be transformed into a radically different organizational configuration—literally overnight.

	Hardware	Software	People
Design	Design of the structures, processes, and systems of organization based on the architecture	Design of the culture, norms, leadership patterns, and required bahaviors based on the architecture	Choice and selection of people for key jobs and roles
Change Management	Planning and executing the installation and movement of assets to implement the new hardware	Planning and executing interventions aimed at bringing about needed software changes	Planning and implementing movement of people into new roles

Figure 10-3 Key Implementation Tasks

Our twelve action steps for managing organizational change pro-vides a checklist of all the things that weren't done at GM. Employ-ees had no idea what was coming; they were desperately short of information. Anxiety and confusion ran high, leading to aggression and outright hostility. Transition management appeared to be an afterthought; the management of internal politics, it seems, wasn't thought about at all. In keeping with the monumental arrogance that led GM to the brink of disaster in the first place, there was an assumption that managers could merely order a massive restructur-ing and that all the pieces would somehow fall into place.

They didn't. Eventually, the chaos subsided. But the reorganiza-tion—mapped out by a tiny group of executives with the aid of out-side consultants, without any participation by the workers and lower-level managers who could have pointed out the pitfalls—failed to achieve its major objectives—efficiency, teamwork, and collaborative efforts among design, engineering, and production. After eight years of costly problems, the CPC-BOC structure was wiped out in 1992 and replaced by the consolidation of the two groups into a single entity, North American Operations.

As time goes on, successful managers will have little choice but to master the design, implementation, and management of change, because redesign is quickly becoming a routine feature of organiza-tional life. Design changes, once rare, have become a normal, ongoing process in the development of most successful organizations. Adaptive organizations are able to respond quickly and effectively to new conditions and are able to reconfigure to support new strategies as needed. And as we're about to see in Chapter 11, the need for practically continuous redesign will have major implications in the coming decade for nearly every organization and for the people who manage them.

Bibliography

Beckhard, R., and R. Harris. *Organization Transitions*. Reading, Mass.: Addison-Wesley, 1977.

Beer, M., R. Eisenhardt, and B. Spector. *The Critical Path to Corporate Renewal*. Boston, Mass.: Harvard Business School Press, 1990.

Collins, J., and J. Porras. *Built to Last*. New York: Harper, 1995.

Finkelstein, S., and D. Hambrick. *Strategic Leadership: Top Executives and Their Effects on Organizations*. Minneapolis, Minn.: West, 1996.

Gabbaro, J. *The Dynamics of Taking Charge*. Boston: Harvard Business School Press, 1987.

Hurst, D. *Crisis and Renewal: Meeting the Challenge of Organization Renewal*. Boston, Mass.: Harvard Business School Press, 1995.

Ingrassia, P., and White, J. B. *Comeback: The Fall and Rise of the American Automobile Industry*. New York: Simon R. Schuster, 1994.

Kanter, R., B. Stein, and T. Jick. *The Challenge of Organization Changes*. New York: Free Press, 1992.

Keller, M. *Rude Awakening: The Rise, Fall and Struggle for Recovery of General Motors*. New York: Harper Collins, 1989.

Kotter, J., and J. Heskett. *Corporate Culture and Performance*. New York: Free Press, 1992.

Miller, D. "Stale in the Saddle: CEO Tenure and the Match between Organization and Environment." *Management Science* 37 (1991): 34–52.

Nadler, D., and M. Gerstein. "Strategic Selection." In D. Nadler, M. Gerstein, and R. Shaw, eds., *Organizational Architecture: Designs for Changing Organizations*. San Francisco: Jossey-Bass, 1992.

Nadler, D., R. Shaw, and E. Walton. *Discontinuous Change: Leading Organization Transformation*. San Francisco: Jossey-Bass, 1995.

O'Reilly, C., and J. Chatman. "Culture as Social Control." In B. Staw and L. Cummings, eds., *Research in Organization Behavior*, vol. 18. Greenwich, Conn.: JAI Press, 1997.

Pfeffer, J. *Managing with Power*. Boston, Mass.: Harvard Business School Press, 1992.

Schein, E. *Organization Cultures and Leadership.* San Francisco: Jossey-Bass, 1985.

Tichy, N., and S. Sherman. *Control Your Destiny or Someone Else Will.* New York: Currency, 1995.

Tushman, M., and C. O'Reilly. *Winning Through Innovation: A Practical Guide to Leading Organization Change and Renewal.* Boston, Mass.: Harvard Business School Press, 1997.

11

Knowing When to Redesign

Consider, for a moment, some of the companies we've focused on in previous chapters and the successive waves of change each experienced in recent years.

Xerox, following a handful of minor restructurings over the previous decade, undertook a fundamental redesign in 1992. The new architecture wiped out the old functional organization and replaced it with a complex, intricately intertwined amalgam of semiautonomous divisions and shared business processes. Just four years later, in the closing days of 1995, Xerox announced yet another reorganization, building on the architecture created in 1992. This time, Xerox combined its nine business divisions into three large business groups, unifying the disparate customer operations divisions under a single executive and eliminating an entire level of senior management.

AT&T, as it fought to succeed in the postdivestiture environment of the 1980s, realigned its structure to focus on long-distance and cellular phone service, network systems, and computers. But six years later, it was evident the new structure was already becoming obsolete as the telecommunications industry continued to explode with new technology, new products, new competitors, and new threats. Facing the inevitability of massive deregulation and the

challenges it would bring, AT&T decided in 1995 to spin off its computer division, NCR, and its network systems and communications
products group, renamed Lucent Technologies, Inc., in the largest
voluntary breakup in U.S. corporate history. General Motors, as we
saw in Chapter 10, tried in 1984 to overcome its sluggish, inefficient,
and incredibly expensive product development process through a
radical restructuring of its automotive divisions, engineering group,
and manufacturing operations. After eight years of occasional chaos,
disappointing performance, and steadily rising costs, the restructuring was abandoned, and GM rejoined the two megadivisions once
again under the single umbrella of North American Operations.
Smaller restructurings followed; in 1996, GM merged its GMC
Truck division with Pontiac in a further attempt to trim costs.

The circumstances behind the restructurings at each of those
companies varied dramatically. Taken together, however, they illustrate an important fact about redesign today: No matter how successful a company might be, no matter how well conceived and
smoothly implemented its most recent redesign, there are powerful
forces at work that make it inevitable that another wave of change
is lurking somewhere in the not-too-distant future.

Unfortunately, most managers are handicapped by notions of
change rooted in the days when a workable organizational design
could last for years. Alfred Sloan's architecture of "divisionalism"
helped fuel GM's market dominance for more than three decades.
But those days are gone. Today, successful managers understand that
an organization consists of a dynamic set of relationships that exist
within a turbulent competitive environment. Operating with a huge
array of constantly changing variables, it's unreasonable to assume
that any design will maintain the organization's viability year after
year and on into the misty future.

As we've already seen, the external environment that shapes an
organization's strategy is constantly buffeted by change in the form
of new competitors, shifting markets, economic trends, legislative
and judicial intervention, and technological innovation. Major
change in the environment typically leads to substantive changes in
strategy, which in turn necessitate new organizational designs.
Moreover, once you accept the notion that design, in and of itself,
provides a major source of competitive strength, then the ability constantly to anticipate, design and implement new designs becomes an
invaluable organizational capability.

Up to this point, we've discussed design in terms of a single
event, or set of events—the design of Corning's newly reopened

Blacksburg plant, Xerox's new architecture of independent business units, the SMH redesign of the Swiss watch industry, and so forth. But recent history suggests that more and more companies are experiencing a pattern of successive redesigns—some successful, some not. Organizations are constantly designed and redesigned. Some redesigns amount to no more than minor tinkering, while others are ground-up efforts to create an entirely new architecture.

In this chapter, we shift our focus to strategic design, not as a static event with an explicit beginning and end but as a dynamic process that occasionally pauses but never stops. Our perspective is on the continuous development of architecture over time. We first examine the factors that propel continuous redesign and, in some cases, make it inevitable. We then turn to the problems typically associated with repeated redesigns. Finally, we suggest some basic propositions about how to perform redesign successfully over time.

The Roots of Redesign

It's virtually impossible to think of any organization that exists today in a truly stable environment. Both within the organization and in its external environment, a multitude of changes make redesign inevitable or, at the very least, highly attractive. We've identified seven factors that push organizations toward redesign, starting with overall environmental change and gradually focusing in on specific issues within organizations.

1. Patterns of industry evolution. Research has established that virtually every industry evolves through a fairly predictable pattern of stages (see Figure 11-1). The details and the duration of each stage vary from one industry to the next, but the general pattern—referred to in professional literature as "the S-curve"—remains fairly constant (Tushman and O'Reilly 1996). Each stage holds major implications for organizations and requires different strategies and different organization designs:

Stage 1: Emerging industries. In the early days of emerging industries or product classes, uncertainty abounds. Technologies, products, markets—all present major risks and challenges for the initial players. At the turn of the century, it was anyone's guess whether the successors to horse-drawn carriages would be powered by gasoline, wood, coal, or electricity, each of which was championed by various inventors and entrepreneurs. The early days of the computer business were just as confusing; in

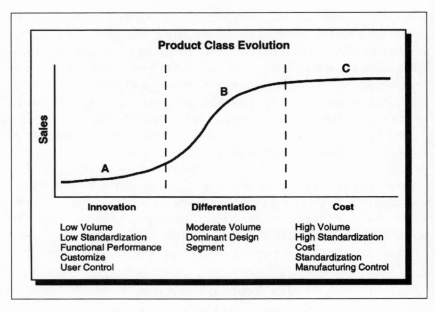

Figure 11-1 Phases of Industry Evolution

retrospect, few people within the industry had a clear vision of how computers might be used and who would want them.

During this early stage, companies compete on the basis of functional performance—what kind of car, copying machine, or computer operating system performs the job best? The emerging competitors learn from trial and error, quickly innovating on the run. Cost is not an issue, and companies are highly sensitive to the customized needs of early users.

Stage 2: Evolving industries. As an industry or product class evolves, increased demand attracts a host of new competitors. The competition between product types (e.g., gasoline versus electric-powered engines for cars, cassettes versus eight-track tapes) eventually leads to industry standardization. At some point, due either to technological or marketing dominance, one or two standard product forms evolve—Polaroid instant cameras, for instance, or Windows and Macintosh operating systems for personal computers. In some cases, the success of a landmark product—the DC-3 airplane, the IBM personal computer, and the Macintosh graphic user interface—provides a dominant design that shapes that particular industry or product class for years, even decades.

The emergence of an industry standard or dominant design signals an important shift in strategic emphasis from major product innovation to more incremental product change and process innovation. Organizations begin to segment markets on the basis of incremental product differences and reduced costs. As products become more standardized, companies shift their focus to process innovation as they seek competitive advantage through efficiency. Marketing, R&D, and production all assume increased importance during this phase. As new markets open up, companies respond with increased specialization, which in turn calls for more complex and interdependent organizational designs. With increasing complexity, size, and volume comes the need for more professional management than the original entrepreneurial organization could provide.

Stage 3: Mature industries. As demand levels off, or even drops, the basis of competition shifts yet again. In mature industries and product classes, competition becomes firmly focused on cost, efficiencies, and incremental product and process innovation. While the mature phase of a product class may be quite profitable, success hinges largely on efficiency, standardization, and innovative marketing and sales. In the auto industry, truly innovative products, such as Chrysler's minivans or the Mazda Miata roadster, are few and far between. Instead, the major competitors have turned their attention to the potential savings to be found in the area of time to market. In the 1970s and 1980s, Detroit typically took anywhere from four to six years (and seven years in the case of the GM-10 project) to bring a new car to market. By the mid-1990s, new cars were being designed and engineered in three to four years, but that still wasn't fast enough: Japanese competitors had set goals ranging from eighteen to twenty-four months. Keeping that development time to a minimum was becoming critical; it represented both important savings in overhead and the ability to get a new product on the market fast enough to respond to consumer demands.

During the mature phase of an industry, companies tend to standardize their product lines and, as we've seen, to invest in incremental product and process changes. These organizations tend to be large, functionally organized, and bureaucratic; they rarely produce radical product innovation, and their cultures emphasize stability, formality, and cost. Technology, politics, legal action, economic developments, social trends—each can and does play an important role in shaping the evolution of any industry. As industries change, so, too, do the dominant competitive issues, requiring strategic shifts by companies that hope to remain viable competitors. And that means periodically reshaping the structures, processes, and operating environment to keep pace.

Moreover, successful organizations must be capable of managing "ambidextrous organizations." Although we've talked about three distinct stages of industry evolution, in reality the stages merge from one to the next. Consequently, managers must be able to redesign portions of the organization while continuing to do the things that have already made them successful.

At the Industrial Gases Division of BOC, for example, C. K. Chow inherited an organization in which some operations— those in the United States, the United Kingdom, and Australia— were doing reasonably well. His challenge was to reshape the overall architecture of the division and make dramatic changes in the country operations in emerging markets, while maintaining the successful operations in others. Similarly, David Kearns and Paul Allaire had to focus Xerox's move into new areas of digital office technology while maintaining the momentum of those operations centered around the production, sales, and servicing of equipment using the traditional reprographic processes.

In other words, management teams have to create the organizational capabilities that will allow them to operate for today as well as tomorrow. Sometimes that means cannibalizing their own product lines or substituting for current products as they move quickly toward the next product cycle, they hope before the competition gets there. They must improvise in the short run even as they innovate for the long run.

2. Discontinuous change. If the S-curve presented the full picture of industry evolution, strategic design would be a relatively simple exercise. But that's just the first stage of analysis.

During the relatively stable periods, most organizations pursue a constant series of course corrections to help them adapt to shifting strategic objectives and maintain good fit among the various elements of the organization. These are *incremental* changes. Incremental changes aren't necessarily small, in terms of the resources involved. But they are minor in the sense that they represent orderly progressions in the organization's current direction and take place within the framework of the existing architecture.

In every industry or product class, however, these periods of gradual evolution are punctuated by periods of upheaval (generally termed "disequilibrium") brought about by a major destabilizing event. That event, or series of events, might be the emergence of new technology, government deregulation, or the appearance of a new competitor with a new offering or process that substantially alters the rules of the game. These are the "shake-out" periods when new competitors emerge; existing companies either adapt to change or fall by the wayside. Organizations caught up in these turbulent periods quickly find that major redesign is virtually inevitable.

A classic destabilizing event was the enactment in early 1996 of landmark telecommunications reform legislation, which radically altered the rules of competition for long-distance carriers, regional phone companies, and cable services. Even before Congress passed the bill, the industry had entered a period of massive upheaval—the AT&T spin-off, the forging of strategic alliances among players such as Nynex and Bell Atlantic, joint ventures by local phone companies and cable operators (such as Ameritech and Jones Intercable in the Chicago suburbs), and the acquisition of small, local phone companies by long-distance carriers seeking entrée into the local phone service arena.

Such periods of disequilibrium—or the anticipation of such periods—typically induce radical or *discontinuous change,* so named because it represents a dramatic shift from the status quo (Nadler, Shaw, and Walton 1995). In its fullest form, discontinuous change affects every component of the organization and involves changes in strategy, leadership, structures, and behavior. The Xerox reorganization of 1992, Nicholas Hayek's restructuring of Swatch, the transformation of two competitors into ABB, and, for that matter, the ill-fated GM restructuring of 1984 all were radical changes brought about by monumental shifts in markets, technologies, and the nature of competition. In order to succeed, each required entirely new strategies, structures, processes, leadership characteristics, human resource systems, and operating environments. As the GM episode illustrates, discontinuous change—particularly when launched in the face of an immediate threat—is often risky, expensive, and, if poorly executed, unlikely to succeed.

The nature of discontinuous change can vary markedly on the basis of timing. *Anticipatory* changes come early in each phase of the cycle, as the industry or product class begins to enter a period of disequilibrium. They result from a strategic scan of the competitive environment and represent a deliberate attempt to either diminish impending threats or capitalize on potential opportunities. Consider AT&T; as early as the fall of 1994, the company was getting signals that its strategic design would become a major handicap in a totally deregulated environment, with the core long-distance company and its network systems operation pursuing conflicting strategies. By mid-1995, management had determined that the breakup had to occur some time in 1996.

Anticipatory changes enjoy a relatively high rate of success, largely because they're implemented with the luxury of time; they take place in a relatively calm atmosphere, with sufficient time for planning and the opportunity to shift gears or modify plans if early efforts fall short of desired goals.

Reactive changes, on the other hand, come much later in the disequilibrium period. They're generally associated with a crisis atmosphere, little lead time, substantial costs, few opportunities for experimentation, and a high risk of failure. GM's 1984 restructuring, for example, came at a time when market share had tumbled to 35 percent, cash reserves were evaporating, competition from the Japanese and from Ford was becoming more intense, and efforts to bring out a new line of autos were going nowhere. In a desperate attempt to right the ship, GM steered off on a new course that had to be corrected by a new management team.

Discontinous change is always traumatic, because it involves simultaneous changes in strategy, structure, power, and controls. Clearly, it's vital for managers to understand the nature of the change in which they're about to engage. Each type of change is driven by a distinctly different design intent, which, in turn, dictates a cascading set of decisions about grouping, linkages, processes systems, and culture, as well as about the implementation and management of those changes.

3. New structural materials. As we saw in Chapters 7 and 8, new "structural materials" emerge over time, leading to the development of new organizational architectures. At a certain point, that growth accelerates and achieves a critical mass—a point at which so many organizations have adopted the new architecture that others feel compelled at least to give serious thought to revamping their own design.

In recent years, the explosion in information technology has provided the structural material for countless new architectures. At the micro level, we saw in our discussion of Blacksburg the key role that the sharing of real-time information plays in the successful functioning of self-managed teams. As long as information was the exclusive, tightly controlled property of management, the role of low-level teams remained severely limited. But the widespread availability of crucial information, particularly to front-line workers who were dealing directly with production and customer service functions, made empowerment more than a hollow New Age concept. Information allowed individuals and teams to exercise independent judgment and to make swift decisions in unprecedented ways. Moreover—giving reengineering its due—information technology provided entirely new ways of thinking about front-to-back businesses processes, reconfiguring people and work in patterns inconceivable within historic boundaries of time and space.

By the same token, information technology opened the door to new ways of designing processes and grouping relationships at the enterprise level. Unconstrained by geography, physical plants, travel times, and interminable delays in getting the right information to the right people, organizations have been freed to forge new relationships with customers, suppliers, and partners.

As more and more companies experience success with new architectures—whether they involve self-managed teams, leveraged business units, or new strategic alliances—it becomes inevitable that other companies will feel compelled to consider using those same "structural materials" for their own redesign purposes.

4. Organizational growth. As organizations grow, they don't just get bigger—they get more complex. Expansion inevitably brings more volume, more differentiation, more specialization, a broader range of offerings to customers, and new geographic locations. As the number of people grows, the number of units proliferates, and interdependence grows ever more intense. Consequently, the organization needs new structures and processes to accommodate the heightened complexity and the increased demands for information processing.

There is a parallel to this in computing, known as "scalability." As you enlarge an image on a screen, it loses its sharpness and clarity; the bigger it gets, the more jagged and disjointed it becomes. That happens because you can't simply make it bigger; you have to "scale it up," adding pixels to provide a proportionate increase in the amount of information fed to the screen. Organizations are much the same; if you do nothing but make them bigger, they quickly grow jagged around the edges. Growth has to be accompanied by appropriate design changes.

The most common example of this phenomenon is the critical period a growing company encounters as it makes the transition from entrepreneurial startup to a professionally managed business.

The two are entirely different, and many startups fail to make the leap, tenaciously hanging on to the informal structures and family-like cultures that spawned their initial success. A quick look at Silicon Valley illustrates how difficult it is—and how essential—to continually match growth with an appropriate strategic design.

5. The "Success Syndrome." While growth presents redesign challenges to every organization, a very special set of problems involves long-time market leaders. Time after time, we have seen dominant companies sow the seeds of their own failure in a self-destructive pattern we describe as the "Success Syndrome."

These successful companies experience all the growth problems we have just described. As they get larger, their systems, procedures, and processes become increasingly formalized in order to handle more complex work flows. Bureaucracies flourish, imposing rigid controls at the expense of flexibility and speed. As the organization becomes more efficient at doing the same things, it becomes less capable of doing new ones.

At the same time, people become more deeply entrenched in the organization. As time passes, their energies become focused more and more on maintaining control and stability. The organizations they run develop standard operating procedures, socialization processes, precedent, history, and culture—a daunting collection of forces resistant to change.

As time passes, market leaders become increasingly arrogant and complacent. The more successful they are—the more dominant within their industry or business—the more they come to believe that what happens outside the organization can't possibly be important. They start to ignore changes among customers and competitors. The inward focus grows, with disproportionate attention to internal politics and power. As success becomes taken for granted, the risk of failure becomes increasingly unacceptable; people grow cautious, experimentation stalls, and innovation dries up.

Moreover, the practices, structures, and processes that contributed to the organization's initial success—or, more accurately, those that corporate lore *perceives* to have been the springboards to success—become formalized, assuming an exalted status as "the things that made us number one." Whenever the company is confronted by a threat, these sacred relics are held up to the masses with the corporate mantra, "Just keep doing what got us here in the first place." In other words, when in trouble, just do more of the same.

Think about General Motors in the 1970s. It demonstrated each and every one of those characteristics: arrogance, a sense of infallibility, conservatism, increased complexity, an obsession with corporate politics, and haughty indifference to fundamental shifts in the marketplace. Small armies of corporate princelings, managers who'd come of age when GM's market share neared 70 percent, rushed through perfunctory rotations in various jobs in their pursuit of top executive positions. The route to the top was to be the stereotypical "company man"—to dress the right way, perform well at meetings, live in the right suburb, belong to the right clubs, get along and not rock the boat. The first tremors in the auto market brought on by the 1973 oil crisis were viewed by these supremely confident executives as a temporary blip; on the fourteenth floor of GM headquarters, it was business as usual. There was total confidence that all GM had to do was keep building its traditional cars, and the customers would soon come back.

In time, the arrogance, insularity, complexity, and conservatism of successful companies lead to some predictable outcomes. Those characteristics squelch innovation, diminish speed, inflate costs, and diffuse customer focus. In short, they produce a seriously dysfunctional organization. During relatively stable periods, successful companies can rumble along with reasonable success despite those problems. But during times of dramatic change—the periods of disequilibrium—those shortcomings become critical, manifesting themselves in poor performance, falling market share, stalled growth, and a sharp decline in earnings. At this point, executives typically engage in deep denial. They blame outside forces—government regulators, unfair competitors, gouging suppliers. They blame the economy, interest rates, and trade barriers. The ultimate symptom of corporate pathology comes when executives blame customers; it wasn't unusual around GM, and at other U.S. automakers, to hear managers decry the hippies and weirdos who would buy Volkswagen Beetles and, later, Datsuns, Toyotas, and Hondas.

Unfortunately, one aspect of the dysfunctional organization is its inability to learn from its mistakes; it just goes on making the same ones. Confronted with critical problems, the all too common response of a company caught up in the success syndrome is: Do more of the same. Over time, this pattern of denial and repetition becomes a "death spiral." There is only one way to escape the spiral: radical and fundamental redesign of the entire organization.

6. Management succession. Not surprisingly, the installation of a new CEO often provides the stimulus for major redesign efforts. In general terms, these redesign processes fall into at least one of these categories:

- *Responding to an inherited crisis.* This reason for redesign is closely related to our discussion of "the success syndrome." The rash of boardroom rebellions in the early 1990s was aimed at CEOs of leading companies who had failed to free their companies from the downward spiral of arrogance, insularity, and "doing more of the same." At GM, IBM, American Express, Kodak, and a dozen other *Fortune* 500 companies, directors sought out new CEOs who could lead radical change, unencumbered by the history, culture, relationships, and loyalties that guided the decisions of their predecessors.

- *Making a personal statement.* Not all new CEOs instigate change because they face an immediate crisis; in many cases, there's simply a natural desire by the new boss to put his or her personal stamp on the organization. Sometimes the new CEO has very specific ideas about changing the overall architecture; other times, there's simply a desire to "make the place run differently"—more aggressively, more collaboratively, more economically—in accordance with the new leader's personal vision and style. That general intent inevitably leads to substantial redesign.

- *Pursuing a new strategy.* The new CEO may assume office with a specific strategic vision in mind. It may involve major portfolio moves, strategic alliances, disaggregation, or the development of a new basis for competition. Obviously, any major shift in strategy will result in serious redesign.

- *Shaking up the place.* There are times when new CEOs, even before they've formulated a new vision or strategy, perceive the need to take dramatic action to shake the organization out of its lethargy. They may want to infuse people with a sense of urgency and, perhaps, some uncertainty about the future. Fundamental redesign is the quickest way to send shock waves through a sluggish organization that is sleepwalking its way through its business.

7. Organizational mutation. At most organizations, there are always some design experiments in the works. They may be going on informally, at a low level or on a small scale, but it's unusual to find a company where someone, somewhere isn't trying something new—working with teams, organizing people across traditional boundaries, or testing new relationships with suppliers.

Every so often, one of these innovations catches on and, in turn, influences the larger organization design. At these junctures, the gradual evolution of an organization's architecture is jolted by a sudden mutation that accelerates change or steers it in a new direction.

Taken together, these seven factors illustrate the enormous forces that constantly push organizations toward redesign. While it's hard to imagine a company that's subject to all seven, it's not at all difficult to find situations where two, three, or more are at work at any given time. What this means is that architectural change—and repeated change—have become a fact of life for most organizations. And as the rate of change continues to quicken, the need for repeated redesign will quickly become the exception rather than the rule.

The Costs of Redesign

There's a joke told around boardrooms about a CEO who has been fired in disgrace. Offering some final advice to his successor, he opens a drawer, pulls out three numbered envelopes, and hands them across the desk.

"Save these," the CEO tells the new fellow, "and open them—in order—only when you find yourself in the middle of a crisis and all else has failed."

About a year later, the company is in serious trouble. In desperation, the new CEO pulls out envelope number one, tears it open, and reads: "Take a huge write-off."

A year or so later, there's a new crisis. The CEO opens envelope number two and finds the message: "Do a major restructuring."

Things seem to get better, but only for a while. Then the CEO remembers the third envelope. Frantically, he searches through his office, finally discovers the envelope under a stack of old files, rips it open, and reads: "Get three envelopes."

The point? All too often, redesign, restructurings, and reorganizations are knee-jerk reactions to corporate crises. Other times they're perceived as gimmicks, rabbits CEOs pull out of their hats to entertain the audience and deflect attention from real problems. And all too often, that's exactly what's going on. The seven roots of redesign that we just discussed can lead to well-conceived, well-executed efforts seriously to rebuild the organization. But they can just as easily be used to rationalize repeated, cosmetic reorganizations that accomplish almost nothing of value, while incurring significant costs.

Let's be clear about this: Up to this point, we've focused almost exclusively on the benefits of redesign. But the very process of redesign carries with it inherent and significant costs. Those costs are present, to one extent or another, every time there's a redesign of major substance, whether it's brilliant or lousy. Moreover, when suc-

cessive redesigns occur in a relatively short period, the costs rise geometrically. The costs include:

- *Disruption.* Major reorganizations disrupt the normal flow of
  business. Long-time relations with customers and suppliers may
  be seriously damaged as personnel, territories, business processes, and strategic priorities are rearranged. Customers often find it
  difficult to do business with companies in the midst of redesign;
  competitors often seize the opportunity to capitalize on the confusion, instability, and intensely inward focus of their rival during these periods. Not surprisingly, the effects of disruption often
  show up in the diminished performance of sales forces, as was the
  case at both AT&T and Xerox during their redesign periods.

- *Stress.* In many cases, the organizational disruption is a collective expression of the personal stress experienced by individuals.
  People are worried about losing their jobs, their friends, their
  working relationships, their career aspirations, their status, their
  routine. They may be assigned to new jobs, in new locations, with
  a new boss and possibly with new subordinates, and have to deal
  with a new set of suppliers and customers. The rules may have
  changed, so people aren't sure what performance is expected, how
  it will be measured, or how it will be rewarded. In these situations, instability and the lack of information provoke anxiety,
  which frequently manifests itself in diminished performance.
  People feel they've lost control of their own destiny; they seek to
  reassert some portion of that power by engaging in intense—and
  often dysfunctional—office politics. As change drags on, people
  tend to focus on everything but their work.

- *Skepticism.* Like it or not, the truth is that redesign—which
  we've portrayed in this book as one of the highest forms of the art
  of management—is almost universally perceived by rank-and-file
  employees as a sign of executive incompetence. Few people—
  very few—like change. The status quo might not be ideal, but
  after a while we get used to it, and we're loathe to let go of it just
  because some bigshot we've never met is assuring us it's the right
  thing to do.
  Within the organization, the general assumption is that
  restructurings are a sign that top executives aren't competent
  enough to manage the organization as well as the old guys did.
  That's the typical reaction to a one-time, well-conceived and desperately needed redesign. Repeated designs that are superficial,
  cosmetic and ineffective inevitably lead to intense skepticism,
  even cynicism, about top management and its ability to run the
  organization.

- *Chronic instability.* Those who like to talk about perpetual restructuring and "adhocracies" where structures and processes are forever fluid ignore the basic human need—both individually and collectively—for stability. Just as industries evolve through long periods of gradual growth punctuated only once in a while by periods of disequilibrium, individual organizations need time after each major change to let people recuperate, take a deep breath, and get back to work. Those periods of normalcy are essential; it takes time for wounds to heal, for people to regain their commitment to the organization and to redirect their focus toward their work and their customers. At companies like Apple, endless waves of restructurings and reorganizations led to enormous anxiety, a loss of continuity, critical defections, and a seriously damaged commitment to the core values that had made the company so successful in its early years.

- *Distracted management.* In previous chapters we've described the enormous amount of time, energy, and attention managers must devote to redesign if it's to be developed well and implemented successfully. Obviously, if managers weren't engaged in the complexities of redesign, much of their time, energy, and attention would be focused elsewhere—on running the core business, improving performance, and dealing with customers. So the full price of redesign should also include some consideration of opportunity costs.

  As we said, these costs constitute substantial hits to the organization even when the redesign is desperately needed, insightfully developed, and efficiently implemented. When redesign is nothing more than a haphazard exercise undertaken in pursuit of short-term gain, the costs to individuals and to the organization become unconscionable. Consequently, it's imperative for managers, first of all, to make sure major redesign is done deliberately and comprehensively the first time around to reduce the need for repeated efforts. Second, they need to resist the impulse to rush to redesign as a quick cure for every problem that arises.

Managing Design over Time

So far in this chapter, we've talked about the factors that are making redesign a more frequent phenomenon than ever before. Some of those factors make redesign inevitable; some make it easy; some make it attractive. At the same time, we've seen the substantial costs redesign imposes on an organization, an issue that argues in favor of using redesign judiciously and with proper planning and sound implementation. Together, these two themes lead us to a set of propositions about how managers ought to think about and plan for redesign as they look to the future.

1. *Without any doubt, every organization's architecture will change over time.* Managers need to come to grips with the inevitability of this change. Incremental change, within the framework of the existing architecture, will go on all the time. Depending on their industry, however, organizations should also expect to undergo a fundamental redesign *every five years or less.* The days when a CEO could reasonably expect to leave the company much as he left it—or to preside over only one major restructuring—are over. This reality is equally important for managers at every level of the organization.

2. *Consequently, effective managers will be constantly thinking about the next round of change.* If you assume that change is on the way and understand the forces that will cause it, then you can intelligently plan for it. Managers who understand the dynamics of change and prepare for it can seriously lower the odds of one day facing the prospect of a frantic, last-minute restructuring in the face of imminent doom. The best managers are always looking ahead, thinking about the next move. At Xerox, Paul Allaire began thinking in 1990 about the sweeping architectural changes that the company would actually implement in 1992.

3. *Managers must relentlessly scrutinize their own design efforts and learn from experience.* Make no mistake: Redesign is an art, not a science. There are just too many ingredients in the organizational mix to allow consistently accurate predictions of how a particular design will work once it moves from the flip chart to the real world.

Given that unpredictability, it's rare for a design to fulfill all its goals on the first try. Borrowing from quality management, managers need to think about design as a "plan-do-check-act" cycle. They should try a design, closely observe how it works in practice, identify what works and what doesn't, and then make the appropriate adjustments. Those concepts apply to redesign at the corporate level, the plant floor, and everywhere in between. At Corning's Blacksburg plant, the design of the High-Performance Work System has continued to evolve over the years, with periodic adjustments. After nearly eight years of experience, managers still see ways the design could be improved.

To guarantee that learning becomes a deliberate process, we strongly recommend that organizations engage in regularly scheduled architectural assessments, particularly in the period immediately following the introduction of a new design. Ideally, these assessments should take place every six months during the initial period and then every year. They should be comprehensive evaluations of how well the redesign is meeting the goals set out in the design intent and of any unanticipated ways the design may be affecting the organization's performance. The result of this process will be periodic radical redesign followed by continuous incremental modifications.

4. *Organizations will develop architectures that are inherently modular, allowing major change without major upheaval.* In Chapter 7, in our discussion of enterprise-level design, we talked about the increasingly popular notion of "organizational Legos," design components that can be added or eliminated to the organization without disturbing the underlying architectural frame. At a time when competition, markets and technology can change dramatically almost overnight, the ability swiftly to redeploy resources without massively disrupting the rest of the organization becomes a major competitive weapon. Sun Microsystems, Xerox, ABB, and SMH have developed architectures characterized by this "inherent modularity."

A key to maintaining successfully this flexible architecture is having a clear design intent. If the purpose of the original design—to enhance speed, accountability, customer focus, technological innovation, flattened hierarchy, or whatever—is explicitly articulated, then there are clear boundaries for adding, deleting, or rearranging design elements. If your organization is already operating with nine market-focused independent business units, adding three new units to accommodate new products and market niches—or shrinking nine to three as the industry shakes out—shouldn't shatter the architectural foundation

5. *It will become increasingly evident that the shortest distance between an existing design and a desired one isn't necessarily a straight line.* Managers intent on moving from the current design to a particular architecture are finding that sometimes it's impossible to go directly from here to there. Moreover, the route you take will have a major impact on how you feel once you get there, a concept known as "path dependence." In other words, it's sometimes necessary to start out with such a radical redesign that it completely shatters the existing architecture; only then can the pendulum swing back to the more moderate design that management was aiming at from the beginning.

Case in point: If Xerox had tried to move in 1992 directly from its traditional, functional organizational architecture to the 1996 design of three large business groups, it would have simply taken all the problems of the original organization and reproduced them three times on a smaller scale. That's precisely what General Motors did in 1984, splitting North American Operations into two smaller divisions that reflected all the structural and cultural shortcomings of the original organization. Xerox, to a large extent, avoided some of GM's problems by first obliterating the structures, bureaucratic complexity, and cultural mind-set that characterized the existing architecture. Then, after four years, it began reassembling some of the elements of the design—but by this point, the organization had new people, new processes, a different focus on customers and markets, and different human resource systems to reinforce the new behavior. Consequently, the resulting organization has a very different look and feel than if the Xerox of 1990 had moved directly to the Xerox of 1996.

6. *Design, because it will be constant and so crucial, will become an essential capability for successful organizations.* We don't mean to imply that massive, fundamental rearchitecting shouldn't involve the assistance of outside consultants who bring valuable expertise and external perspective to the process. (In fact, we might be among the last to suggest such a thing.) But as we've seen, repeated redesign on one scale or another is inevitable. Therefore, organizations that are constantly looking to the future will realize the importance of having their own people who have a sufficient grasp of design constantly to assess the adequacy of the current design and to start planning what comes next. And given all we've said about the importance of implementation, the organizational capability should include the skills to put new designs in place as well as to develop them.

7. *As design becomes increasingly important, organizations that are design innovators will enjoy significant competitive advantage.* Successful organizations will regard the activity of design as an essential management process and an important source of competitive strength. Design innovation will be seen as an essential competitive activity. To succeed, organizations will have to engage in constant experimentation, widespread use of pilot programs, and continuous benchmarking, particularly with companies outside their own industry. Innovation requires learning, which in turn demands specific processes for deliberately studying both successful and failed designs and then applying the lessons learned to a new

round of experimentation and incorporating the results into the existing design.

Summary: The Role of Leaders

These propositions have particular significance for CEOs and other organizational leaders. Executive leadership requires more than driving current performance while "drawing down the account." To the contrary, true leaders manage, develop, and grow organizational capabilities. And doing that requires personal attention to the thoughtful development, over time, of the organization's architecture.

Senior executives can, and often do, delegate much of the responsibility for planning and executing incremental change. But when it comes to radical change and the articulation of a guiding vision for the architecture of the organization as a whole, leadership can't be delegated; the CEO and the most senior people simply have to be involved.

Increasingly, the true test of outstanding leadership lies in the ability to envision, articulate, and launch radical change in the absence of an immediate threat. In reality, few executives possess the combination of courage, commitment, and vision to subject their organizations to all the horrendous costs of major redesign—all in anticipation of change.

Our focus in this chapter has been on the relationship between architecture and change and on the fundamental nature of strategic design as a dynamic, never-ending process. Tomorrow's most successful leaders will be those who deliberately develop innovative design as a distinct organizational capacity. That ability will rest on learning the skills, concepts, and tools of design. The practice of design, as we've described it in this book, rests on some very basic principles, which we present, with some final discussion, in Chapter 12.

Bibliography

Barnett, W., and G. Carroll. "Modeling Internal Organizational Change." *Annual Review of Sociology* 21 (1995): 217–236.

Barton, D. L. *Wellsprings of Knowledge.* Boston, Mass.: Harvard Business School Press, 1995.

Eisenhardt, K., and B. Tabrizi. "Accelerating Adaptive Processes." *Administrative Science Quarterly* (1995): 84–110.

Foster, R. *Innovation: The Attacker's Advantage.* New York: Summit, 1987.

Huber, G., and W. Glick, eds., *Organization Change and Redesign*. New York: Oxford, 1993.

Hurst, D. *Crisis and Renewal: Meeting the Challenge of Organization Renewal*. Boston, Mass.: Harvard Business School Press, 1995.

Kanter, R. *The Change Masters: Innovation and Entrepreneurship in the Corporation*. New York: Simon & Schuster, 1984.

Morone, J. *Winning in High-Tech Markets*. Boston, Mass.: Harvard Business School Press, 1993.

Nadler, D., R. Shaw, and E. Walton. *Discontinuous Change*. San Francisco: Jossey-Bass, 1995.

Tushman, M., and P. Anderson. "Technological Discontinuities and Organization Environments." *Administrative Science Quarterly* 31 (1983): 439–465.

Tushman, M., W. Newman, and E. Romanelli. "Convergence and Upheaval: Managing the Unsteady Pace of Organization Evolution." *California Management Review* (Winter 1986): 29–45.

Tushman, M., and C. O'Reilly. "The Ambidextrous Organization: Managing Evolutionary and Revolutionary Change." *California Management Review* (Summer 1996): 8–30.

Tushman, M., C. O'Reilly, and P. Anderson. "Levers for Organization Renewal: Innovation Streams and Ambidextrous Organizations." In M. Tushman and P. Anderson, eds., *Managing Strategic Innovation: A Book of Readings*. New York: Oxford University Press, 1997.

Tushman, M., and L. Rosenkopf. "On the Organizational Determinants of Technological Change." In B. Staw and L. Cummings, eds., *Research in Organization Behavior*, vol. 14. Greenwich, Conn.: JAI Press, 1992.

Utterback, J. *Mastering the Dynamics of Innovation*. Cambridge, Mass.: Harvard Business School Press, 1994.

12

The Lessons of Design

If any theme should have emerged by now, it's that there is nothing easy, automatic, or formulaic about organizational architecture and design. Each situation is unique. Let's return one last time to our metaphor of physical architecture. Every time an architect takes on a new assignment, the creative challenge is shaped and constrained by a staggering array of variables—geographic location, topography, size, function, structural materials, exterior design, budget limitations, zoning constraints—the list goes on and on.

Organizational architecture, if approached from a truly thoughtful perspective about the organization's long-term growth and success, is just as complex—in some ways, even more so. While architecture rests on certain immutable laws of physics, engineering, and mathematics, the basic building blocks of organizational architecture are the intangible concepts of group dynamics and human behavior.

You can build a scale model of a house, factory, or skyscraper and get a clear, concrete representation of how it's going to look and how the basic components will fit together. But an organizational model is nothing more than a conceptual framework for imagining and predicting the interrelationships of individuals, groups, their work, and the overall goals of the organization. It represents an educated best guess of how a given design, implemented in certain ways in a particular cultural and competitive environment, will affect the ability of people to perform the kinds of work required to meet the organization's strategic objectives. There are never any guarantees that people will act according to plan or that unforeseen external events won't necessitate a shift in strategy—in fact, they probably will.

Nevertheless, the notion of architecture as a framework for organizational design and the fundamental concepts we've presented concerning the function, development, and implementation of design are essential tools for any manager hoping to guide an organization through this new era of perpetual change. Without those underlying ideas and guiding vision, managers are left to frantically steer an uncertain course from one crisis to the next.

Throughout this book, we've attempted to support this view through a melding of contemporary theory and current practice—both good and bad. Some of the information might have been particularly relevant to certain kinds of organizations, or to managers at specific levels in their organization. But throughout, we've attempted to develop certain propositions about architecture and design that apply equally to managers at every level, at practically every kind of organization. This, then, is how we would summarize the ten basic themes that capture the essence of this book.

1. Organizational capabilities represent the last truly sustainable source of competitive advantage. Until fairly recently, in a historically stable business environment, there were all kinds of ways in which companies could develop and maintain sources of competitive advantage. Those might have involved exclusive access to customers or capital, outstanding product lines, unique technology, unmatched production processes, or unrivaled distribution channels. No more. Information technology, global markets, and changing customer demands have changed all that. Recently, the CEO of a major international corporation told us he'd come to believe that his people were the final source of competitive advantage, and we had to disagree; even that's not true any more. In these times of diminished loyalty between employees and their employers, the most talented people can vanish in an instant.

Instead, we are firmly convinced that the last remaining source of genuine competitive advantage that any organization can sustain over time is its ability to organize and motivate people in unique ways to achieve strategic objectives. During the 1990s, for instance, Chrysler has developed the organizational capability to develop and bring to market more innovative products, in less time and at significantly lower cost, than either of its Detroit rivals. That doesn't mean that Chrysler's specific strength is technological innovation, expert engineering, or low-cost production. Instead, the company's newly found competitive strength lies in its ability, through new working relationships and processes within the company, as well as through unique alliances with major suppliers, quickly and efficiently to meet a constantly changing set of strategic targets.

2. Organizational architecture provides a conceptual framework for employing strategic design to develop organizational capabilities. In effective organizations, design is more than a series of unrelated attempts to restructure departments and modify reporting relationships. The Xeroxes, AT&Ts, and ABBs of the world think in terms of their overall organizational architecture—the collection of formal structures and informal relationships that give their company a particular feel and functionality. For them, design is a process for configuring social and technical components in ways that fit the architectural framework and focus the organization's capabilities.

Essential to this concept is the idea of organizations as both social and technical systems. The process of strategic design falls heavily on the "hardware," or technical side of the organization, and that has been our emphasis here. But we've also tried to make it clear that effective strategic design acknowledges and addresses the relationships between formal structures and the informal patterns of values, beliefs, and behavior norms that make up an organization's culture. It is the unique mixture of strategy, structure, work, people, and culture that together dictate the architecture of each organization.

3. At every level of the organization, design constitutes one of the most powerful tools for shaping performance. Of all the techniques managers have at their disposal, design is one of the most potent and appealing. Major shifts in strategy, staffing, and culture are difficult, destabilizing, time-consuming, and, in some cases, the responsibility of only a small number of senior executives. But design is a process available to managers at every level of the organization. It can take the form of sweeping, enterprise-level redesign as a spearhead of radical change, or it can—and frequently does—occur almost constantly at lower levels in the form of incremental improvements.

The immense appeal of design is also what makes it so dangerous. From the outside, it seems deceptively simple. But poorly conceived design is at best ineffective and at worst truly dysfunctional. Using design as a quick and easy solution to every organizational problem erodes managers' credibility and builds widespread cynicism about the organization's commitment to change. Redesigns that merely rearrange the boxes and lines, without producing fundamental changes in governance, create instability and divert attention from important work but provide few off-setting benefits. And managers who engage in free-lance redesign in pursuit of short-term goals run the risk of doing serious damage; design, at each and every level, has to start with the organization's or the unit's strategic goals, not someone's desire simply to "shake things up."

4. Regardless of its scope or scale, there are certain fundamental concepts that apply to design at every level. Whether you're talking about redesigning a department of fifty people or a factory of 500 or a global corporation of 150,000, the fundamentals of design remain the same. Design at any level involves a series of decisions about grouping and linking aimed at enhancing the organization's ability to process information and coordinate interdependent work that crosses formal grouping boundaries.

Implicit in those concepts is the notion that the primary work of modern organizations is the gathering, channeling, and processing of appropriate information. The increasing complexity of competitive demands and strategies has been matched by growing interdependence within organizations; all along the value chain, each group of people is increasingly reliant on others for information about technology, suppliers, customers, and competitors. At the same time, as the limited rote jobs of the assembly line give way to more complex jobs requiring individual judgment, there's an infinitely greater need for information to flow directly to people in front-line jobs. In each case, the result is the same: a heightened need for the swift, focused, and efficient flow of information.

Designers can take those basic concepts—the configuration of groupings and linkages to enhance information processing and interdependence—and apply them to any strategy, organization, or workplace. Whether they're designing Corning's factory work teams or Xerox's independent business units or Kaiser Permanente's customer service areas, the fundamental concepts remain the same.

5. There is a logical sequence of actions and decisions that applies to the design process at any level of the organization. As we have pointed out, organizational design tends to be done badly because, at first glance, it seems so simple and intuitive. That's absolutely wrong. Even at the most basic level, effective design is more than drawing boxes and arrows; it flows from a thorough understanding of strategic objectives, takes into consideration both the formal and the informal elements of the organizational units involved, both directly and indirectly, in the redesign, and weighs the potential impact on the rest of the organization and its ability to fulfill strategic goals.

We've talked about organizations—Xerox, Corning, and Kaiser Permanente, for example—that engaged in full-blown, step-by-step redesign projects involving scores, even hundreds of people. We've also encountered small companies in which redesign was effectively handled by a handful of people. What each of those efforts had in common was an orderly thought process that led to the final design. Generally speaking, that process begins with a preliminary diagnosis of the obstacles that stand in the way of the organization's achievement of its strategic goals. That leads to a design intent—the stated purpose of the redesign—fleshed out by design criteria, specific requirements that the redesign is supposed to meet. Then comes a deliberate process of developing and assessing a wide variety of grouping alternatives, matching the most promising ones with appropriate linking mechanisms and submitting the remaining "feasible set" of alternatives to an impact analysis, assessing their potential effect on the rest of the organization, and surfacing problems that must be addressed during implementation.

While that process can be pursued with widely varying degrees of detail and formality, what's really important is the basic sequence of decisions. That process involves the articulation of concrete goals, the development of the widest possible range of alternatives, and the construction and assessment of feasible sets of grouping and linking patterns.

6. There are no perfect designs; the design process requires the weighing of choices and the balancing of trade-offs. The fundamental choice in design—the selection of grouping patterns—involves inherent trade-offs. As soon as people and activities are grouped together to enhance their communication, goal orientation, and information flows, they are, by definition, distanced in those same ways from other groups, activities, and information sources located outside their own structural boundaries. Moreover, grouping decisions go on at every level of the organization; in large corporations, the number of possible permutations is enormous. And each alternative offers different strengths and weaknesses, different points of emphasis, different priorities, each attaching varying levels of importance to strategic objectives and core competencies. As business environments become more complex and organizations find it necessary to focus simultaneously on several strategic objectives, matrix designs become increasingly popular. But they, too, involve trade-offs; while attractive on paper, they are considerably harder to manage than simpler, more traditional grouping arrangements.

The notion that all designs involve trade-offs merely underscores the importance of a design process that emphasizes the development and consideration of a wide range of feasible alternatives. Some of the most effective processes are those that begin with the question, "If you were going to invent this company from scratch today, what would it look like?" and then go on to challenge every aspect of the status quo. The perfunctory consideration of a single alternative just doesn't provoke that kind of creative process.

7. The best designs draw upon the knowledge, experience, and expertise of people throughout the organization. Design expertise rarely resides exclusively in the executive suite. Indeed, our experience clearly shows that design efforts benefit not only from widespread participation but from the insights shared by people who understand both the day-to-day workings of the organization and the network of relationships in the informal organization. As we mentioned earlier, one of the critical shortcomings of the GM restructuring of 1984 was that it was devised largely by GM executives, far removed from the organization's hands-on work. Many had spent so little time in each of their management jobs that they'd failed to grasp the nuances of the informal organization. There were thousands of people lower down in the corporation who could have explained to them how things really worked—and undoubtedly could have suggested ways to make them work better—but were never asked.

The redesign process at Kaiser Permanente's Northern California Region, on the other hand, was practically a textbook case on involving the right people. The original design team included third- and fourth-level managers—people with a fairly broad perspective who were still fairly close to the front lines. They represented different geographic regions and professional disciplines and harbored both an intense loyalty to the organization as well as a recognition that it wasn't working as well as it should. As the process moved on to the operational design stage, the circle of participation grew wider and deeper, with more and more knowledgeable people being brought in to help reshape the grouping structures and business processes.

8. Even the best designs can be derailed by ill-planned, poorly executed implementation. Time after time, entirely reasonable redesigns have stumbled at the starting gate because managers somehow believed that announcing a design would automatically make it happen. Implementation is a complex process that requires careful planning and intense management. Successful managers often think in terms of the organization moving from a current state to a future state through an inherently unstable period of transformation called the transition state. As we've seen, the transition state presents a full range of potential nightmares. Normal management processes break down. Feedback, more crucial than ever, becomes hard to find. Anachronistic reward systems can penalize those who embrace the new behavior patterns. In the face of uncertainty, anxiety spreads, politics run rampant, and performance suffers.

Managers of effective change provide their staffs with as much information as possible about the necessity of change, the shape it will take, and the benefits it offers. They do everything possible to encourage participation in the planning and implementation of change, thus building personal commitment and a nucleus of political support. And when necessary, they employ specific structures and mechanisms specifically designed to manage the difficult but critical transition period.

9. As continual redesign becomes a fact of life, successful organizations will learn to create flexible architectures that can accommodate constant change. In recent years, we've seen companies that have undergone as many as half a dozen restructurings in ten years. The immediate assumption is that they weren't doing it right— either the basic strategy, the details of the redesign, or the implementation were somehow fouled up. That's entirely possible—but not necessarily true.

If we accept the proposition that constant change is the hallmark of the competitive environment as we head into the next century, then strategies will need to change if they're to keep pace. And changes in strategy will invariably dictate changes in design—in the structures, processes, skills, and working relationships necessary to pursue the strategy. If that's the case, then constant redesign will become a fixture in the workplace.

At that point—and the fact is, we're already reaching that point—the real challenge for organizations will be to develop flexible architectures that allow for continual redesign without massive trauma. In terms of physical architecture, they'll be able to renovate the third floor without demolishing the rest of the building in the process. Already, some managers are thinking in terms of "organizational Legos," modular components that can be removed or attached without disrupting the rest of the organizational design. An obvious example that we've already discussed in some detail is the Xerox architecture of independent business units linked by strategic, technical, and customer-focused processes; depending on strategic shifts and competitive emphasis, Xerox can easily add or remove individual business units without affecting the others. It's important to note that the concept of flexible architecture involves more than clever design. It represents a dramatic rethinking of the classic approach to design that has guided organizational management throughout most of this century—a reliance on the machine bureaucracy to maintain control in a stable environment. Today, designing for stability is a recipe for disaster; architectures that allow people, processes, and structures quickly and easily to incorporate change will become essential.

10. Flexible architectures and designs that leverage competitive strengths will themselves become the ultimate competitive weapons. It's our firm belief that the intense search across the global marketplace for competitive value and new customers will lead organizations to rethink their basic architectures. The successful competitive architectures will feature not only flexible internal designs but porous external boundaries. These architectures will embrace a broad range of organizational arrangements capable of leveraging each company's core competencies while expanding its access to new technology and markets.

Some organizations, including Sun Microsystems, have redesigned their architectures to allow each component of the value chain to become a semiautonomous business. Each subunit draws from the parent company's pooled resources but is sufficiently independent and entrepreneurial to seek out new markets for the goods, services, and business processes once provided exclusively to their own company. Others, like Chrysler, are lowering their external boundaries in order to develop unique relationships with suppliers; in Chrysler's case, selected suppliers are now becoming key participants in the earliest stages of design and engineering, dramatically slashing the time and cost of product development. And others, most notably Corning, have become particularly adept at stretching their boundaries to create dozens of strategic alliances and joint ventures to leverage their core technology into new products and new markets.

Each of these organizations, and others like them, have focused on the singular importance of architecture—the grouping boundaries and linking processes, the patterns of personal and cultural relationships that get work done in certain ways, the interaction of the social and the technical sides of the organization. They have seized on the immense possibilities that lie ahead for organizations that grasp the potential of an organization's architecture as its paramount source of long-term competitive advantage. In a very real sense, they have embraced the powerful concept of competing by design.

Index

235